Doug Clark's
Loose Clark Journals

To Sherry, a wife who shares my dreams,
and the only editor I've ever slept with.
And to Ben and Emily,
thanks for being part of the adventure.

DOUG CLARK'S LOOSE CLARK JOURNALS

A Collection of Columns

by

Doug Clark

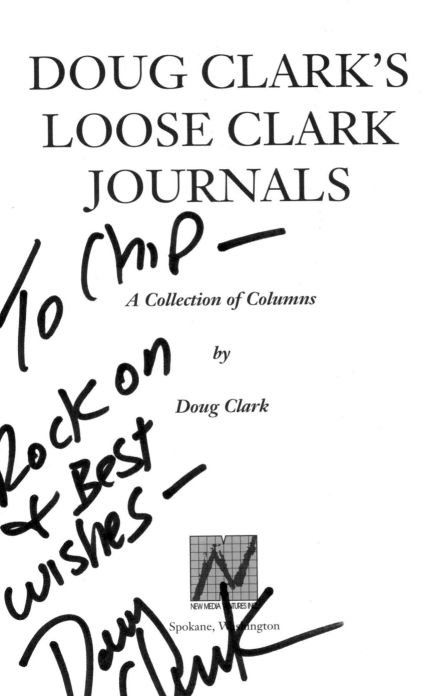

NEW MEDIA VENTURES INC.

Spokane, Washington

To Chip —

Rock on & Best wishes —

Doug Clark

A Spokesman-Review Book
from
New Media Ventures, Inc.

Doug Clark's Loose Clark Journals

1. Non-fiction   2. Social commentary   3. Humor
4. Newspaper columns   5. Spokane, Washington

ISBN 0-923910-10-7

I. Doug Clark

New Media Ventures, Inc., Spokane, Washington

Series Editor: Shaun O'L. Higgins
Production Coordinator: Laura B. Lee
Typography and Design: The Oxalis Group

Printed by Lawton Printing Company, Inc., Spokane, Washington,
on Georgia-Pacific 70-lb. Valorem Natural Book paper.
Bound at the Lincoln and Allen Bindery, Portland, Oregon.

Doug Clark's
Loose Clark Journals

Contents

Introduction

During a recent night out at a Spokane brew pub, my friend John paused between forkloads of jambalya to exclaim, "Dang, you've got a great job!" We had been talking about eccentrics, and his unsolicited remark came at the finale of telling him about my 1987 encounter with a wacky guy who calls himself Accordion Joe. As you can read for yourself in this book, Joe made good on a promise to play his infernal squeeze box while water skiing backwards and blindfolded. The point of all this is that John couldn't have been more on target. I have a dream job. Writing three columns a week for my hometown paper for the last dozen years has allowed me to meet people and subjects no fiction author could make up.

I'm not the kind of columnist who writes endlessly about his own life and family members. I've done some of that, as you'll see, but I believe focusing on what other people do is far more interesting and entertaining. The highest praise I ever received professionally was the year I won second place for humor writing in the annual awards competition of the National Society of Newspaper Columnists. Better than the award were the comments of one of the judges who wrote, "Finally, a columnist who will get up off his butt and do some real reporting!"

This then is a compilation of some of my favorite adventures. You'll find Richard Butler and his band of Hitler-heiling Neo-Nutsies of North Idaho. You'll find my day on the job with a topless house cleaning service and the time I took my minister brother to a nudist camp. You'll find Thomas Budnick, who found the Spokane County Auditor's Office to be the only agency willing to file his mining claims for the planet Mars. You'll meet heroes like Holly Caudill, who not only went on to graduate from law school but became the nation's first quadriplegic United States Attorney. You'll find bureaucratic boondoggles, family feuds, tragedies, triumphs and politicians gone mad.

As you'll note, an entire chapter has been given to Billy Tipton, the woman jazz musician who spent a half-century successfully masquerading as a man. Tipton remains the most amazing tale I've ever stumbled upon and among the biggest stories in *The Spokesman-Review*'s long history. After I broke the news in Spokane, the story appeared on front pages around the world. Magazines, tabloids and television had a field day for months. Movie deals were discussed. And in perhaps the most bizarre twist of all, an opera was written in which the tenor was a columnist named Doug Clark.

It's not widely known, but I turned down a $50,000 offer to take a year off and write a book about Tipton. Why? I told everybody it was because I was just too burned out on writing about Billy Tipton. I figured nobody would believe the truth, but here it is: Writing three columns a week is just too damned much fun.

Doug Clark
Spokane, Washington

The Loose Clark Journals

PINK HOUSE HOLE, IDAHO – Under a scalding July sun, 26 dugout canoes, hewn by hand from 1,500-pound logs, slip into the fast-running Clearwater River.

The plucky souls piloting these crude, tipsy craft wear buckskins and tunics of another era, although some of these pseudo pioneers are lacking in the authenticity department. One lanky gent sports too-tight polyester tan pants with brown fringe sewn down each leg.

Could fate have a fashion sense? The canoe he paddles makes it 10 feet before swamping like the Edmund Fitzgerald.

The crowd lining the shore jeers with approval.

Lewis and Clark had it plenty rough, sure, but I'll bet the Nez Perce Indians never sat on the banks hooting at them.

"Sounds like we're at a demolition derby, not a historical event," remarks one of my shipmates. We soak in the spectacle from the dry safety of a food-laden media jetboat.

The canoe ride is part of the *Lewis and Clark Experience*, a historical tribute to America's intrepid explorers. The event climaxed Sunday night in Clarkston. Documentarian Ken Burns, of *The Civil War* and *Baseball* fame, premiered excerpts of his new film on the fabled expedition.

Being a Clark supposedly related to famed explorer Meriwether Lewis made me a natural to witness all this.

At least I grew up thinking old Meriwether was kin. My father uttered this so often I accepted it as fact. True enough, his mother's maiden name was Lewis.

But when I called my own dear mother for confirmation, my link to the greatest feat of westward expansion began crumbling like a sand castle in a gale. My late father, she reminded me, once told her he had won the Silver Skates award. She later learned the closest he had been to ice was an occasional bourbon on the rocks.

Maybe my Meriwether tie is a crock. But I set out anyway, enjoying the same thrill the unknown Lewis and Clark experienced in 1803 – when President Thomas Jefferson commissioned them to explore the wilds.

Like Lewis and Clark, I decided to chronicle my exploits in a diary historians will no doubt call the "Loose Clark Journal."

Day One – July 25, 1997

Lewiston-bound. A late start makes the task ahead formidable. We must obtain press credentials before the *Lewis and Clark Experience* office closes at 5 p.m.

Lewis and Clark found help from Sacajawea. I have my wife, Sherry.

She is not related to Sacajawea, but claims a direct descendance from Pocahontas. "Let's not go down that road," I say, somewhat surly from post-Meriwether letdown.

Progress comes to an aggravating halt outside Colfax. Road construction creates a half-hour delay. No espresso stands in sight. Lewis and Clark would undoubtedly have turned back. We press on.

More trouble. This time at Lewiston's Grand Plaza Hotel. The press office is still open, but our room, a shocked maid discovers, has been given to a CBS reporter.

"Dan Rather?" I ask. She shakes her head no.

"Throw the louse out."

The maid leaves muttering. At the front desk, I tell the manager I don't appreciate the view of the Skipper's from our replacement room.

"Aren't you supposed to be roughing it?" says Robin Spencer, rolling her eyes.

I crank up the whining. Spencer agrees to let us have the Governor's Suite. "Last weekend," she says, "Richard Gere stayed in it."

My wife suddenly becomes extremely interested. "*The* Richard Gere?" she says. "*The* Richard Gere was here?"

"He was buying an appaloosa horse for his girlfriend," adds Spencer.

We take the Governor's Suite on condition we will be out early the next day before professional golfer Chi Chi Rodriguez plays through.

The suite is very luxurious, even by Lewiston's high standards. It comes with silk flowers, an empty wet bar and a chess set. My wife examines the bedspread hoping to find whatever is left of Richard Gere's cooties.

We take a *Pretty Woman* bubble bath in the Jacuzzi, dropping a history book from our press packet in the water. What happens next is none of your business.

Day Two – July 26, 1997

Fresh aiiiiir . . . Yikes! I haven't been to Lewiston in years. I forgot it often smells like Grandma died in the outhouse.

"It's the smell of money," explains Lorraine Roach, a perky member of the *Lewis and Clark Experience* crew.

More like the smell of Potlatch, a behemoth pulp mill that fumes like Frankenstein's lab at one end of town. Lewiston residents tolerate Potlatch the way a poor family endures a rude, rich uncle.

We board a quirky-looking maroon jetboat called a Duckworth. It's loaded with enough Oreos, pistachios, sandwiches, pop and assorted goodies to feed a Third World nation, or Orofino.

Captain Perry Heinecke, who owns the Duckworth company, powers us miles up the Clearwater to the launch site at Pink House Hole. The sandy patch of beach is lined with dugout canoes. A couple hundred spectators are here to watch the re-enactment.

Hungry visitors may buy a Lewis and Clark continental breakfast. For the thirsty there is bottled water called Lewis and Clark Clearwater Ice.

My appetite weakens. That disturbing smell of money hangs over the food court like a decaying lynch victim. This time we can't blame Potlatch. Some idiot put the food tables downwind from the chemical toilets.

The idea to celebrate Lewis and Clark in a big way was hatched last year by Lewiston car dealer Jock Pring and two marketing men, Jim Soyk and Steve Leroy.

"People live here all their life," says Leroy, who later took over the event, "and the only thing they know about Lewis and Clark is what they see in neon signage."

A quick skim of the Yellow Pages reveals the Sacajawea Motor Inn, Lewis-Clark Karate, Meriwether's restaurant, Lewis Clark Federal Credit Union . . .

After some windy speeches, the canoes take to the water. They are led by an advance group pretending to be Lewis and the gang.

Each canoe took about 150 hours to build. But despite all the effort, the Clearwater is soon bobbing with swamped canoes and riders hanging on for dear life. Those dugouts not dunked must be frequently bailed out as the choppy water spills in.

Even Lewis and Clark lost a canoe near the Big Eddy, a mean-spirited, frothy section that upends all but a few of today's voyagers. Life jackets and quick-acting sheriff's deputies on Jet Skis keep the day tragedy-free.

After a couple of hours of floating fun, the log armada reaches Myrtle Beach. Latter-day explorers will camp overnight and prepare for the final journey to Clarkston in the morning.

The pioneer life is indeed hell. My jaws ache from scarfing Oreos all day in the Duckworth.

Captain Perry motors us to Lewiston in time to hear rock 'n' roll legend Randy Bachman perform in the grass behind our hotel.

Anyone fool enough to hop a log down a river would appreciate the sentiment contained in one of Bachman's best-known hits: "Ride, ride ride, won'tcha let it ride."

Day Three – July 27, 1997

Potlatch is my pal. We learn that the CBS interloper who stole our room took one snort of the smell of money and left town.

We strike out on a mission to find Ken Burns at the sprawling *Lewis and Clark Experience* site in Clarkston. The festival features tepees, Native American dancers, mountain men and a food court where you can barter for a Lewis dog ($2.50) or a Clark dog ($2).

At another booth an Indian gentleman offers "Ancient Nez Perce Astrology" charts for $11.50. I don't know how ancient it can be. He's using a computer.

After traversing the dusty, parched grounds with no sign of Burns, we retire to the air-conditioned comfort of the nearby Quality Inn bar.

Bartender Rena McCully has the pioneer spirits. She recently invented two drinks: The Lewis (Amaretto, whiskey and sour) and the Clark (vodka, peach schnapps, cranberry and orange juice).

This area is suffering from historical hysteria.

Burns eventually comes out of his room. He's a slightly built, bearded man in jeans and a blue work shirt. He'd be completely normal except that every time he moves his lips, Hal Holbrook's voice comes out.

Ha, ha. Just a little documentary humor.

We walk from the hotel to the *Experience* site where Burns autographs books before showing his film on a 30-foot outdoor screen to a crowd of about 500.

Nightfall soon plops over the land of Lewis and Clark like a musky horse blanket. Time to saddle up the Ford and head for the hills.

I think I just got another whiff of that money.

Billy Tipton

Chapter One

Jazz musician spent life concealing fantastic secret

For more than half a century, jazz musician Billy Tipton kept guard over a fantastic secret.

It was a secret none of his many fans, his friends, his fellow musicians or even his three adopted sons knew. The Billy Tipton they saw was a popular Spokane entertainer. He was a doting father who at one time was a Scoutmaster and who lived for years with a wife in a modest South Hill home.

But things are not always as they seem. And on January 21, 1989 – the day 74-year-old Tipton died of a bleeding ulcer – the secret could be held no longer.

Billy Tipton, physicians discovered, was a woman.

"I'm just lost," said a stunned Jon Clark, one of Tipton's sons, when he learned of his father's deception.

Clark shook his head in disbelief and described how he had been handed the truth.

"The guy at the funeral home showed me a little yellow piece of paper where it was marked 'female' under sex. I said, 'What?' and he said that it was true."

Since hearing the news, he said, he hadn't been able to sleep and had been drinking. "I don't know what I'm gonna do. I don't even know who I am any more. I don't know what to think. I just feel deceived."

He tried to smile but it came off as more of a grimace.

"For 26 years I've thought I had a dad. Now I find out this. I know there's no way from stopping a thing like this from getting out. No way. People are already starting to ask me about it.

"I just want a chance to say how it really was. I can honestly say in front of God that my brothers and I never knew."

Because Tipton was so accomplished at his role reversal and because so many years have passed, a full insight into his motives and some of the details of his life may never be known. So far, even the Spokane County Coroner's Office hasn't been able to confirm Tipton's vital statistics, such as name, place and date of birth.

The only thing known is that Tipton probably began this sexual masquerade in the 1930s as a way to pursue a career in jazz.

According to information given funeral directors by Kitty Oakes, the woman Tipton said was his wife, Tipton was born December 29, 1914, in Oklahoma City, Oklahoma. Tipton was reared in Kansas City, Missouri, a town well-known for its freewheeling style of jazz.

In a 1974 interview with *The Spokesman-Review*, Tipton said he was something of a musical prodigy who gave a violin concert at the age of 7. He said he graduated from a Kansas City high school, the Kansas City-Horner Conservatory of Music, and the Oklahoma State Junior College in Stillwater, Oklahoma.

What Tipton didn't talk about was the considerable obstacle that stood between him and a musical career during the Big Band Era.

Unless you were an attractive "girl singer" in those days, *a la* Doris Day or Helen Forrest, performing in a swing band was strictly for men. With the exception of a few examples – Margie Hyams on vibes and pianist Mary Lou Williams – women, regardless of talent, rarely bridged the gender gap.

Tipton apparently considered the social milieu and prejudice of the times and made a life-altering decision to put career before identity.

"He gave up everything," said Oakes, who separated from Tipton 10 years ago. "There were certain rules and regulations in those days if you were going to be a musician."

After the transformation, Tipton apparently broke off ties with family and played the role of a man so well that neither close friends nor fellow band members had a clue.

"No one knew," Oakes said. "It was the best-guarded secret since Houdini." Other than a few comments, Oakes refused to talk about Tipton and her life with him.

"The real story about Billy Tipton doesn't have anything to do with gender," she said. "He was a fantastic, almost marvelous, and generous person."

Tipton spent the 1940s building a reputation as a fine player who could sight-read with ease the most difficult jazz arrangements. He traveled and played with some of the best in the business: heavyweight acts like the Jack Teagarden, Russ Carlyle and Scott Cameron orchestras.

By the 1950s, Tipton had settled on more intimate nightclub work. He formed a trio and traveled throughout the West, playing mainly in fraternal clubs. To supplement their income, the Tipton trio made two albums featuring him on sax and piano.

"Whenever I go to Denver or Phoenix or Seattle – even back East, people know Billy Tipton," said Clark. "People loved him."

One such person, Dick O'Neil, considers Tipton the best friend he ever had. O'Neil joined the trio in 1951 and played drums with the group for almost 10 years.

In the early days of the trio, O'Neil recalled, some listeners made cracks that Tipton looked too feminine to be a man. His high singing voice and baby face, O'Neil said, no doubt fueled the comments.

"But I would almost fight anybody who said that," O'Neil said. "I worked with him for 10 years. I never suspected a thing."

"I was 23 when he gave me a job as a drummer. I hardly knew my right hand from my left, but he had the patience to put up with me."

"With Billy, friendship came before professionalism."

Those who knew Billy Tipton remember him as caring and generous.

"He was probably the first person I met when I came to Spokane in the mid-1950s," said Don Eagle, who for the last three decades has entertained Spokane with his own popular jazz combo.

Tipton, like Eagle, had been drawn to Spokane because of its reputation as a "little Reno." Slot machines were everywhere, which made for some salad days for the area's entertainers.

Tipton found regular work at the Tin Pan Alley. It later became the now-defunct Vic's Showcase. During that period, he presented himself as the husband of a woman named Mary Ann.

Whenever a musician fell upon hard times, Eagle said, it was Tipton who rented out Spokane's old Post Theater after hours and staged a benefit concert.

"Everybody owed him little favors, so he could pull it off," he said. "I can't say enough good things about him."

In 1958, when the slot machines disappeared, Tipton filled gaps between engagements by working as a talent agent with the Dave Sobol Theatrical Agency. It was a natural transition. Sobol had been booking performances for Tipton's trio since 1951. He considered the entertainer a close friend.

Tipton's job as an agent kept him closer to Spokane, where he bought a house on the South Hill. "Billy Tipton Trio" became familiar words on the marquees of the Ridpath and other major clubs.

Sobol said in 1958 he introduced Tipton to Kathleen "Kitty" Flaherty, a dancer and entertainer he represented. According to Sobol, the two liked each other and, in 1960,

Tipton told Sobol that he had divorced Mary Ann and married Kitty.

Sobol, who spends his winters in Arizona, said he had known Tipton for more than 30 years and had worked with him daily much of the time.

The retired agent said he suspected Tipton had something to hide. Sobol said he could never get a Social Security number from him. "I asked him about it and he said there was a reason, but he would never confess to me what it was."

Although rare, such charades aren't unheard of. The November 1988 issue of *MD Magazine*, for instance, featured the tale of British surgeon James Barry.

Barry (1795-1865) was called one of the most skillful physicians of his day – graduating as a teenager from the University of Edinburgh Medical School and serving with distinction in the British Army medical service for nearly half a century.

Yet with Barry's death at age 70, wrote *MD* editor Donovan Fitzpatrick, "came the astounding revelation that James Barry was, in every essential respect, a woman."

Some people who knew Tipton think his story should be buried with him.

Oakes said she saw no reason to dredge up the past. Tipton died with the secret, she said, and that should be respected.

Several of Tipton's close friends, and his 19-year-old son, William, share that view.

But others, like Sobol, see no harm in talking about it. "At this point, I don't think it makes any difference who knows."

Tipton's oldest adopted son, Scott Miller, 27, is trying to understand the pressures his father faced.

"Now I know why I couldn't get him to a doctor," Miller said. "He had so much to protect, and I think he was just tired of the rat race, tired of keeping the secret."

In recent years, Tipton lived in a mobile home in the Spokane Valley, playing infrequently around town. Miller and others close to Tipton, say the aging musician died broke and beat.

"You can imagine the pressure he lived with," said Clark. "Who knows? Maybe that's what gave him the ulcer that ended up killing him. He had so much to protect."

Both Clark and Miller say they had a normal father-son relationship with Tipton.

"I haven't seen any difference in what he did and other fathers did," said Miller. "He took us in and he cared for us."

"Mentally he was a father."

Clark agreed, but added that some of the things he accepted as normal during his childhood look different today.

"Now I know why he would never take off his shirt and go swimming with us," he said. "I thought he was just shy. But we were in Cub Scouts and Boy Scouts, and he was always there for us."

At Tipton's funeral friends and loved ones paid their last respects to an exceptional human being, more exceptional than most of the mourners knew.

But for some, the memories of Billy Tipton can't help but be bittersweet.

"He'll always be Dad," Clark said. "But I think that he should have left something behind for us, something that would have explained the truth."

If anyone has any answers, he said, he would appreciate hearing them.

"We loved our Dad, but we would have liked some honesty. I don't think that's too much to ask."

Jazz musician's sex masquerade fuels family feud

Six weeks after his death and the discovery that Billy Tipton was a woman, the story of the popular Spokane jazz musician has taken on an unpleasant life of its own.

In contrast to Tipton's gentle ways, the surviving family has become split into two camps that are feuding over the estate, the rights to the musician's story and the details about his life.

On one side is Kitty Oakes, a former striptease dancer who lived as Tipton's wife for about 20 years, and Billy Tipton, Jr., 19. He is the youngest of three sons Oakes and Tipton said they adopted while they lived on Spokane's South Hill.

The other two sons, Scott Miller, 27, and Jon Clark, 26, make up the other camp. They say they are angry and bitter with the rosy picture of family life that Kitty has painted.

"It's a mess," said Miller, adding that he and his brother wouldn't be surprised if some aspects of the dispute end up in court.

"She (Oakes) was the reason we moved out of the house and lived on the streets when I was 15. She treated us horribly and, after we left, she took it out on Billy until he couldn't take it any more and left, too."

Oakes declined to comment directly, instead letting her agent, Barron Stringfellow, speak for her. Stringfellow said his client had always wished the best for her children and had been deeply hurt by attacks from Miller and Clark.

"Inside, she's a mother," Stringfellow said. "She doesn't understand why the other two boys have been playing so down and dirty."

Although the family members apparently have harbored hard feelings for years, it was Tipton's death and subsequent publicity that fueled the current venom.

Tipton, 74, died January 21, 1989, of a bleeding ulcer. A musician and entertainer, Tipton had for at least half a century lived in the guise of a man.

After the news that he was a woman broke in this column, the story made headlines from *The New York Times* to the *National Enquirer*. *People* magazine devoted two full pages; *Time* magazine's article was shorter, but carried a 1950s-vintage publicity photo of the Billy Tipton Trio in its heyday.

Journalists weren't the only interested parties. For days, Tipton family members were deluged by inquiries from TV and movie producers, talent and literary agents and others looking for story rights and a piece of the action. So far, Unistar, a Hollywood-based independent production company, has signed Clark and Miller for the rights to their story. Unistar representatives say a deal for a television movie about Tipton is all but guaranteed.

"We're really close," Mike Valverde said on Thursday. "We're still negotiating on a couple of deals, but we're really close."

Oakes and Tipton, Jr., who originally protested that my column had invaded their privacy, have been anything but private.

They have hit the talk-show circuit hard. They sold their "world exclusive" story for the February 21 edition of the *Star* tabloid.

"Oh, Billy! You poor baby," opened Oakes' first-person article for the *Star*. "How you must have suffered – but I bet you're having a glorious laugh on us all now! That was my reaction when I learned the truth."

As of yet, however, Oakes and Tipton, Jr. haven't signed away their story rights.

"We haven't talked any money with anybody," said Stringfellow, adding that Oakes and Tipton, Jr. are examining a number of serious offers.

"It comes down to accuracy," he said. "How much accuracy they are interested in. Kitty would rather let the Billy Tipton story be shelved if it isn't done right."

After all, said Stringfellow, "She and Billy, Jr. are the story. Without them there is nothing."

There is plenty of disagreement on that point.

According to Unistar's Valverde, Oakes and Billy, Jr. have practically talked themselves into motion picture irrelevancy. Their appearance on talk show and tell-all interviews, he said, has them overexposed and has greatly diminished their worth to a producer.

"Most of her story is common knowledge now."

The *Star* article is detailed in Oakes' depiction of life with Tipton. In it, she claims to have been as unaware of Tipton's sexual identity during their marriage as her children were.

Oakes, who met Tipton in 1959, writes that she never had sex with the musician. Nor did she ever sleep in the same room with Tipton or see her husband naked. She attributes their lack of intimacy to her own health problems and a story Tipton told her about being rendered impotent after a car accident.

Miller and Clark find much of this to be hogwash. They also question her claims of not knowing Tipton's secret and the descriptions of a happy family life.

Miller says the *Star* article has a number of inconsistencies.

For one, Oakes claims to have married Tipton on "St. Patrick's Day, 1962, by a justice of the peace in Spokane" and to have divorced him in 1982.

No such records exist at the Spokane County Auditor's Office. That fact, said Miller, proves that Oakes was involved in some kind of cover-up from the beginning.

Likewise, Miller and Clark say they have proof that their adoptions were never legal, either.

Stringfellow agreed that it was possible that Oakes and Tipton were never officially married. As for the adoptions, "Kitty herself says they (Miller and Clark) were never adopted," he said, adding that he has seen legal documents on the other son's adoption.

Adding to the mess is a dispute over two wills supposedly left by Tipton. One, handwritten and not notarized, leaves everything to Tipton, Jr. The other will, this one notarized, leaves everything to Clark.

In the meantime, the two Billy Tipton entourages invaded the East last week and proved that even in death, the Spokane jazz musician is star of the show.

In Pennsylvania, Clark and Miller were guests of *Pittsburgh Talking*, a citywide television call-in program.

In Connecticut, Oakes and Tipton, Jr. taped a segment for the nationally televised *Sally Jessy Raphael Show*, to be aired in mid-March.

As divided as the Tipton household is, they are in agreement on one thing: The world has offered them a chance to cash in on the mystery of Billy Tipton's sexual masquerade.

Billy Tipton: An improvised life

Oklahoma's summer of 1935 was a scorcher. A popular country swing band called The Cavaliers sweated away nightly in stifling, crowded dance halls in towns like Shawnee, Seminole and Muskogee.

But the heat is not what band leader Lavoy "Son" Wallin remembers most about that summer.

To help his seven-piece band stay cool, "I decided we'd wear matching T-shirts," says Wallin, 76, who lives in Oklahoma City. But one member refused, the 5-foot-4, babyfaced saxophone and piano player named Billy Tipton.

"We all liked Billy," says Wallin. "He was really the life of the whole band, but the boys were a little irritated."

So The Cavaliers, minus Billy, took the matter to D. L. Hickman, a booking agent who had discovered the 19-year old musician living in Enid, Oklahoma, in 1934.

Hickman offered a simple explanation: "That's 'cause Billy's a girl."

Wallin could not have known that this secret would not be revealed again until Tipton's death – nearly 54 years later.

January 21, 1989, at age 74, Billy Tipton died inside his Spokane Valley mobile home of a bleeding ulcer. Only after paramedics had attended to the body was it discovered what The Cavaliers had learned back in 1935.

The strange story of Billy Tipton was reported first in *The Spokesman-Review* and *Spokane Chronicle* on January 31, 1989. Soon after, it made news around the world – in newspapers from Tokyo to Paris to New York; in *Time, Newsweek, People* and *Vanity Fair*; in supermarket tabloids and on television talk shows. A movie and book are in the works.

This widespread fascination with the Billy Tipton story is not hard to understand. For more than half a century, Tipton carried out a male masquerade so successful that it fooled his three adopted sons, at least three ex-wives, a score of fellow musicians and nearly everyone else who ever knew him or heard him play.

Today, after a two-month investigation, much of the mystery of Billy Tipton's life has been solved. Still, one question remains unanswered: Why did Billy do it?

Billy's brother, one of his former wives and some musicians say Tipton's decision to live as a man was strictly a career choice, that Billy changed his identity to cross the unspoken sex barrier that kept women from playing in the big bands of the '30s and '40s.

Two other women who were married to Tipton have a different view that takes into account the musician's erotic interest in women.

"We were never shy about making love," says Betty Cox, 61, one of those former wives, who lives in the Midwest. "We did it every day."

Keeping the secret was Tipton's greatest performance. It was a complex, intricate solo that overshadows anything his career as a minor-league jazz musician achieved.

"After Hickman told us the truth about Billy, nobody brought it up again, but Billy knew that we knew," says Wallin. "We decided to let Billy be one of the guys, but I think Billy was uncomfortable about it.

"Billy didn't stay with us too much longer and nobody who knew the secret ever heard from Billy again."

Her real name was Dorothy Lucille Tipton.

She was born in Oklahoma City at 2 a.m. on December 29, 1914. Her father was George William Tipton, a machinist. Her mother was Reggie Tipton, who listed her occupation as housewife on the birth certificate.

At the time, George was 21; Reggie was 20. Dorothy was their first child.

William T. Tipton, Dorothy's brother, would come along seven years later, also born in Oklahoma City. Now living in Arkansas, Tipton, 68, is a retired superintendent of a Missouri public utilities company.

As the last living member of George and Reggie's family, William holds the key to many details about his parents and, of course, the other Billy. William, however, is under contract with Interscope Communications, a Hollywood production company that plans a motion picture based on his sister's life. Therefore, William says, he is legally limited in what he can say.

But he does say his family eventually moved to Kansas City, Missouri, where he entered the school system as a first-grader in 1928. About a year later, he says, George and Reggie separated and then divorced.

William moved with his mother to Oklahoma. He refuses to discuss what happened to his father or Dorothy, but school records indicate she remained in Kansas City with her uncle and aunt, G. W. and Bessie Coffey.

From 1930 through 1932, Dorothy Tipton attended Southwest High School, at the time Kansas City's most well-to-do school. Dorothy had studied music at an early age and played alto saxophone in the school orchestra.

Maybe the most remarkable thing about Dorothy Tipton's high school career is how unremarkable she must have been. Records show she was an average student. Thirteen of

Dorothy's classmates who were contacted have no recollections of her.

A possible clue to what might have been going on inside Dorothy Tipton lies in the 1932 Southwest High School yearbook. Dorothy, a junior, is listed as secretary of the school's drama club – The Masqueraders.

In 1933, Dorothy didn't return to Southwest for her senior year. Instead, she pursued a new life as a musician and applied for a Social Security card using a name she borrowed from her brother: Billy Tipton.

Fellow musicians describe Billy Tipton as a competent journeyman, a musician who spent his career playing watered-down jazz numbers and dance tunes in a string of roadhouses, nightclubs, social organizations and hotels.

Although he never hit the big time, he often bragged to his friends about playing with swing-era bandleaders Jack Teagarden, Russ Carlyle and Scott Cameron. The national television show *A Current Affair* has implied that Tipton played with jazz giant Duke Ellington. The claim is based on a photograph that pictures the two musicians together.

As it turns out, the truth doesn't live up to the myth.

"Yeah, Billy played with Duke Ellington," chuckles Ron Kilde, who played bass and violin with the Billy Tipton Trio from 1954 until 1960.

He explains: "In '54, we were playing in Albany, Oregon, and the Duke was playing at the Elks Club. After he finished, he came over and was in the audience. It was his birthday. We threw a big party for him and he sat in with us."

In 1956, the Billy Tipton Trio recorded two albums, *Hi-Fi Piano* and *Sweet Georgia Brown*, under an independent label. The records, Kilde says, were sold mainly in discount racks in drugstores and some department stores.

Far more fascinating than a musical legacy is how Billy Tipton maneuvered his way through what must have been a social mine field, dotted with situations that could have led to his exposure.

As a father, Tipton tried to live the life of a solid family man. In Spokane in the 1960s, Tipton and his fourth wife, Kitty, adopted three boys.

"Many of the things I did, he copied," says Kilde. "When I bought a trailer, he bought a trailer. When I bought a pony for my kids, he bought a pony for his kids. When I bought a house, he bought one in the same neighborhood."

Kilde laughs, "I used to think it was one of those, 'keeping up with the Joneses' things, but I think he used me as a role model of what a married man should be. Billy tried to act masculine. He'd get real mad if anybody said he wasn't masculine enough."

During his earlier days on the road, Tipton improvised ways to keep his true identity hidden. Even World War II became a problem, musician George Mayer wrote in a letter before his 1990 death in Texas.

At the time the Japanese attacked Pearl Harbor in 1941, Mayer and Tipton were playing in Joplin, Missouri. "We began losing men from the band as the draft caught up with us," writes Mayer. "I was 4-F because of a heart condition."

As the war effort grew, Tipton realized he would have to explain away his own non-involvement. One day he came to Mayer with an important announcement.

"Good news, George," said an excited Billy. "I'm 4-F, too!"

Thanks to that stroke of luck, Mayer's band was able to muster a trio that included: "Billy, myself and a woman drummer who weighed at least 300 pounds."

Tipton also had to guard against injury. A trip to the hospital could mean the end of his secret. Mayer recounts one occasion when Tipton gave up a good-paying job to keep out of harm's way.

"Corpus Christi (Texas) was a Navy town. There were a lot of free-for-all fights among the sailors who came to the

Palmero where we played," writes Mayer. "When a fight broke out, beer bottles flew in all directions. Billy was ready to quit. The manager put up a screen of chicken wire to protect us from the flying bottles.

"That calmed Billy down until one night a shot rang out and a bullet whizzed by the bandstand. Billy said, 'That does it!' and he quit the band on the spot."

Mayer sent his letter last June to Unistar International Pictures, a Hollywood production company that is trying to get a book written on Tipton's life. Mayer had hoped to turn his Tipton reminiscences into cash, but died before anything could come of it.

While Tipton lived, Mayer never knew the secret. Their musical partnership lasted from the late 1930s into the early 1950s.

"He was an excellent pianist," writes Mayer of his friend, "much in the style of Teddy Wilson, a style that went well with my clarinet since I was playing the Bennie Goodman style in those days."

Tipton's musical talent is one thing to evaluate. What drove Dorothy to become Billy is something else.

"It was career," Billy's brother says firmly. "Girls in those days didn't play in bands. Especially if you did instrumental work, you couldn't find work as a woman. After she started it, there was no turning back."

Kitty Oakes, who also has signed with Interscope, agrees.

Oakes lived as Tipton's wife in Spokane from 1960 until they separated in 1978. She says she didn't know her ex-husband's secret until after their separation and is adamant that Billy did what he did for music.

"He gave up everything," she said after his death. "There were certain rules and regulations in those days if you were going to be a musician."

She says her life with Tipton was sexless. "There was an attraction between us, but it wasn't physical," she wrote in the

February 21, 1989, edition of the *Star* tabloid. "I was attracted to his gentle warmth and compassion."

But, like Betty Cox, another of Tipton's wives acknowledges a sexual relationship with the musician. Mary Ann, 69, who lives near Portland, says, "Billy was very, very affectionate. Women always found him attractive."

Shunning publicity, Mary Ann asked that her last name not be used.

Cox lived with Tipton from 1946 to 1953. Mary Ann was with the musician from 1954 until about 1960, when she says Tipton dumped her for Kitty, a voluptuous stripper 16 years younger than she.

"Let me put it this way," she says. "Anybody that's 16 years younger, well, you can't fight the odds."

Betty and Mary Ann, who have never met or talked, have similar stories. They both met Tipton in nightclubs. After their years with Tipton, each woman married a man and had children.

And both say they never knew their lover was a woman.

"How did Billy do it? That's something only the good Lord will ever answer for me," says Cox.

"Both of my brothers are truck drivers. I came out of a family of six. If my brothers had ever in their wildest dreams thought that their little sister was living with a woman, they'd have knocked me and Billy into the middle of the next county."

Betty says her brothers liked Tipton, who loved to work on his cars and swap jokes with the boys.

Tipton, in fact, was perceived by many who knew him as something of a ladies' man. Wallin recalls that Tipton always had a girlfriend hanging around him during his days with The Cavaliers. And Cox says Tipton dumped his first wife, June, to take up with her.

Cox met Billy when he was playing in the Heidelberg Club in Joplin, Missouri, in 1946. She wasn't quite 16, but says she was well developed and serving drinks there.

June was a singer in Tipton's band and supposedly Tipton's first wife, although Mary Ann says Tipton never really married anyone. The wives were part of the masquerade.

"During breaks, he'd come into the kitchen and drink coffee," says Cox. "That's how I got to know him and we fell in love. The next thing, June was leaving to sing with another band. I don't think they were getting along very well anyway."

Cox says she was with Tipton for seven years, yet never knew the secret. She left Tipton in 1954, when her father got sick and she decided to go back home.

"I know it sounds incredible, but I'm a normal, healthy woman who enjoys her man. And if that little Billy was still alive today, well, I'd still enjoy him."

Cox and Mary Ann say they never saw Tipton naked and that he kept his chest wrapped. Cox says Tipton wore T-shirts and underwear and used sexual devices when making love.

It's not as implausible as it sounds, says Allan Berube, a researcher with San Francisco's Gay and Lesbian Historical Society who has documented several cases similar to Tipton's.

"The question seems to be, are women like Billy Tipton really lesbians who want to hide it? Or are they women who identify as men so strongly that they are actually heterosexual in their relationships with other women?"

Sometimes, says Berube, there is no definitive answer.

"How Billy interpreted his life and how others around him interpreted it might not fit into any category."

Of the cases Berube has studied, he has found no single reason that prompted women to try to pass as men.

"Some were actors who portrayed a male role and found how easy it was," he says. "Others applied for jobs that women couldn't get. Still others were girls who ran away from home and realized they'd be hassled a lot less if they were male."

If exposure came, says Berube, it usually came by being jailed, hospitalized or through death.

Berube says career could have been a motivation for the change from Dorothy to Billy. But Tipton's relationships with women indicate that there were other motivations at work.

Dr. Lillian Faderman, a UCLA professor and author of *Surpassing the Love of Men*, says there is a large spectrum of lesbian relationships and that Billy Tipton was at one extreme.

"When I've been asked about Billy Tipton, I give the standard feminist speech," says Faderman. "I think women had a very hard time making it in music, and I imagine Billy Tipton was devoted to her profession.

"But I think with Billy Tipton there were two things going on: Her career would have been an important consideration, but her erotic interest in women would have been just as important."

Faderman says most people caught in such an identity crisis today would opt for sex-change operations.

Tipton, she says, was an anachronism. "For much of her life she was in the midst of not only a feminist movement, but a feminist lesbian movement. Yet she kept her mindset of the '30s and '40s. I'm sure she had a very, very hard life."

Mary Ann has some idea of the emotional toil.

After Tipton had left her for Kitty, Mary Ann says she began re-examining her relationship with the musician and began to suspect the truth. During a phone conversation in the early 1960s, Mary Ann says she confronted Tipton.

"I said, 'Why didn't you tell me years ago that you were a woman and not a man?' But he didn't say anything. He didn't want to talk about it."

Tipton was too consumed with keeping the secret. In the end, it cost him his life.

"There was no reason anybody should die of a bleeding ulcer," says Mary Ann, who became a licensed practical nurse after Tipton left her. "We kept in touch with each other, and I even offered to send him to a doctor a month before he died. But he wouldn't go. He didn't want to see any doctors."

So Billy Tipton died, holding onto the one thing he valued more than his own life. In death, however, Tipton became what he never was in life – a star.

The truth about Tipton has sparked a much-publicized family feud. Oakes and 19-year-old Billy, Jr. side against her other adopted sons, Jon Clark and Scott Miller.

A lawsuit against the Tipton estate has been filed by Patricia Clark, Jon's natural mother. She claims she was defrauded when she gave her baby up to the Tiptons and that the revelations of Tipton's gender have caused her emotional harm and damaged her relationship with Jon.

Even Tipton himself has not been allowed to rest in peace. After cremation, his ashes were divided between warring family factions.

Mary Ann says watching all this has been hard to take. She noted that her former lover died broke, living in a mobile home that a friend had bought for him. Tipton's fear of exposure kept him from filing for Social Security payments.

"It's all been so sad," says Mary Ann. "He didn't have to die a pauper. If he had come forward with the story of his life, he would have been rich and famous. But he didn't. He chose to take his secret to the grave.

"And the saddest part is that everybody found out anyway."

Opera not over until writer sings

OLYMPIA – It ain't over 'til the columnist sings.

And what a fine-looking columnist he is: Thick mane of blond hair. Slim build. *GQ* looks. Clear tenor voice . . . .

That's how Troy Fisher portrays me in *Billy*, an original opera based on a story I broke in 1989.

"So, what do you think so far," I whisper to my daughter, Emily, toward the end of the first act.

"You have hair," she whispers back, giggles barely suppressed.

So much for art imitating life. Of course, when you're dealing with the life of Billy Tipton, is anything ever as it seems?

Born Dorothy Lucille, Tipton stole her brother William's name to play jazz as a teenager and kept up the male masquerade for 54 years. Tipton settled in Spokane, took a wife, bought a South Hill home, adopted three sons and played the role like a virtuoso. Tipton was a coach, a Scoutmaster and, as one of his musician pals said, a "man among men."

Then Billy Tipton died of a bleeding ulcer January 21, 1989. A day or two later, Spokane County Coroner Graham McConnell handed me the scoop of my career.

The wild thing about Billy Tipton wasn't that he was a she, it was that nobody had a clue. Not sons. Not band members. Not friends. Even three Tipton ex-wives I managed to track down claimed they didn't know.

Keeping that incredible secret is what *Billy*, the opera, is all about.

"I wanted to examine why somebody would do that," says Bryan Willis, the Seattle playwright who wrote the text. "The more interesting aspect is the burden of keeping that kind of secret for over half a century and how that kind of secret would affect your life."

The opera centers around Tipton's last moments, as he wrestles with whether "To Tell or Not To Tell." Tipton argues musically with his alter egos and ignores a former wife, who urges him to call a doctor.

The wisdom Tipton refuses to accept is that nobody checks out of life's hotel without settling up. People paw through your mortal baggage. Paramedics. Doctors. Undertakers. Coroners.

The first law of journalism is that somebody always spills the beans.

34

Enter stage left: Doug Clark, *Spokesman-Review* columnist, sits at a glowing word processor and begins to sing the story he types.

"For more than half a century, jazz musician Billy Tipton kept guard over a fantastic seeee-cret."

Hearing words you wrote on deadline sung to you by a tenor with hair is a very dissonant experience, let me tell you . . . But I wasn't the most unsettled Clark at the opera. Not by an aria.

"It brought back a lot of memories I didn't think I'd have again," says Tipton's son, Jon Clark, who was so shaken he left the theater for a few minutes. "I guess I expected something a little more subtle."

The Billy Tipton transgender saga is tailor-made for the over-the-top theatrics of an opera.

Timothy Brock, who wrote the rich, haunting score and directs the 37-piece Olympia Chamber Orchestra, says he wanted to immortalize Tipton through opera within days of hearing of the musician's death. He was so taken he bought a trailer similar to the one Tipton died in and composed the music there.

Overall, *Billy* is wonderfully entertaining stuff with a few flaws. The second act is a bit jumbled and doesn't live up to the promise established by the dying Tipton in the first.

And, believe it or not, this Doug Clark character is way too noble. Willis has me turning down offers to write books and film scripts because I don't want to be sensational. That works for opera but, in truth, I rejected a book deal mainly because I was beginning to see Billy Tipton in my sleep.

As for having my part played by a guy with killer looks and flowing blond locks, yeah, that seems pretty darned accurate to me. (See dust jacket photograph for verification – that's me on the right.)

Politics and Your Government at Work

Chapter Two

Reagan could find better room rate if he'd shop around

Don't get me wrong, a presidential visit seems like a swell thing for Spokane, and I'm sure Mr. Reagan would have dropped in to see us even if there hadn't been this nasty old election business.

But I am a little concerned by the excess surrounding our leader's much publicized, one-night stand.

Reports of how the presidential entourage will take over the posh Sheraton Hotel and the president's prissy predilections for fancy silverware and antique furniture seem a bit highfalutin to me.

Reagan is, after all, a fiscal conservative, the man who encouraged good Americans everywhere to tighten their belts and "trickle" down upon one another.

(Er, economically speaking, that is.)

I realize the GOP and, in particular, Senator Slade Gorton's war chest will cough up the estimated $30,000 to $50,000 to pay for the visit.

But this is of no comfort to taxpayers. These are hard times for a lot of folks and the Great Communicator shouldn't be blowing his frugal image for the sake of room service, little bars of perfumed soap and towels nice enough to hide in your luggage.

With no offense to the Sheraton – which has a lovely view of the Spokane River to the north and the Union Gospel Mission to the south – I have taken it as a personal challenge to cut Mr. Reagan a better deal on a room in a hotel with, shall we say, a more conservative ambiance.

If the guy's willing to hold a rally in our armpit of a Coliseum, he can't be too particular about atmosphere, right?

Frankly, I'm amazed at what a few hours of careful comparative shopping will accomplish. I've found no fewer than three Spokane hotel managers who would be tickled silly to put up the prez – and at a fraction of what the Sheraton will charge.

"Oh yeah, we'd love to have him, he's a helluva good actor," said Pete Presta, who owns and runs the Starlight Motel four miles west of downtown Spokane off Interstate 90 exit 276.

"As long as they all behave like gentlemen and the women show a little class, they're welcome to stay here."

True, the Starlight is out of town, but it is close to the airport, where Air Force One will touch down. And you can't sneeze at Presta's $27.95 price for a room with two double beds.

On the down side, Presta refuses to dicker on a package deal for more rooms.

"Reagan's money spends the same as anyone else's."

There's no room service at the Starlight, but Presta agreed to deliver Reagan a Coke should the commander-in-chief get thirsty, "as long as I'm not busy or there's nothing good on TV."

J. E. Flynn of the Otis Hotel, South 110 Madison, says he can outbid Presta, no problem.

The president can have a room with a double bed for $11.86. Of course, he'd have to share a bathroom at the end of the hall, but if he springs for four rooms, the total drops to an even 30 bucks. That should make the savings worth any inconvenience.

"We'd be glad to let him have a room," said Flynn. "The big benefit is that we're right downtown, just five minutes from Riverfront Park. Plus, the president would be able to hang around a lot of his constituents.

"We've got a lot of old war veterans and retired people on Social Security – the ones he's done so much to help. I think President Reagan would really want to come down and socialize with them."

Which brings us to Accommodation No. 3, and my favorite: Al's Spa Tub Motel on Division.

For $40, Gary Frey will let Mr. Reagan have the establishment's VIP Suite, which includes a waterbed big enough for three, a 4-by-6 hot tub and an adjoining bedroom for two.

It's a little more money, but this is, after all, the president we're talking about.

I figure Reagan, Chief of Staff Donald Regan and Press Secretary Larry Speakes will want to sleep together in the waterbed to maintain that vital White House communication link. If the Rooskies invade Europe, Speakes won't have to go far to wake up his boss.

Secret Service agents can have the smaller bedroom.

It sounds uncomfortable, but I slept two and three to a bed on several college band tours and you get used to it as long as nobody snores.

"We have an apartment behind us filled with low-income minority people," Frey said. "Staying here would give the president a chance to observe the welfare state firsthand and then he could report what he saw back to Congress."

According to Frey, the president won't have to mess with limousines or the aggravating Division Street traffic snarl.

"City buses come every half hour and stop right outside. And since the president is a senior citizen, he won't have to pay full fare."

If none of these lodgings meet with Mr. Reagan's approval, my 8-year-old son, Benjamin, has graciously offered our spare bedroom.

With one condition.

"He has to stay and go trick or treating with us. That'd be neat."

Now and then, New Bob sounds a bit like Old Bob

The "New and Improved" Bob Dole stepped lightly from his private jet Monday and, after a bit of walking, slid into the red leather interior of a virginal white Ford limo.

A take-charge guy, this New Bob Dole. No back-seat posturing dignitary here. The man who would be president (and is a leading Republican senator) ignored a clean-cut aide, who respectfully held the left rear door wide open.

Offer declined, Dole ambled around the car, opened the front door and plunked himself down. Next stop, a press conference at Cavanaugh's Inn at the Park in downtown Spokane.

Until then, however, the man was mine. The Dole people had been gracious enough to let me ride along, which may give you a bit of insight into the caliber of mental processes making up the good senator's campaign staff.

I wasn't too proud to sit in back. I made myself quite comfy, in fact, turned on my tape recorder and stared ahead at what just might turn out to be the presidential bald spot. The time had come to expose the truth about Bob Dole's newness.

We know, of course, that Dole is a hot new item from all the ink he got in the September issue of *Life* magazine.

"I haven't even looked at that one," grumbled Dole from the front.

Dole might've been sore that he didn't get the cover. That went to a silly grinning Prince Charles and the loud, yellow caption: "Good Guy or Wimp?"

Not much of question, if you ask me.

On Page 63, though, a pensive-looking Dole stared ahead at the headline:

"A Loner's Quest; As he reaches for the presidency, can the NEW Bob Dole put the Old one behind him?"

Apparently, the Old Bob Dole was sort of, well, grumpy. Stories about him remind me of a former neighbor, Frank

Knowles, who used to aim his sprinklers at the sidewalk to keep me from riding my tricycle near his house.

"I was fascinated," wrote former Dole speechwriter George Gilder for *Life*, "by this strange stormy figure who, in approaching the pinnacle of American politics, made little effort to control his temper, relate to his staff, research his positions or uplift his rhetoric."

Not exactly a portrait of presidential material.

In 1980, as Gilder points out, Dole won less than 2 percent of the vote in the Iowa Republican party caucuses. Iowa, by the way, is right next door to Dole's home state of Kansas, which makes coming in behind one of the all-time loonies – Lyndon LaRouche – even more embarrassing.

But now a change has allegedly occurred. He may not be Pat Robertson, but Dole is Born Again. Like laundry detergent, Dole's formula has been upgraded with a secret formula.

If you can believe *Life* magazine, the senate minority leader has been to – are you ready for this? – charm school.

"Of course," says New York image consultant Dorothy Sarnoff in the article. "I changed him. He was the best student I ever had. A nice, nice man. I took away his snide."

That quote got the New Bob Dole's attention. If he bothered to read *Life* magazine, he probably would have dropped his subscription somewhere out the limo window along I-90.

"I think I spent about 30 minutes with her," he said. "I don't go with that garbage. I didn't take any course from Dorothy Sarnoff, and George Gilder is a (Jack) Kemp activist. They assigned him to write a piece on me, and you wonder why people get upset with the media . . ."

This New Bob Dole sounds a lot like the old one.

Aside from earning a few paychecks as one of Dole's speechwriters, Gilder is a former consultant to President Reagan and an admitted proponent of supply side economics. He's written seven books, too.

"Nobody's read 'em," groused Dole. "He's one of those who believes you can get a free lunch."

Ah, the joys of politics.

But this is kid stuff compared to what happened in Iowa the other day.

While George Bush was out campaigning in the farm-lands, an unsubstantiated rumor cropped up that the vice president had a mistress. Shades of Gary Hart.

All that's no skin off Dole's nose. What bothered him was the word coming out of Bush forces that Dole's troops had started the ugly rumor-mongering. Dole was righteously steamed, and a Cable News Network camera caught the senator chewing out George Wittgraf, the Iowa Bush for President chairman.

"This is about the third thing we've caught him doing," said Dole. "He put out a memorandum attacking my agriculture record. Wittgraf put it out, but it was probably orchestrated by Washington. And Bush had to apologize for it and say that Bob Dole has always been a leader in agriculture.

"We had a lot of trouble with the party there that was in Bush's pocket, so they were giving us a hard time."

Dole never said what Wittgraf's second offense was. The third thing, however, "was when this rumor started and we had nothing to do with it. But some people enjoy that kid stuff."

The trick to overcoming all of the nastiness, the political cartoons, the *Life* magazine articles and what-have-yous, said Dole, is simple.

"I don't read much of it," he laughed. "That's one thing I learned from Nelson Rockefeller. He said, 'Never read all the stuff that people write about you, or you'll spend all day react-ing and you'll never get anything else done.'"

I guess that lets me off the hook. Chances are he won't read this, either.

Clinton laments old friend

Inside a drafty English row house during the fall of 1969, two bearded and shaggy-haired Rhodes scholars lounged on mismatched cushions and warmed themselves with heated discussions about the Vietnam War.

One was a 23-year-old from Hope, Arkansas, named Bill Clinton. The other was Frank Aller, 22, of Spokane.

The two roommates agreed America's role in Vietnam was morally wrong, but each man chose his own philosophical road to travel. Their destinations couldn't have been more divergent.

Clinton's path took him into politics and, should he win the November election, the presidency of the United States.

Aller's journey led him to resist the draft as a fugitive. It also led him to an early grave.

On September 12, 1971, ten months after he returned to Spokane and gave himself up, Aller shot himself in a friend's apartment. He was a Vietnam casualty as much as any soldier who died on a battlefield.

"I think he thought it was his duty to change the world," says his mother, Anita. "When you saw him watching the news about Vietnam on TV you could see how he suffered. He was just overwhelmed."

Clinton, campaigning in Spokane, says he still thinks about his old friend. "I'm glad I knew him, and I'm glad I lived with him. That's the first thing I thought when I landed, was I miss him and I wish he was still there."

Aller was one of Spokane's brightest lights, a whiz kid who skipped the fourth grade and was barely 17 when he graduated valedictorian of University High School's Class of '64.

His brilliance continued at the University of Washington. He graduated *summa cum laude* in Far Eastern studies in 1968. He was one of four Pacific Northwest students given a Rhodes scholarship that year.

At UW, Aller had also become a fierce opponent of the Vietnam War. By the fall of '69 – when Clinton took up residency with Aller at a poorly furnished flat at 46 Leckford Road in North Oxford – the Spokane man had already decided what to do about the draft.

"The purpose of this letter is to inform you that I cannot in good conscience accept induction into the armed forces of the United States," wrote Aller in a three-page letter to the Spokane draft board on January 20, 1969.

"To do so would involve not only a violation of my own moral position on the war, but would also help to sustain policies which I feel are harmful to the citizens of the United States and disastrous for our relationships with much of the rest of the world."

Aller's father, Herb, who worked for the Internal Revenue Service, took the news of his son's defiance hard. "I almost had a heart attack right then," he says.

Clinton was also in turmoil. He had been given a draft deferment after he promised to enroll in the ROTC program at the University of Arkansas.

After many long and intense talks with Aller, Clinton decided to break that promise. On December 3, 1969, Clinton wrote Colonel Eugene Holmes, ROTC director at his school. He explained that he had decided to take his chances with the draft "to maintain my political viability within the system."

Two days before he wrote to Holmes, Clinton drew a high number (311) in the draft lottery. He was never called for service. In the letter (excerpted in the February 24 issue of *Time* magazine), Clinton referred to Aller:

"One of my roommates is a draft resister who is possibly under indictment and may never be able to go home again. He is one of the bravest, best men I know. His country needs men like him more than they know. That he is considered a criminal is an obscenity."

What happened to Frank Aller was obscene. Today, in the Allers' modest, neat-as-a-pin home in the Spokane Valley, Herb and Anita are still trying to recover from their son's suicide.

Anita believes the stress of their loss brought on a series of heart attacks that Herb suffered a few years later.

Until last week, Herb was not willing to talk openly about what had happened. Many of his son's letters and personal papers had been put away, unread. Anita first saw his letter to the draft board on Friday.

"I think it helps to finally talk about it," concedes Herb, who was born in Spokane in 1912.

From January 1969 to late November 1970, their son stayed in Europe as a federal fugitive. Shortly after Thanksgiving in 1970, he flew to Spokane and surrendered to a U. S. Marshal.

"His sunny, jovial personality was completely gone," says Anita, 75.

Aller was torn by his convictions and the effect they had on his parents. There had been many arguments and tears shed over his resistance, says Anita.

"I made that pretty plain that I thought it would ruin his life," says Herb. A moment later, he softly adds, "I had a gut feeling that his would end in tragedy."

Shortly after his arrest, Aller was released on his own recognizance. He was allowed to travel to Los Angeles where a job waited for him with the *Los Angeles Times*.

They wanted him to cover the war in the newspaper's Vietnam bureau. He came back from his training more depressed than ever.

"I think events moved him along," adds Herb, shaking his head. "That he was going to Vietnam, of all places in the world."

Aller had received medical help on several occasions. Nothing could pull him out of his emotional fog. He took his life on a Sunday, the day before he was to fly back to Los Angeles and then ship out for Vietnam.

Today, Anita and Herb respect their son's decision to resist the draft. It was, they say, heartfelt and completely sincere.

Clinton, too, respects Aller. But being a conscientious objector wasn't for him. "No," he says quickly. "I didn't think it was the right thing to do."

Despite their grief, the Allers share a happy memory of both Clinton and their son: during a visit to the row house on Leckford Road in May 1970.

Herb remembers Clinton as a warm, fuzzy-faced and friendly young man with intense views.

Looking back, Anita says she isn't at all surprised that Bill Clinton took to the campaign trail. "I got a little irritated with him," she says. "Here I was there to visit Frank, and Clinton wouldn't stop talking about politics."

Anita smiles and laughs heartily. "He sure did talk a lot."

Road kill bill runs head-on into controversy

Good evening, madame et monsieur.

Welcome to Representative Steve Fuhrman's Roadside Grill, where Stevens County elite come to eat meat off the street.

Please be seated at one of our luxurious window tables and enjoy the view of U.S. Highway 395.

The logging trucks will be thundering by soon. So pay close attention. If you're lucky, you might see tomorrow's meal being prepared.

Now, may I start you both off on a nice cockapoo-tail, or would you rather order something from our whine list?

Excellent choice, monsieur.

The chateau d'opossum was squeezed underneath a radial near Colville in '88. A very Good-year. Our customers never tire of it.

Tonight's entree, "skunk du jour," is a dish specially grilled by our master chef, Bubba. He even used his own grill. A Ford Escort, I believe.

Ah, too bad the Fuhrman Roadside Grill is only a dream.

But if the representative's Road Kill Bill passes, who knows what lurks ahead?

The Kettle Falls Republican has always been about five trout short of a daily limit. He just might see the commercial possibilities in a restaurant offering such nouvelle cuisine as braked Alaskan Husky or flat cat au gratin.

This week, Fuhrman proposed legislation that would make state wildlife employees responsible for scouring county roads for any 18-wheel meal deals. The hapless critters they collect would then be offered to landowners or prisons for consumption.

Road pizza. Mmm, good!

According to published reports, Fuhrman's bill (HB-1668) was a response to some of his constituents who have complained about all the animal carcasses that go to waste along Stevens County roads.

These constituents, says Fuhrman, are afraid of touching the road kill for fear of being accused of poaching.

Joe Bob: "Jethro. Jethro. I seed a Bigfoot whut got kilt by a truck. Wouldn't that Bigfoot be tasty with a mess o' taters?"

Jethro: "You betcha, Joe Bob. But we best don't tetch it lest we get 'rested like the time we shot the horse you thought wuz a moose."

Joe Bob: "Ah know. Ah'll call ole' Fuhrman, the wisest man in Stevens County. He'll make us a bill."

State wildlife officials aren't exactly wild over the prospect of being saddled with Fuhrman's road kill distribution plan.

"It's absurd that Fuhrman would come up with this," says Captain Mike Wharton of the wildlife department's Region One enforcement division. "This is our state legislator? No wonder they laugh at us on the East Side."

In Wharton's mind, this is tantamount to making Washington State Patrol troopers responsible for retreads thrown by trucks or hubcaps that fall off cars.

"We might as well get rid of our patrol cars and put in for some dump trucks," grumbles the captain.

The contact wildlife officers already have with dead animals is burdensome enough. Figure there are only 16 agents to cover the 10 counties of Eastern Washington.

In a year, these agents write nearly 2,000 tickets and patrol thousands of miles. Now, Fuhrman thinks they should take care of all the chickens who don't quite make it across the road.

"It would be an incredible drain of manpower," Ron Pegrin, assistant chief of wildlife enforcement, told a reporter.

Under the very best conditions, there isn't much difference between an animal felled by a bullet or a Buick. Some road kill, in fact, is already served up to inmates at a couple of state prisons.

But how many crunched critters are actually fit for the table? "Maybe one out of 100," says Wharton.

Most of the time, animals thumped by oncoming cars or trucks end up with scrambled innards. Intestines break loose. Potentially deadly bacteria is spewed about the body cavity.

Not a pretty picture.

No, the best plan is to leave the Washington's wildlife department alone and pay Fuhrman to open a Roadside Grill in Stevens County. That would get him out of Olympia, where he can only do more damage, and satisfy his constituents' demand for squashed weasel ala mode.

Bon appetit!

Foley's liberal, vintage Buick goes up for bid

Tom Foley may be a bit high on miles, but at least his gears don't slip.

Which should be of great comfort to whoever wins today's bid on Foley's vintage 1965 Buick Riviera.

The political wheel's wheels will be put on the block as part of the Silver Collector Car Auction, beginning at noon at The Coeur d'Alene Resort.

As a special bonus, Foley – speaker of the House of Representatives, third in the line of presidential succession – will be present to encourage the bidding and to bid bon voyage to his beloved Buick.

But there's more:

Buy his car and Foley will toss in, at absolutely no extra cost or hidden agenda, an autographed, U.S. Congress key chain.

This may sound like tomfoolery. But if former Speaker Tip O'Neil can crawl out of a piece of luggage in a TV commercial for a major hotel chain, our man Foley can do a little schmoozing to get his old car sold.

"My uncle drove Buicks," say Foley, who paid a Spokane dealer about $4,300 for the car in 1965.

"When I finally got the chance, I had to get one. I had enormously good luck with it."

It shows.

Foley's car is a '60s gleam machine, a beautifully kept automobile in midnight blue, black vinyl seats and glossy chrome. Why, there's even real wood in the console.

As soon as I heard it was for sale, I couldn't resist revving up Foley's Riviera for a test spin.

By the way, this baby has a 425 cubic-inch engine under the hood, which creates 360 horsepower and makes the speedometer's range of zero to 140 miles an hour not wishful thinking.

Don't worry. I didn't treat Foley's car with any accelerator-tromping disrespect. I cruised it gently east on I-90 and then south to the home of my little niece and nephew, Kristen and Stephen.

"This is Tom Foley's car," I told them.

"Wow!" said an enthusiastic Stephen.

I asked Stephen if he knew who Tom Foley was.

"Nope!" said an enthusiastic Stephen.

Auction organizer Mitch Silver, however, believes the Foley fame could boost the car's value from $2,000 to perhaps $3,500.

Foley isn't so sure.

"Uh, probably five dollars," he said, when I broached the subject with him.

Foley isn't what you'd call wild about selling. After 25 years and 111,000 miles, he's grown rather attached to his Buick.

But he is also a man used to facing facts.

"I don't get my hand on the wheel much any more," he said. "I'm sorry to part with it, but I believe cars should be driven."

Being on top of the political food chain, Foley spends most of his drive time being chauffeured from place to place. He'd take a government jet, but John Sununu always beats him to it.

So the Buick must go. A car auction, Foley decided, would be a fun and fitting way to say goodbye.

But let the bidder beware:

• The car is a two-door hardtop, which makes it more collectible than a four-door. Government studies have shown that four-doors are mostly bought by frumpy, middle-aged Republicans who need space for their bratty nuclear families.

• The car has an automatic transmission. That lessens its value as a muscle car, but it fits that Foley would drive an automatic. Democrats don't like people to shift for themselves.

• Foley's Buick naturally pulls to the left. Actually, it's the old-fashioned tires that cause the car to drift with the contours of the road.

The politically-correct solution would be to stop at any of Duane Alton's five tires stores and pick up a set of radials.

A conservative, Alton staged two unsuccessful election bids against Foley. Alton may be a loser, but he's sure to have enough right-thinking radials to get the Foley vehicle back on a truer course.

Other than that, the '65 Buick is a wonderful car. Oh, sure, it takes an Exxon spill to fill the tank, but there are some benefits that can't be measured in mere octane.

Planted in the driver's seat, where Foley has often sat, I imagined the heady thrum of political power coursing through my pants.

I gripped the wheel. I thought of sending vast sums of foreign aid to undeserving Third World nations.

Suddenly, I began to filibuster.

"Tax the rich!" I yelled out the window. "House the homeless! Socialize the medicine."

"Spend, spend, speeeeeeeend!!!"

Tom Foley's Buick is not just a car, it's a political machine.

Like it or not, we Republicans are stuck with Dole

The Clark political juggernaut was humming like a fine Japanese import.

Big Mo had pitched her pup tent in my campsite.

And for a fleeting, seductive moment at Tuesday night's GOP caucus I tasted the heady brew of power.

Phew! I spat it back.

Call me an ingrate, but I turned down a golden opportunity to attend the county Republican convention as a delegate representing my Spokane South Hill precinct.

Although I'd never before caucused in public, I gave it a shot, thinking it could be a springboard to better things:

First, there would be caucus delegate Doug, then Senator Doug and then on to the White House. Catchy campaign slogan: "President Doug – Hey, it could be worse!"

But the cost of assuming this delegate mantle was too high.

A majority of the seven who showed up to represent my precinct clearly wanted Dole supporters representing them at the April 13 county convention.

In fairness to these very nice and thoughtful people, I pulled a Phil Gramm scram and dropped out of the race.

Sorry, I'm not yet ready to jump on the Dole train.

My political enthusiasm flopped like an underdone souffle months ago, when Jack Kemp chickened out. Now, like many conservative-minded voters, I find myself in a queasy quandary.

Forbes and Alexander are burnt toast. Buchanan is a jackal. And this latest edition of the Dole-For-President campaign is as thrilling as a cold bowl of gravy.

Seeing Dole run again is like watching another Bob Hope TV special. You kind of admire the geezer. You just wish he'd get off the stage before he falls down and busts a hip.

"I'm not excited about him, either," said Dave, a member of my precinct. "But who else do we have?"

The caucus is a crude instrument for seeking truth. Most states wisely have scrapped these outdated gatherings that consist of, well, anyone who bothers to show up.

Even my own wife wouldn't come with me to the caucus. Sleeping with me was one thing, she said, but "I won't be any part of your political machine."

"It's a dumb system," agreed Jon, another of my fellow precinct members.

Some precincts go unrepresented. Because of the small numbers, the meetings can be railroaded by political sharks.

Some of those in my precinct, for example, are still hacked off at the highly organized Pat Robertson fanatics who hijacked the GOP caucuses in 1988. The entire state went for Robertson that year. How embarrassing.

"Basically we took a vote. Each candidate received about 30 percent," recalled another precinct member and the lone Forbes supporter. "Some guy all of a sudden declared Robertson the winner."

No ugliness could be found Tuesday night. A dozen or so precincts crowded into a room where the group discussion on issues was quite civil. After listing our various concerns – taxes, crime, abortion, welfare reform, etc. – we huddled for brief precinct meetings to elect delegates.

With Dole finally mopping up in the state primaries, the Republican situation is clear. If we are to toss out Bubba, the philandering Arkansas weasel, Dole is our guy.

But we don't have to like it.

Dole made a sour impression on me in 1987, when I interviewed him in a limousine after he blew into Spokane during that year's quest to be prez.

The senator reminded me of a cranky neighbor who used to aim his sprinklers at the sidewalk to keep kids from riding their trikes near his house.

You know that cop who woke up from a coma the other day?

The first words out of his mouth were: "It's been seven years. Everything's changed. Except Dole."

Who needs science? You'll never use it

Boy, did we ever dodge a speeding bullet with that highfalutin' Pacific Science Center deal.

The final ballot count released the other day by the Spokane County Elections Office shows the nays had it by a whisper: just 350 votes.

Saints be praised! The last thing we need is for the city's youth to start stuffing their heads with the wonders of the universe.

Newton. Einstein. Archimedes . . .

No good can come of this.

Start kids thinking lofty thoughts and before you can holler "Eureka!" they're moving their overgrown brains out of town for meaningful careers.

While they're curing cancer or plugging holes in the ozone layer, where does that leave us?

In an IQ-barren hog wallow. A place that would make the dim lights on our current county commission look like NASA technicians.

Kids don't need to set their sights on the stars. They need to keep their eyes fixed and dilated on reality.

You don't need to know a lick of physics to get a perfectly good job right here in River City.

All you have to learn is how to say a few words:

"Paper or plastic?"

Or, "Would you like the curly fries or the regular ones?"

Of course, I didn't always feel this way.

I'm ashamed to admit I actually voted to stick a science center in the Riverfront Park Pavilion.

I foolishly figured such an addition would be more uplifting than the petting zoo, so cherished by our toothless hill folk.

I was deluded into believing our young people would get more out of conducting hands-on science experiments than playing Boom Ball in the Pavilion's sweaty amusement gallery.

Anti-City Hall activist Mamie Picard showed me the fly in my ointment.

Mamie is one of the stalwart Gang of Nine – a tireless group of citizens devoted to dumping sugar into the gas tank of progress.

The Gang can't take all the credit for the vote, certainly. But it deserves a standing O for tossing grenades whenever it could.

Mamie dropped by the newspaper to see me the other day. She was aglow with the heady thrill that comes with clubbing a science center to death.

"We didn't get enough information," she kept telling me. "Too many unanswered questions."

That's the greatness of the Gang of Nine. These people can spot an unanswered question a light-year away.

No concern is too microscopic to be ignored. No detail is too trivial to overlook. There is always a need for MORE INFORMATION.

The Gang wages a holy crusade against all the misguided efforts to supposedly improve the conditions of this community.

Well, things are just fine the way they are.

It's just a sloppy shame these vigilant warriors weren't around 20-some years ago. They would have scuttled Expo '74 quicker than an O. J. jury.

What business did we have to think we could host a world's fair? All Expo '74 did was ruin Spokane's vibrant railroad industry.

Our city once was crisscrossed with a maze of majestic concrete train trestles. They weren't pretty, but the sheer weight of their presence thrummed with power and wealth.

The vast area around the clock tower was a wonderful sprawling railroad yard.

There were freight cars dripping diesel into the black earth. And wine-soaked riders of the rails that Spokane residents referred to lovingly as "bums."

It was a grand and gritty place and now it's a grassy, crowded park. Thank the arrogant dreamers who dared turn this modest town upside down.

Count your blessings we dodged the science center. I grew up without a science center. Look how smart I turned out.

Duh, would you like the curly fries or the regular ones?

Dreamer bets life savings on campaign for presidency

One day Tom Shellenberg realized that he could take his $80,000 life savings and:

A. Light it on fire.

B. Scatter it off a cliff. Or . . .

C. Blow it all running for president.

Shellenberg chose C. when his parents, Fred and Vi, agreed to loan him their 22-foot motor home for the summer.

Look out Clinton, Dole and Gramm – the Shellenberg for President campaign is on the road!

"I've always been told that in America any kid can grow up and be president," says the affable candidate, who rolled into Spokane the other day for a press conference at Riverfront Park.

Towing an old Ford Escort behind the Tioga, Shellenberg has embarked on a whirlwind tour of the contiguous 48 states.

He should be finished by the end of August, when his grubstake runs drier than a Death Valley creek bed.

This is the Forrest Gump – "Stupid is as stupid does" – approach to seeking higher office.

Shellenberg, 43, doesn't have loot enough for an entourage. He's all alone except for a couple of public relations flacks he pays by the hour to answer telephones back in Colorado.

To fuel his presidential pipe dream, Shellenberg sold the prosperous Boulder, Colorado, accounting firm he established nine years ago.

In April, he moved back to Livingston, Montana, so he could launch his candidacy from his hometown.

"I tried to talk him out of it," says Tom's dad, Fred, a retired photographer. "I always give advice, but he always has that faraway look in his eyes when I'm giving it."

Even Shellenberg's dear mother figures her son's chances of success at somewhere "between slim and none."

He's put everything he has on the line, adds Vi. "That's hard for a mother to accept. I hated to see him give up everything he'd worked so hard to acquire."

Hmm. So what you two are saying is that Shellenberg is stubborn and doesn't listen to reason. Hey, maybe this guy does have what it takes to be president.

Shellenberg claims to be a Republican, but has no party support. Why should he? The man has never held public office or even tried to hold one.

Being president, he explains, "is something I wanted all my adult life."

He says he's as qualified to be commander in chief as Bill Clinton except "there's no Gennifer Flowers, I'm sorry to say."

So what makes Shellenberg run?

A burning desire to balance the federal budget, he says.

The divorced accountant came up with a detailed plan he spelled out in *Balance the Budget Now & How, The Silver Lining*. Shellenberg paid $50,000 to research, write and publish this book.

Unfortunately, due to technical problems, the book wasn't ready in time for his campaign.

It should be out in a month, says Julia Herz, who runs the Shellenberg for President effort from her office back in Boulder.

Some office. During our telephone conversation I heard a dog barking in the background.

"I wouldn't hook on with any wackos," says Herz, a bit touchy at defending this lost cause.

Shellenberg isn't a loon. He's a sincere man doing something extremely looney.

Too bad Fred and Vi couldn't stop him. Book or no book, nobody is going to take this guy in a motor home seriously.

Sure, he'll get a lot of press coverage. Quirky political stories are great summer journalism fare.

At end of the trail, he'll have a thick scrapbook filled with all the news clippings reporters wrote when the bargain basement candidate blew into town.

Then he can move back to Livingston with his parents and write his second book: *How I Spent My Summer Vacation and All My Money*, by Tom "I Need My Head Examined" Shellenberg.

Pricey pedicure peeves patron, nails taxpayers

Al Krafft is sore as a bruised bunion over a $51 bill that was charged to Medicare.

For cutting his toenails.

By my deft calculations, this works out to $5.10 per tootsie, which the 75-year-old Spokane man contends is an outrageous clip job.

"Ridiculous," grumbles Al, a retired Safeway worker. "It took longer for me to take off my shoes and socks than it did for the guy to cut my nails."

To begin our adventure in proper foot care, we must travel back in time to the February day Al sprained his knee. That put him in the unenviable position of not being able to bend over and trim his toenails.

Al's doc referred him to the Northeast Community Center. That non-profit organization offers a small clinic that caters to the elderly and needy.

So on Valentine's Day, Al took his piggies to market to get his tootsies some TLC. Tender Loving Clipping.

There wasn't much of that. Al says a rather terse physician's assistant performed a no-frills clipping in less than five minutes.

The experience didn't mean much until mid-April, when Al received his eye-popping Medicare statement. Medicare agreed to pay 80 percent of the $51, which means we taxpayers shelled out $40.80 to clip Al's toes.

Even that amount seems like highway robbery. "If I'd have known how much it was going to be, I never would have gone for it," says the piggies' papa.

"What's worse," adds B. J., Al's wife of 49 years, "is you know this kind of thing goes on everywhere."

Few would disagree the national health care system is a bloated, Ted Kennedy-sized tar pit oozing with fraud.

But not at the Northeast Community Center, says an employe, who claims Al wasn't overcharged one dime. The 51 bucks is the standard fee submitted to Medicare for an office visit.

Besides, she adds, as part of the visit Al would have surely been weighed and had his blood pressure checked.

"Nothing like that happened," says Al, scoffing at the suggestion. "The guy just came in and undid his scissors." Al adds that he told the clinic what he was there for from the get-go.

I tried to call the Medicare people to learn the fair market price of a toenail clipping.

This is a very relative thing. For example, I ain't touching Al's ol' dogs for less than a grand.

After I was put on hold for about a fortnight, a recorded voice told me any actual telephone conversations would be "monitored for quality."

When I finally reached a human, he told me to call someone else. I dialed that number and listened to Nat King Cole sing "All in the Game," which set my own toes a tappin'.

I gave up and found the answer in the Yellow Pages under manicures and pedicures.

"Fifty-one dollars? Oh, good gracious," says Peggy Dial at A Perfect 10 salon at 206 East Wellesley.

For 21 bucks and change, Peggy guarantees "an hour of bliss:" toenail clipping, buffing, polishing and massage up to the knee. For $15 more, she will customize your toes with bright colors and designs. Maybe a rhinestone or two.

"It would really impress me if Al did that," says B. J.

Al, however, discovered the toenail-clipping bargain of the century. It's at the South Hill Senior Center at Lincoln Heights.

He went there in April and got clipped, a foot massage and a hot soak. For six bucks.

It's part of the center's pedicare program offered once a month by licensed nursing home workers. Charlotte Bjurstrom says the waiting list is so long she can only book people every two months.

Of course, if B. J. has her way, Al will spend the extra money and have Peggy give him the flashiest set of toes in town.

"Wow," says Al. "I'd start wearing sandals."

Public forum is best part of boring council

At their best, Spokane City Council meetings are as thrilling as watching cold gravy congeal.

This is a world-class collection of sleepwalkers led by Mayor Jack Geraghty, a guy I'd wager could win a staring contest with a corpse.

And now Mayor Monotone and his Snooze Patrol want to pluck the lone maraschino cherry from atop their dish of dietetic vanilla ice cream.

They want to pull the plug on the public forum.

Oh, say it ain't so.

The public forum is a rude, crude half-hour of rambunctious hilarity where citizens face the council to air various gripes, concerns and delusional outbursts.

Last summer – in a rare flash of brilliance – the council moved the forum from the end of their snorefests to the beginning.

Our beloved leaders thought this to be a swell idea only because they never really expected more of the public to show up. If there's anything guaranteed to make an elected official sweat bullets, it's a more-involved public.

But use the public forum they do.

The preamble to every council meeting now is an unparalleled parade of fruitcakes. The best part is you don't have to buy a ticket or get committed to a nuthouse to enjoy it. The show is broadcast to our homes on Channel 5, thanks to the unblinking eye of the Cox Cable TV rabble-cam.

I tune in whenever I can. The public forum has more belly laughs than *Seinfeld* or *Simpsons* reruns because it is totally live and unrehearsed mayhem.

One of my favorite episodes involved a wild-haired, messianic loon who kept warning the council that "judgment day" was nigh.

Speaking in a they'll-never-take-me-alive tone, he said he would no longer tolerate abuse from police and, presumably, all the voices he hears through the fillings in his molars.

No public forum is complete without a cameo appearance by Jimmy Marks. Spokane's Gypsy poohbah storms the podium with the constipated countenance of an Old Testament prophet or an IRS auditor.

Jimmy loves to mutter, "An a-nudder ting," while wagging a stubby finger at the council members he loathes and invariably refers to as "poor babies."

Jimmy is the one visiting jackal who can twist Geraghty's normally tofu expression into something resembling the throes of an obstructed bowel.

I once turned on the public forum to hear one of the Gang of Nine snivelers suggest that a column I wrote caused one of his cronies to suffer a heart attack.

Hey, I'm good, but not that good.

A reader of mine, Jim, called recently to say he was going to the public forum to protest a parking ticket.

Jim has spent days memorizing all the vagaries and nuances of Spokane's parking code. He has prepared what is sure to be one brain-numbing harangue.

"I don't know if I should go now," said Jim, "or wait until after the first of the year," when new council members are sworn in.

Hurry, Jim, hurry. Our Sominex City Council has threatened to banish the public forum next month to the untelevised, catatonic finale of its meetings.

This will be the biggest crime against comedy since the canceling of *The Gong Show*.

I'm sick of all those politically correct sissies who whine for polite, safe and sane government.

Government works best when it doesn't pretend to be anything other than what it is: a cross between a carnival peep show and an autopsy.

We need more, not fewer, public forums. We need to go back to electing bloated, cigar-chomping characters who swagger and wear watch fobs and have nicknames like "Big Tuna" and "Kingfish."

Maybe government wasn't pretty back in the old days. Maybe it wasn't polite or squeaky clean. But it never put you to sleep and, you know, things got done.

Cops and Robbers

Chapter Three

Major bust! Mom takes trip to jail

Thanks to one of Spokane County's finest, citizens can sleep easier at night.

Criminal case No. 1100941 has finally been solved.

On March 22, 1989, justice caught up with Teresa Bradley, a 27-year-old mother of three. She was also nine months pregnant, but that didn't keep sheriff's Deputy Doug Marske from making this big bust.

As Teresa's three pre-schoolers watched in befuddled fright, Marske told their mommy to get into his patrol car. He graciously decided not to snap on the cuffs, probably because Teresa was so great with child that she wouldn't waddle very far if she tried to escape.

But at the county jail, the Spokane Valley woman was treated like any other suspect. Teresa Bradley was booked and fingerprinted. They took a mug shot and searched her for concealed weapons or drugs.

Teresa's husband had to leave work to tend the kids. Three hours after her arrest, Teresa's mother-in-law drove in from Tum Tum, Washington, to pay the $79 bail to get Teresa out of the slammer.

The charge: failure to pay a 1981 unlicensed dog citation.

Yes, you heard me right.

"This just about tore me apart," said Shirley Bradley, Teresa's mother-in-law. "My thinking was that the county must have an empty jail and they are trying to fill it up.

"I've never heard of anything so ridiculous."

Neither have I.

The incident began when a neighbor called the sheriff's office to complain about Teresa's children. Teresa said she is involved in a running feud with the neighbor and that this isn't the first time bad blood has surfaced.

That's neither here nor there, although when officer Marske responded to the scene, he found no evidence to verify the complaint. But he did, as police officers are trained to do, run Teresa's name through the law enforcement computer.

Up popped an 8-year-old bench warrant stemming from an unpaid $37 ticket for an unlicensed dog.

The sheriff's department declined to set up an interview with Marske, but his boss, Lieutenant John Simmons, backed the officer's decision to haul Teresa to jail.

"Anytime there's a bench warrant," said Simmons, "it's our job to produce the body."

Anybody who believes that old "going-by-the-book" garbage doesn't know much about cops. Police officers make judgment calls all the time, decisions that take human considerations into account and don't necessarily follow a strict interpretation of the law.

Marske was fully aware of the insignificant nature of the warrant. Rather than putting Teresa in jail, he could have asked her to take care of it on her own.

One might think there are more pressing things for Officer Marske to do with his day.

"Sometimes you just have to look the other way because of the nature of the beast," said Sargeant George Schee, who heads the sheriff's warrants department. "If I had been there, I probably could have looked the other way."

Schee laughed.

"I wouldn't want her to go into labor in my patrol car," he said.

Teresa hadn't known there was a bench warrant for her arrest. The dog in question, she said, had belonged to a friend who was staying with her. Teresa supposedly gave the $37 ticket to the friend, who agreed to take care of it.

Apparently, the friend never did. And a warrant with Teresa's name joined 20,000 others filed in local law enforcement computers. Once they are entered, they linger in a kind of clerical purgatory until some resolution is made.

Warrants are issued by judges in cases where a defendant fails to appear in court or pay a fine. They range in severity from homicide to something as trivial as an unpaid dog citation.

"We've got six or eight filing cabinet's worth of warrants," said Sergeant Schee. "They used to issue between 200 and 300 a month out of district court alone."

But after a warrant is issued, a lot can change.

In 1983, for instance, dog citations were decriminalized. Instead of being a misdemeanor, an unlicensed pooch is an infraction, much like a parking ticket.

There's a good chance that Teresa's case, to be heard April 14, will be dismissed.

The humiliation of her arrest, however, will take a long time to go away.

"I've never, ever in my life had a record and now I do," she said. "It was so embarrassing.

"How do you explain to your kids why their mom is being taken to jail?"

Desire to cover for two bad cops epitome of sleaze

So the Spokane Police Guild will pay a thousand bucks to find out who snitched on poor Homer "Rusty" Jackson and Larry E. Peterson?

Too bad I can't offer a reward.

If I could, I'd give it to thank whoever identified Jackson and Peterson as the off-duty cops accused of hiring two teenage prostitutes outside the Rainbow Tavern on March 21, 1992.

Whoever gave their names to the public did this community a huge service. These officers were caught in the deep end of the sleaze pool. Their identities should have been exposed as early as possible.

What a shame the weasels at the police guild don't know this.

Unfortunately, these officers are more concerned with protecting their shaky image rather than the public they are sworn to serve.

Shortly after Jackson's and Peterson's names appeared in *The Spokesman-Review*, angry guild members voted to put a $1,000 bounty on the head of whoever leaked the names to reporters. No questions asked.

As a point of distinction, the police guild is the union that represents Spokane police. The Police Guild Club is a benevolent organization of cops and their cronies.

But these organizations are closely tied, and for both smut and stupidity go together like a finger and a trigger.

Back in 1986, about 60 police officers crowded into the Police Guild Club to attend a memorable bachelor party for one of Spokane's finest. The featured attraction was a nude woman who sprayed whipped cream on the audience before she simulated intercourse with a variety of sex toys.

The guild got quite haughty when information about their little party made headlines.

Three years later, police union leaders were forced to cancel their "wet-clothing contest" when word reached the press. That year's police officers' ball was to include "a wet T-shirt contest for the ladies and a wet gaunch contest for men."

What a class act this police guild is.

But as outrageously dumb as the guild's new "Stooling for Dollars" program is, it isn't the worst thing about this story.

The worst thing is that Police Chief Terry Mangan knew about the bounty but did nothing to discourage it.

Quite the contrary. In a recent news story, Mangan made it perfectly clear that he, too, would love to discipline whoever leaked the name. Like the guild, the chief is fried that someone in his department spilled the beans.

"It was a violation of rules and regulations," he told a reporter, "a violation of professional ethics and a disservice to the city."

What a load of garbage.

One of the disturbing characteristics of Herr Mangan's regime is the way complaints of police misconduct rarely see the light of day. Internal investigations are conducted behind closed doors. That's pretty much where Mangan wants to keep them.

The less the public knows, the better. It's not surprising, then, that the chief has consistently resisted attempts to have a Citizen Review Board as a watchdog over his troops.

But his support of the police guild's witch hunt shows how desperately Spokane needs a review board. And I mean one with teeth.

You'd better believe the public had a right to know the names of the officers involved in this sordid case.

Ask 65-year-old Jean Oton, a bona fide member of the public.

"I think what the police guild did shows that law enforcement in this city is still nothing more than a good old boys network," says the woman, who called the newspaper to express her views.

"You bet we have a right to know about this."

Court documents accuse Jackson and Peterson, who have since resigned and have been charged with offering two teenage hookers $50 apiece for sex.

At Jackson's home, the girls – one a pregnant heroin addict – performed oral sex on the men. After that an argument

71

ensued. According to reports, Jackson and Peterson tried to get their money back.

One of the girls was scared enough to dial 911, which brought Patrol Officer Brenda Dahlstrom to the scene.

"Look Brenda," Jackson reportedly told her, "it gets down to we paid for (intercourse) and didn't get any."

Can you imagine any police organization wanting to cover for these two clowns?

"What the guild members are saying is, 'We're like the Mafia. We don't squeal on each other,'" says Oton. "Well, I think that's rotten to the core."

WSP's Royal Order of the Fly takes back seat to no one

It wasn't the sort of thing a person would normally dare yell at a cop.

"Hey, are you one of the ones with a fly on your ass?"

The question was blurted by a fan during the Apple Cup. The target was a Washington State Patrol trooper who was part of the security for the November 21, 1992, football game between Washington State and Washington.

Hearing the words, however, the trooper didn't get mad. He grinned and pointed a finger at WSP Sergeant Kris Goness.

"I'm not," replied the trooper. "But he is."

It's true. Though all WSP law officers wear the silver shield, about 20 select troopers, sergeants and even a lieutenant sport a second badge of honor where the sun doesn't shine.

The Royal Order of the Fly.

To be a member of this (formerly) secret club, a person must:

1. Work for the WSP within the Spokane district,

2. Be personally invited, and

3. Have the group's gawdy mascot, "Nuclei the Fly," tattooed on the right cheek of his derriere.

"It's a mark of distinction," say Dan Davis, president of the Washington State Patrol Trooper's Association and a founding father of the Royal Order of the Fly. "We just don't take anybody. You have to be one of the chosen."

Last month, seven new members were inducted in a mass buttocks-engraving ceremony at Spokane's River City Tattoo, North 709 Monroe.

Getting Nuclei the Fly emblazoned on your fanny takes 20 minutes and 35 bucks. The tattoo is silver dollar-sized and drawn vividly in red, blue, green and black.

"It's quite colorful," concedes tattooist Constance Eller-Doughty, who designed Nuclei and has planted the fly on each and every ROF member. "But then, these are colorful guys."

They are indeed.

"I think that woman's seen more bare trooper butts than any other woman in the world," says Pete Powell, who got his own Nuclei last winter. He had Eller-Doughty add his badge number, 641, and the letters "RET" to signify his recent retirement from the force.

Some background is in order.

Nuclei the Fly was hatched a dozen years ago in Dan Davis' backyard. "I was sitting there when Ken Lofquist shows up and says, 'Let's go get a fly tattooed on our butts.'"

Neither man has a canny explanation. Lofquist, now a sergeant, simply says, "I dunno, I just always wanted a tattoo on my butt."

With that lofty goal in mind, the pair enlisted Boness and two others. By nightfall, five of WSP's finest had embarked on a journey that would evolve into legend.

"There were a few wives left crying on the doorstep that night," says Boness, who works out of Ritzville.

At River City, Nuclei was tattooed on all except one rebel. That trooper, who now practices law, insisted that his buttocks bear a buzzard. "He had little kids back then and he told them it was an American eagle," adds Boness, laughing heartily.

The Royal Order of the Fly didn't really take wing until last year, when word leaked out among some of the new rank and file.

"The new guys found out and they thought it was neat," says Davis. "We were obviously flattered."

Today the Royal Order of the Fly boasts a membership of about 20. Davis says female troopers have so far resisted invitations to join.

The highest-ranking member to turn the other cheek is Lieutenant Wayne McDowell.

"I'm over 50, I voted for a Democrat and now I have a tattoo on my butt. What does that say about the kind of year I'm having?" says McDowell.

ROF members are worried that exposure may put their colorful behinds in a sling. Some fear they will be viewed as a bunch of party animals who have demeaned the WSP.

Captain Jim LaMunyon, who commands the Spokane district, says what troopers do during their off-hours is their own business. The Royal Order of the Fly, he adds, doesn't affect the integrity or efficiency of the state patrol.

Years ago, however, LaMunyon was invited to join. He declined.

Let's face it. Getting a large multicolored fly indelibly placed on your posterior probably won't put you on the express lane to WSP advancement. But as Davis says, it's definitely a kick in the pants.

"We've been hoping we can all go to the WSP Academy some day and pose for a group photo."

That would positively give a new meaning to the old police phrase, "assume the position."

Columnist was sick over preferential ticket policy

I spent several hours Friday feeling sick to my stomach.

The queasiness began when I learned that a Spokane Police corporal had telephoned *Spokesman-Review* reporter Bonnie Harris to give her a disturbing addition to her front page story that morning. Public officials like Spokane Mayor Jack Geraghty aren't the only people who get preferential treatment when they crack up their cars, he said. In fact, added the corporal, columnist Doug Clark benefited from one of these so-called favors. Police brass, not wanting to get on the newspaper's bad side, quashed an investigation and decided against writing me a ticket after a fender-bender.

Harris made an appointment to check out the officer's evidence.

When I walked into the newsroom, I found myself the gossip of the day.

"Have you been in any accidents?" my editor asked me after closing his office door. "Well, there have been a couple of minor ones," I told him, beginning to sweat. I'm not the world's best driver.

"Let's just let the reporter do her job and see what they have," was his reply.

Everyone deserves a ticket now and then. When those tell-tale blue lights flash, it's only normal to hope that the driver of the cruiser behind you is a fair-minded cop who will at least thoughtfully consider your side of the story.

The public isn't served well by robocops who go strictly by the book. Police officers should always be able to weigh the circumstances and use their discretion to decide when and when not to issue a ticket or make an arrest.

But politics should never factor into the equation.

The criminal justice system is degraded every time people are given breaks because of who they are, how much money they have, where they work or what office they hold.

How can we respect those who enforce the law if the law isn't enforced evenhandedly?

Mayor Geraghty, Harris reported in her story, would have received a ticket had he been an ordinary Joe when he collided with another motorist two months ago in downtown Spokane. One officer at the scene thought the mayor had run a red light and deserved a citation.

"Private citizens," wrote Harris, "are either given tickets at accident scenes or mailed one later. The decision to write a ticket is up to the officer."

The Mayor wasn't cited because of a misguided policy that, at best, has the appearance of unseemliness. City officials don't get tickets until the traffic cop writes a recommendation to a boss who either says yea or nay.

This review process found that the traffic light Geraghty ran was probably green.

Maybe that's exactly what happened. But doesn't such a process put out a stink?

Likewise, doesn't it scald you to know the police would nix my ticket just because I write a newspaper column?

Harris kept her Friday appointment with Corporal Harry Kennedy. Corporal Tom Sahlberg and Sergeant Mark Sterk were there, too.

While I wandered the streets worrying, the officers presented these details:

In January 1992, Doug Clark ran his car into another car on the North Side. After exchanging information, Clark left the scene although the other driver wanted to call a cop.

The angry motorist called for an officer, who investigated the accident and sent his report up the chain of command. Corporal Kennedy and Sergeant Sterk wanted to write me a ticket. The police decided I left the accident scene afraid the cops would be out to get me because of past columns critical of their behavior.

Then word came down from on high to drop the matter.

"I was trying to do what I thought was right and I was told differently," says Kennedy, who refuses to reveal who made the decision. Police superiors ordered Kennedy to leave me alone because they wanted to "keep media relations smooth" and didn't want to "ruffle any feathers."

Isn't that a system worthy of our trust?

The story Kennedy and the others told shocked me, all right. Especially because it involved a different Doug Clark.

Nobody down at the station bothered to verify the driver's identity. A higher-up leaped to a false conclusion and interfered with legitimate law enforcement. For two years, Kennedy and other police officers have been steamed, thinking I got away with something I shouldn't have.

They should be steamed, but at their leaders who put political concerns ahead of justice.

In the future, Spokane Police, I'll take what's coming to me. Please don't do me any more favors.

Sobering thoughts on a career

He was the man most likely to become Spokane's next police chief.

He had worked his way up the hard way, from beat cop to motorcycle patrol to SWAT commander, finally becoming the department's No. 2 man. He served in high-profile posts on the proper civic boards. Intelligent and congenial, he earned the respect of the rank and file.

Then one night as he drove home from a St. Patrick's Day party, Assistant Police Chief Dave Peffer saw the familiar blue lights of a police car. This time, they were winking in the dark behind his white Jeep Cherokee.

A breath test showed his blood had more than twice the legal alcohol limit. And that was that. Peffer's ride to the top had just swerved over a cliff.

It is a gloriously warm evening. Peffer, 53, sits in the declining sunshine, sipping iced tea on the deck of his home in the Spokane Valley's upscale Painted Hills.

He looks fit and remarkably at ease for a man who a day earlier bid an emotional goodbye to the profession that happily consumed him for nearly 30 years.

Peffer has agreed to speak candidly about his life since two state troopers caught him driving drunk on Dishman-Mica Road.

"I can tell you when that happens, you see your life flashing before your eyes," he says. "I knew it wasn't going to be another drunk-driving arrest. I knew it was going to be big news."

He makes no excuses. He knows his job set him up for a bigger fall than the average citizen.

He also says politics played a part in Chief Terry Mangan's decision to demote him. After Peffer had been assured his punishment would be determined after his treatment for alcoholism, Mangan publicly demoted him "on my fourth day in the program."

Peffer's uniform these days reveals a new passion: a green ball cap advertising Big Dog golf clubs sits slightly askew over his brown hair. The front of his white T-shirt depicts a golfer in full swing. More golf time aside, he admits, retiring was a gut-wrenching decision that caught the department off guard.

With Mangan retiring soon and Peffer leaving, an air of frustration hangs over the Police Department. Despite objections from his men, however, Peffer believes he made the correct move.

In the weeks after his humiliating demotion, he realized he had thrown away his chances of replacing Mangan. He was damaged beyond redemption. The prospect of returning to work as a captain grew less appealing with each day. "Been there, done that," he says.

Peffer says he was no hard-core drunk, sneaking shots during the day to keep the shakes at bay. He says he rarely drank before 5 p.m. His slide into alcohol abuse took years, beginning with an innocent beer or two at home after work.

Without realizing it, "I increasingly began to rely on alcohol to calm me down and soothe me," he says. "With an alcohol disorder it seems to always take a crisis to bring it out in the open." That "I could be that intoxicated and driving a car and not even thinking that I'm intoxicated" terrifies him.

There was a time in the not-so-distant past when police brass driving drunk may never have made the news. The unspoken Brotherhood of the Badge would have kicked in. The inebriated officer would have probably been driven quietly home. Case closed.

Peffer has nothing but praise for the two troopers who, he says, did the right thing. "I know how (heart)sick they were," he say, "but they had absolutely no options. They were professional. They were sympathetic. They were very nice and they did exactly what they should have done."

Police work came unexpectedly to Peffer. An Indiana native, he moved to Spokane with his wife, Bitsy, in 1967 with plans of going to Gonzaga University's Law School.

When his financing fell though, Peffer landed a job stacking bricks during the winter. Someone told him the city was giving tests to join the police force. Peffer showed the natural brilliance that would make him a leader: "A cop drives a car. A car has a heater. That's the job for me!"

Peffer scored first on the civil service exam and first on every police promotional test thereafter. There are few jobs within the Spokane Police Department he didn't try.

Like most police officers, Peffer never had to fire his weapon in the line of duty. He pauses. No, that's not right. He did fire his handgun once.

"It was a head shot, too," he says, not bothering to conceal his pride.

It happened when a meat packing plant caught fire in the late 1960s. The blaze sent burned animals scattering wildly.

Peffer ended up hanging on a fence as two officers chased a charred sow his way.

"Shoot it, shoot it," they screamed. Like *Dirty Harry*, Peffer whipped out his revolver and fired once as the hog bellowed by. The bullet went straight into the suffering animal's brain, dropping it like a side of bacon.

Peffer theatrically blew smoke from the gun barrel and holstered his weapon. "Then I turned off my radio and hid," he says, laughing. "I'd had enough of that."

Humor is one of the reasons for Peffer's popularity. He has an earthy side that probably dates to his days playing drums as a teenager in road shows and strip joints.

His wedding night was marred when he couldn't find a replacement drummer. He had to leave his bride at their new apartment while he backed the two girls who billed themselves as the "Stripping Singing Sisters."

"You can imagine what they did when they found out it was my wedding night," he says.

Peffer and Bitsy have four grown sons. They are still married and good friends, he says, although they have been living apart for several years.

Dealing with his alcohol problems, he adds, is bringing his family closer than they have ever been. Peffer is going to Alcoholics Anonymous meetings a couple of times a week, but working on his sobriety a day at a time.

"Had I made it home that night, I'm not sure it would have ever registered how I was driving," says the man who would have been chief.

"I feel good," he says. "I feel peaceful. Even during my first week of treatment, I knew there would come a time when I would look at that arrest as the best thing that ever happened to me."

Lengthy jail term really brings out ol' time religion

Let me be first to holler "Hallelujah" at James Barstad's conversion to Christianity.

Yes sir, there's nothing like the prospect of growing aged inside four drab prison walls to give a fella one righteous dose of that ol' time religion.

Do I hear an "amen" out there?

Brother Barstool, who snuffed out two unsuspecting souls last Memorial Day weekend, was in a Spokane courtroom the other day to receive 50 years – the stiffest drunken-driving sentence ever.

But before Superior Court Judge Thomas Merryman performed this refreshing judicial slam-dunkectomy, Barstad was allowed to spew Bible verses and proclaim his newfound faith with the screechy zealousness of an Old Testament prophet.

The Reverend Jimmy's rap, however, came off sounding as self-interested as a call for bucks by a televangelist flim-flammer.

In between Scripture passages, Barstad said he feared becoming a victim of "those seeking revenge rather than justice."

Victim?

Time for a Bible lesson, Jimbo.

The Good Savior didn't wipe out two lives at Mission and Hamilton. He was blameless and yet they nailed him to a cross.

Now that's injustice.

Barstad, however, is as guilty as original sin.

Like a drunk firing a pistol into a crowd, he got tanked out of his gourd and then gunned his macho truckster through the intersection with disregard to any humans in his way.

He slaughtered Julie Allen, a 14-year-old North Pines Junior High student on her way home with her mom, who was critically injured in the crash.

He slaughtered Karen Sederholm, a 26-year-old woman who handled lost-baggage claims for Southwest Airlines.

81

For this heinous act he got 50 years.

Barstad should stop complaining and count his blessings. His sentence is still so much more merciful than the cruel fate he meted out to his victims.

Now he's lost his tie-dyed haircut and bad boy attitude and gives interviews about how he wants "to be an inspiration so others won't drink and drive."

"Please, in the name of Jesus, stop running those red lights," Barstad wrote in a letter to *The Spokesman-Review*.

Please. Few things are so predictable and lame as the jailhouse conversion, and I'm sick of hearing from these clowns. Prisons are packed with felons who conveniently find Jesus as they await judgment.

More often than not, like Barstad, they yank out their born-again status as a thinly veiled attempt to mitigate their sentence.

"I know I was bad, judge," they snivel, "but I'm way different now. I got Jesus in my heart."

These frauds sing "I'm a believer" more than the Monkees ever did.

It seems to me that a real Christian would emulate Christ and take his lumps in silence. There's no whining to be found in the story of the crucifixion.

The time to assess the legitimacy of a jailhouse conversion is years after the fact.

Regardless of what anyone thought of Nixon hatchetman Chuck Colson, who went to prison for his dastardly Watergate deeds, nobody can say his turning to Christ was phony baloney.

More than two decades later, Colson still lives a godly life beyond reproach.

Let's see if our pal Barstad's bringing in the sheaves 20 years from now.

Here's hoping he celebrates a Merry Christmas and ushers in the first of many, many, many, many more Happy New Years.

Behind bars, right where he belongs.

Oddsville

Chapter Four

For sale: Spooky South Hill mansion

The mansion on the hill comes with secret panels, hidden passageways, ghosts, buried treasure and a bloody past.

It is where the notorious abortionist, Dr. Rudolph A. Hahn, once lived and played. And worked.

It is where a bullet ended the life of Hahn's young wife, Sylvia. It is where Hahn held wild parties, engaged in druken brawls with his wife and feuded with his neighbors.

To owner Pat Stiley, the dark and sprawling stone house at 2526 East 17th is a fascinating piece of Spokane lore.

"When I was a kid, we used to play in the woods behind the place," said Stiley, a 44-year-old attorney. "We would dare each other to see who would run down and touch what we called the haunted house."

Years later, Stiley would discover that the spooky reputation was well founded.

In 1980, Stiley fulfilled his childhood interest in the Hahn house when he bought it the first day it went on the market. His plan was to restore the estate to full glory, but the job was bigger than he thought and has forced him to sell the three-story house and its four-plus acres.

The asking price is $250,000 and it needs at least $50,000 more in repairs. But whoever buys it will get a lot of history for the dollar.

The story begins in 1916, when Sarah Hecla Smith, recent widow of the chief stockholder of the giant Hecla silver mine, paid $75,000 to have the palatial home built. An old newspaper account and a floor plan in Stiley's possession indicate that

85

at least part of the house was designed by famed Spokane architect Kirtland K. Cutter. It is fitted with gold leaf carvings, mother-of-pearl inlays and beamed ceilings.

Smith divorced her new husband in 1918 and sold the house to druggist William Whitlock. Hahn bought it from Whitlock in 1924.

Hahn was a true eccentric, a man who dressed in flashy clothing but wore bedroom slippers in public. He was 59 when he moved into the house with his second wife, Sylvia, who was 32 years his junior.

Born in Chicago, Hahn came to Spokane in 1899. Here he made a name for himself by racing cars and boats and practicing dubious medicine.

Newspapers would later dub him "the mad doctor," but he wasn't a licensed physician. He was a former barber and portrait painter who had found wealth by administering quackish electro-therapy and performing illegal abortions for the rich.

"Dr. Hahn was somebody high society needed at the time," said Stiley, who has compiled a lot of research on the man. "He was somebody society knew about, paid princely sums to and hobnobbed with. Dr. Hahn didn't make his money servicing the families of the poor."

Not long after moving into the South Hill mansion, Hahn sank $50,000 in landscaping and other touches. Outside, the grounds were filled with Japanese gardens, a swimming pool, ornate statues, fountains and pastoral walkways. Inside, he added secret panels and tunnels presumed to be escape routes – a practical consideration for a man in Hahn's line of work.

On a recent tour, Stiley knocked on a piece of mahogany paneling in the spacious living room. A hollow sound thudded back. "The panel used to be spring loaded so you could open it quickly," he said with a grin. "It's big enough to hide a body in there."

For two decades, Hahn and his home and his troubles were the talk of the town. During the Roaring Twenties, nights were rare when there wasn't a loud party going on, attended by a least 50 people. The well-to-do guest list included flying ace Jimmy Doolittle, who stayed in the house for a week during a 1926 air show.

Hahn let his race horses graze in the front yard. Prohibition meant nothing to the doctor and his wife, who frequented speakeasies and let the liquor flow generously at their parties. During one drunk, it's said that Hahn drove his car into his swimming pool and later had the pool filled with dirt so it wouldn't happen again.

Hahn's love of radio started a neighborhood feud in 1929. After mounting large speakers in the tall pines behind his house, he started booming his radio from early morning to well past midnight.

Complaining neighbors circulated petitions to make him stop. Hahn, a smooth talker, rounded up other neighbors to attest to the radio's healthful and soothing effects. "If they can stop my radio, they can stop them in the houses," railed Hahn to a reporter.

A judge disagreed and Hahn turned his radio off. But he would make headlines many more times.

• In October 1929, Hahn was acquitted of performing an abortion on a 17-year-old.

• In September 1932, Sylvia won a divorce after testifying that Hahn had chased her out of the house with a sword.

• In June 1933, the Hahns remarried. They said their long-distance phone calls to each other were getting too costly.

• In August 1933, they were jailed for being drunk and beating each other. "She's a mighty good girl and a good worker, but she is awfully rough," said Hahn, nursing broken ribs.

• In March 1934, Hahn filed for divorce, claiming he was not physically able to combat Sylvia during her rages. They reconciled within days.

• On May 2, 1940, police found Sylvia, 42, dead in her bedroom. She had been shot in the side of her head. Although an inquest would rule suicide, many believed the doctor had pulled the trigger.

Hahn had previously threatened Sylvia with a gun. The bedroom where she lay was riddled with bullet holes. The door lock had been shot off.

But Hahn explained that the bullets were from target practice. A witness testified that Sylvia had talked of suicide. The doctor was off the hook.

• In January 1945, Hahn was charged with manslaughter when a woman died after getting an abortion. That case was later dropped, but Hahn, 80, was convicted on two other counts of abortion. Because of his age, he was fined $1,000 and put on probation.

A broken man, Hahn sold his dream house for $21,000 and moved to room 503 in the New Madison apartments.

But Dr. R. A. Hahn was not a man to quietly fade away.

• On August 6, 1946, Hahn was found dead in his apartment, a bayonet sticking out of his heart. After an extensive FBI manhunt, an ex-convict named Delbert "Frenchy" Visger (pronounced Vee-jay) was arrested and confessed to killing Hahn during a robbery.

To this day, legends remain about Hahn's wealth. Stiley said he has been visited many times by people who believe Hahn buried thousands in gold on the property. "I've let them check the grounds with metal detectors, but I've never really searched the house."

Then there are the ghostly manifestations that supposedly haunt the place.

The caretakers Stiley has living there say they have heard unexplained noises and seen shadows moving across the walls. The owners before Stiley told him of seeing a woman at the top of the stairs.

Was it Sylvia, wanting to set the record straight about her death?

Sitting at a table in the Hahn house, Stiley laughed at the thought.

"I can't speak to ever seeing any apparitions here. But hearing the stories makes the hairs stand up on the back of my neck. But considering all that has happened here, I guess anything is possible."

Everyone's got a creepy tale about sinister Rock Lake

You can have your Bigfoot, your Loch Ness monster and your unidentified flying objects.

Who needs 'em?

When Homer Dickerson wants to tell a good spooky yarn – the kind that makes the goose bumps do the boogaloo up and down your backbone – he just draws on one of his childhood memories of Rock Lake, without a doubt the creepiest place in the Inland Empire.

"That is a lake with a lot of mysteries," agreed Homer, 61, an affable Cheney plumber who grew up near the stony shores of the cold, murky lake.

Fabled train wrecks, sunken treasure, unexplained disappearances, an elusive underwater creature . . . Not even Homer knows why the lake has fostered so many bizarre tales.

"Oh, there's lots of weird stuff all right. It's just got stories all over hell and I guess I've heard 'em all."

One reason for the bad reputation could be in the seemingly sinister shape this narrow body of water has adopted. Only a half-mile across at its widest, Rock Lake stretches nearly 10 miles, a skeletal finger clawing the northwestern corner of Whitman County.

Another possibility may lie in the fact that the ghostly town of Rock Lake was platted and planned, yet, for some reason, never built.

But Homer says the Indians felt queasy about the place way before the white man moved in.

According to the legend, Indians would camp in the flat area at the lake's foot but would rarely be seen floating about on it. They believed that the lake was home to a leviathan who would think nothing of upending a defenseless canoe and then snack on the inhabitants like they were cheese curls.

One story involved three Indian women who suddenly fell through the bottom of their canoe and disappeared, presumably into the monster's innards.

As the years went by, the Rock Lake monster survived, if not in fact, then certainly in conjecture. Sightings of the log-like sea serpent persist to the point that a recent airline magazine included Rock Lake with the famed Loch Ness as a home for monsters.

Homer chuckles at that.

"Now I spent practically most of my boyhood on the lake and I was never scared of it," he said. "I heard of a farmer who planted sturgeons and I suspect the creature is one of those.

"But my uncle and his friend swear that they stood on a ridge overlooking the lake and saw the thing swimming along. They all swear it's a great big monster."

If creatures don't grab you, perhaps the great Rock Lake train wreck will. Somewhere between 1908 and 1925, as the story goes, a hapless train derailed and sent a couple of boxcars skidding down a steep embankment and into the lake.

The boxcars were filled with brand new Model T Fords that supposedly are still waiting to be found.

A number of diving expeditions have failed to locate this automotive gold mine. So far, no records of the rail companies that used the track can confirm the wreck. Ditto the newspaper's trainwreck file.

Admittedly, though, information from those days is pretty sketchy.

What is verifiable is that this account, like the monster, won't go away. Spokane Public Library employee Nancy Compeau said she gets frequent inquiries from scuba divers seeking historical information on the alleged wreck.

To add to the mystery, the library's Rock Lake files (pause for ghostly organ music) seem to have disappeared just like the Model T's.

Homer doesn't buy the wreck story, either. A more chilling happening, as far as he's concerned, involves the fate of four young men in the spring of 1956.

The men were believed to have been racing each other in two small boats during the night of March 19. Nobody ever pieced together how calamity struck; the bodies were never recovered.

Even that doesn't worry Homer.

Like the hapless Indian women, victims have been known to forever vanish into the icy water that is well over 300 feet deep.

No, what gives Homer the creeps is the weird envelope that arrived at the St. John Post Office a few weeks after the accident. Inside was a detailed drawing that pictured two of the men in the water clinging to their boat while the two others stood watching on shore. No name or address accompanied the odd letter that bore a Coulee City postmark.

It could've been a hoax, but Homer isn't so sure. A third boat was seen on the lake the day of the drowning although no witnesses ever came forward.

Not only that, said Homer, "The drawing showed a duck blind that was on the point. Now you wouldn't know about that unless you were well familiar with the lake."

And so the legends grow.

Even Spokane fisherman Mel Hill has one of his own.

His motorboat once struck a submerged rock and over-turned. Hill said his son and his 8-year-old grandson went into the water and probably would have died of hypothermia had they not been rescued by another boater.

"It was one of those damned freak things that could have ended tragically. I've never been so cold in my life."

Mel said he never saw the rock that sunk him.

"At least I thought it was a rock," he laughed. "Maybe it was the tail of the monster."

Oh, curse! Gypsies jinx entire city

"Thinner," the old Gypsy man whispers, and caresses his cheek, like a lover. Just one word. . . but six weeks later, and 93 pounds lighter, Billy Halleck is more than worried.

— From Stephen King's novel *Thinner*

Feeling a little, shall we say, strange lately?

Bad luck breathing on your bones? Lost any family pets in freak trash-compactor accidents?

If so, there could be a perfectly plausible and scientific explanation.

We're doomed.

Word is out that Spokane's Gypsy community – disgruntled over a June 1986 IRS and police seizure of some $2 million in cash and jewelry – has laid a 50-megaton curse on the city.

That's one Big Mother of a Gypsy curse we're talking about here.

And although lawyers defending the Gypsy leaders have advised them to keep away from the press, accounts of the hoodoo have been passed along through several of their friends and employees.

"I talked to Jimmy (Marks) and he confirmed that a curse has been put on the city," said Chris Tweedy, a longtime friend of the Gypsy family. "He didn't want to say too much about it, though."

Small wonder the Spokane Valley wants to avoid annexation.

Look what happened the last time the Marks clan brought out the whammy. After losing a civil case over the ownership of a bag of gold, Marks and several of his family members got down to business and cast just your teensy run-of-the-mill pox in Judge Richard Ennis' courtroom.

"They told us 'Look behind you because the Gypsy hex will be on you forever,'" recalled the businessman who won the lawsuit.

Then, two days after the state Court of Appeals upheld Ennis' ruling – *TWANTG*! – the judge's $250,000 South Hill home mysteriously burned to the ground.

The cause of the fire was determined to be:

"Mysterious."

Friends close to the Gypsies say the current curse was made shortly after their run-in with law enforcement and tax officials. Since that time, they say, Gypsies have watched the spellbinding string of scandals at the Spokane Police Department – that brought on the early retirement of Chief Robert Panther – with a certain sense of accomplishment.

There was the controversy over the departure of an undercover narcotics detective with an addiction to cocaine, the police corporal fired for collecting explicit evidence photos of sex crime victims, the lewd conduct of officers who hired a stripper, recent accusations of police brutality on members of certain minority groups and the four squad cars that disappeared in a blinding flash.

OK, I'm kidding about that last one. But you add it all up and it looks pretty suspicious.

"It almost looks as if it (the curse) were coming true," said Bob Wilson, a psychologist who has been working with the Gypsies and plans to co-author a book with Jimmy Marks. "But I guess it depends on how superstitious you are."

According to Assistant Police Chief Dick Jorgenson, none of the city's finest are much worried about voodoo. At least, nobody's started clipping good luck charms onto their gun-belts – yet.

"I'm personally not too superstitious," he said. "But I always read my horoscope at the end of the day so I can see if it had any meaning.

"If they have laid a curse on Spokane, though, I hope they laid it on individuals rather than all of us."

Other city officials are maintaining cavalier attitudes.

"My older brother used to tell me that the Gypsies left me on the doorstep when I was a baby," said Mayor Vicki McNeil. "I'm not superstitious, but I pay attention to my gut feeling. I do that."

"I haven't felt cursed, but I've been cursed at," chuckled Assistant City Manager Bill Pupo. "I'm not superstitious, but when I play softball I don't step on the chalk lines, and I always look both ways when I'm driving through intersections."

Likewise, U.S. Attorney John Lamp doesn't want to credit a Gypsy curse with having anything to do with the broken water line that caused thousands of dollars damage to the U. S. Courthouse, including IRS phone lines.

"I don't think I'd better comment on that," he said. "But it was probably just an old pipe."

Just an old pipe? Hah!

We know better than that, don't we?

Actually, when you think about it, having a Gypsy curse hanging over our heads is the best thing that could happen to Spokane. It's the perfect excuse for everything that could possibly go wrong.

"Er, sorry I was late boss, but while I was driving to work this Giant Evil Eye came out of nowhere and . . ."

And what about the potholes, and the Davenport Hotel that won't sell, and Big Time Wrestling coming to the Coliseum?

Or how about the miserable way the Spokane Indians play baseball? If that's not the product of a curse, I'll eat my rabbit's foot.

So you see, there's a positive side to everything.

"You bet," said City Councilman Dick Gos. "I was aware of the curse on the city and I'm glad to see that the Gypsies are willing to take credit for some of these problems.

"Nobody else has wanted to."

Psychics discover bald spot in aura of columnist

And now for the latest news from the Great Beyond:

My insides are swimming with magic plankton, the inventor of something called "The Pod" wants to use my forehead for advertising space and there appears to be a disturbing hole in my aura.

I found all this out Saturday inside the Body, Mind, Spirit and Earth Expo at the Spokane Convention Center – a sort of K-mart for the cosmic consumer.

Here are booths that boast the most powerful woman in the world, a man who photographs nature spirits, crystals to ward off the dangers of fluorescent lights, fortune tellers, healers, palm readers and, of course, the Jerry Brown for president booth.

"We're sort of the political speed bump here," says Michael Watson, co-director of the local Brown for president campaign.

Well, they didn't call Brown "Governor Moonbeam" for nothing.

But enough about one of our nation's leading airheads. Let's talk about bigger concerns, such as electromagnetic energy directly above the bald spot.

This hole in the Doug-zone was revealed after I had a photograph of my aura taken. "I see some growth going on, but it's sure not hair," says JoAnne Ward, who took one look at my photo and broke into a fit laughter.

My concern is that every other aura photo I examined shows the subject positively shimmering with brightly colored light. JoAnne's auragraph, for example, is lit up like a Chinese New Year. She is surrounded by an impressive and intense white brilliance.

"It means I'm a highly evolved person," explains JoAnne.

I guess we can all figure out what that makes me. Fortunately, for those of us with non-evolved, Cro-Magnon auras, there is help a few booths away.

Yes, I'm talking about the wonders of MOLDAVITE.

According to Pamela Barclay, Moldavite, which naturally looks like dirty glass from a broken Seven-Up bottle, came from space 14.8 million years ago and landed in Czechoslovakia.

Nobody knows what the Czechoslovakians of yore thought of this. But a hunk of it ($5 a gram) is said to be a sure-fire aura boost. There are some side effects, however.

Pamela says she gave a piece to her left-brained friend David, who was an accountant for the government. Not long after carrying the Moldavite, she says, David's job became intolerable and he had to quit.

So Pamela started hauling Moldavite and guess what? She had to quit her job, too.

To test this theory, I bought a sliver of Moldavite for $7.56 and put it in my back pocket. So if my column suddenly disappears from this newspaper, we'll know Moldavite really works.

As you can probably tell, I'm a bit skeptical when it comes to the purveyous of the paranormal. I'll become a believer the day I see a headline that reads: "Psychic Wins Lottery."

But I wasn't the only one who managed to wade through all this telepathic residue. "Just in the booths I've passed, I figure it'd cost me 2000 bucks to become a more complete person," says Lee Manning of West Richland.

Manning came to Spokane for the event with his girlfriend, Darlene Tracy, who is a believer. "There is so much more to what we can see and feel and touch and taste," she says.

Especially when the taste we're talking about is a nice juicy glass of spirulina, the magic blue-green plankton. Yech!

Lisa Spector, at the spirulina booth, sold me a 25-cent gulp of her powdered plankton drink she claims is a miracle food. "It's made me a better person. You may be beyond help."

Doug abuse seems to be rampant at the Body, Mind, Spirit and Earth Expo.

Gordon Wendlandt, for instance, poked a finger into my fatty mid-section and said, "I used to have one like that." Then he tried to sell me some tea to help unclog my intestines.

A little later, Dick Meden, inventor of a $500 hanging cage/chair he calls "The Pod," invited me to sit in his contraption. When I did, he threatened to write the word "specimen" across my forehead if I fell asleep.

This all goes to prove that making your way through the powerful forces of the unknown is a long and dangerous journey. Only my incredible inner strength let me live to tell the tale.

Ouch! I just sat on my Moldavite.

Spirit warrior wreaks havoc on woman's life

She had a lovely home on the South Hill, a good career as a middle school English teacher and a comfortable marriage to a professional man.

Then a friend one day invited the soft-spoken Spokane woman to watch "an exciting" New Age videotape.

That, says Betty Nunnery, was the start of how she lost her piece of the American Dream to a 35,000-year-old spirit warrior from Atlantis named Ramtha.

Between January 1985 and August 1989, Nunnery says she was sucked ever deeper into the bizarre world of J. Z. Knight – a Yelm, Washington, medium who channels Ramtha to anyone who can pay her steep fees.

Nunnery paid dearly.

Believing Ramtha's teachings were her only hope, she says she quit her job, divorced her husband and spent thousands on at least 27 of Knight's channeling sessions, tapes, literature and travel expenses.

"I sacrificed everything for Ramtha," Nunnery says sadly. "My husband, my savings, my retirement fund, my house, my self-esteem. It cost me my emotional and mental health."

The middle-aged woman pauses a second and adds in a frail, halting voice, "I think it was psychological terrorism."

Now trying to rebuild her shattered life, Nunnery realizes she could never recover a fraction of what she gave up. Getting back some of her money would be a good start.

A lawsuit filed in May 1993 in Thurston County contends Knight's "fraudulent and unlawful conduct" compelled the Spokane woman to throw away all she held dear. The action was amended later, adding criminal racketeering to Nunnery's claims against the channeler.

In a statement issued by her Puyallup attorney, Knight vehemently denies the allegations.

"I want the public to know and understand that I categorically deny being involved in violations of any law, let alone racketeering," says Knight, "and that I intend to aggressively defend these preposterous charges."

Nunnery isn't the first to call into question the phenomenon at Knight's $3 million, 50-acre ranch compound in Yelm.

"I'm convinced there is some kind of mass hypnosis going on," stated Carl Raschke, a University of Denver religion professor, in a 1986 *Time* magazine story on Knight and her channeling.

Knight, a former cable TV executive, has told reporters that Ramtha first spoke through her in 1977 while she was experimenting with crystal pyramids.

She moved to Yelm in 1983 and received a cosmic boost by being mentioned in Shirley MacLaine's best-selling autobiography, *Dancing in the Light.*

Knight says her multimillion-dollar enterprise is an emerging religion. Over the years, hundreds of her followers – dubbed "Ramsters" by cynical locals – have immigrated to Yelm. Among them is Linda Evans of TV's *Dynasty* fame.

When Nunnery viewed the videotape in 1984, she glimpsed what Ramsters pay between $400 to $1,500 to see: Knight as human conduit for Ramtha, spouting platitudes and messages from beyond in a husky transcendental voice.

Already a believer in metaphysics, Nunnery "felt a tremendous amount of love and concern for humanity" in Ramtha.

In January 1985, she decided to experience the spirit warrior first-hand. That workshop led to another in April and another in May.

But Nunnery says it was the July seminar in Phoenix, where Ramtha predicted her death before 1990, that caused her undoing.

"That was just a disaster to me, just incomprehensible. But I believed this person so much; I didn't doubt it."

With a death sentence hanging over her head, Nunnery says she lost focus. Ramtha became the center of her universe, and she began to rid herself of everything else: friends, family, career . . .

Then 1990 came and went. Betty Nunnery began to emerge from the haze. She found herself destitute and alone.

The shame and the guilt have, at times, overwhelmed her. Nunnery still finds it difficult to express anger at anyone but herself.

She's getting wiser, though.

"I can see now that my mind became so bent that I failed to see what I was giving up," she says. "I hope whoever reads this will see that we don't need psychics to tell us the truth."

Professor hopes to turn Bigfoot into big profit

To heck with catching Bigfoot.

I'd rather catch the big groans coming from Washington State University academics and administrators when they learn their Professor Sasquatch is making news again.

He is Grover Krantz, instructor of anthropology at WSU.

To the university's dubious distinction, Krantz also is the nation's most accredited scientist to openly embrace Bigfoot as something more than a hairy Northwest legend.

Bigfoot and Elvis sightings have been depressingly off lately, but Krantz has embarked on a novel way to put the giant apeman back on top.

Attention Christmas shoppers! Get ready for the ultimate in size 25 triple-E stocking stuffers: The Bigfoot Collection.

Collaborating with a Kennewick artist, Krantz is peddling genuine mounted reproductions of plaster Bigfoot tracks.

This is basically the same concept as the jackalope – those antlered rabbits hung up in North Idaho bars – only a lot prettier and more expensive.

"The Cripple," for example, is a beautifully framed set of two tracks allegedly made by a physically challenged Bigfoot. Price – $350.

For $295, you can buy "Patterson 1." This is from the historic actual cast taken by Bigfoot hunter Roger Patterson. The 16mm movie filmed by the Yakima man is one of the Holy Grails of sasquatchery.

Patterson and a pal supposedly were searching for Bigfoot in Northern California when – surprise, surprise – they stumbled onto one.

Patterson fell off his horse, grabbed his camera and – perhaps after helping his friend climb into a gorilla suit – shot some amazingly incoherent and fuzzy footage. So blurry is the film that the woolly figure could be either Jerry Garcia or an ungroomed mastiff.

The plaster cast was made after the beast had shambled away. Or maybe after the two had caught their breath from laughing about the big hoax they were pulling.

"I think there's a market for this," says Lori Morey, the artist who convinced Krantz to hawk his Shaq-sized footprints.

Those not flush enough for a wall hanging can get a Bigfoot coffee mug ($7.95) or T-shirt ($12.95-$15.95) or Krantz's book *Bigfoot Prints* ($14.95).

Weird science for fun and profit.

Since the 1960s, Krantz has tried to legitimize the elusive Bigfoot with the stubborn conviction of Captain Ahab hunting Moby Dick.

"A belief is an opinion held because it makes you feel good," says Krantz. "Once I decided (they) were real, I never wavered."

This stuff seems pretty danged deranged to me.

Krantz claims there are as many as 2,000 seven-foot-tall, 800-pound creatures lumbering within the tall timbers of the Pacific Northwest.

Maybe they are great at hiding. But where are the mountainous piles these brutes surely would leave?

Someone should have stepped in some. The forests practically are crawling these days with hunters and hikers and loggers and tree-spiking environmentalist psychopaths.

Most of Richard Clear's radio talk show listeners live in tunnels deep in the woods.

They always are telephoning Richard to report federal black helicopters and battalions of United Nations soldiers who are training in secret to take us over.

Yet none of these unwashed hillfolk is yammering about Bigfoot.

I find this significant. By now, a Bigfoot should have been captured, taken to Portland and given a huge shoe deal by Nike.

The sad fact, however, is that even so-called Bigfoot experts disagree on these things.

Canadian Rene Dahinden, who dumped his wife to trail sasquatch, accused Krantz of using his professorship to "promote and glorify himself and his wild, unbalanced ideas."

Krantz says Dahinden is just plain mean. Besides, he adds, he will cut off this footprint-marketing scheme should publicity become too wild.

Professor Sasquatch has his standards. He is, after all, a man of science.

Body bags? Squeamish he's not

Most of you haven't met Ray Corkrum. Yet.

Hang around Spokane long enough and odds are there'll come a day when this soft-spoken, pleasant man will drive up and, well, get to know you.

Ray runs a most unusual escort service. His job is one probably 99.9 percent of the population couldn't perform.

Ray Corkrum picks up dead bodies.

Murders. Suicides. AIDS. Deaths by natural causes. Deaths by accidents. Deaths by dismemberment. Deaths by car wreck, plane crash, hit-and-run . . .

From the quiet, almost blissful passing of the elderly to the most vile, bloodsoaked homicide scenes, this 51-year-old man encounters practically every way there is to check out of this mortal motel.

Last week, Ray passed a personal milestone, picking up his 6,500th, er, client.

"Of course, that's just since I started counting," he says. "I was working a few years before I decided to keep track." Ray is an independent contractor on call for every funeral home in the Spokane area.

It's his job to go where someone has died and load the remains carefully into the back of one of his inconspicuous station wagons. He owns blue and tan wagons, each equipped with the necessities of his trade: body bags, stretchers, plastic sheets, rubber gloves, disinfectant . . .

The trip ends when the body arrives at the proper mortuary or morgue. Then Ray waits for the next call.

His brother, Ron, often helps. But Ray is available 24 hours a day, seven days a week.

Although death is a squeamish subject for most, there's nothing ghoulish or macabre about Ray Corkrum. He is actually a gentle soul who believes the service he provides is more for the living than the dead.

"I enjoy working with families the most," says Ray, who always wears a suit and tie to make a good impression. "Being able to help people in their most devastating time is very satisfying."

Ray is paid $40 for each body he transports. Considering death never takes a holiday, the man obviously does quite well.

But there must be more to this than mere money. Why else would a man endure constant interruptions?

"He has the patience of Job," says Jack Riggins of Riplinger's Funeral Home. "We keep expecting him to drop. There are nights when he doesn't sleep."

When your life revolves around death, leisure becomes an alien concept. On a recent Friday, for example, Ray made six runs after midnight. "Maybe it was seven," he adds. "I'll have to check my book."

Last Christmas, as youngsters tore into their presents, Ray's pager sounded and he was off.

Ray went to see *Forrest Gump* recently. He bought some popcorn and found a seat. Thirty minutes into the movie, his pager went off.

On August 1, he took his wife, Michelle, to Patsy Clark's restaurant to celebrate their first anniversary. After dinner they took a romantic stroll in the park across the street.

Guess what happened.

Fortunately, Michelle Corkrum understands. She should. She is a trained embalmer.

In fact, Ray met his second wife "over the embalming table," she explains. "He used to bring the bodies in and we got to know each other."

She often accompanies Ray on his journeys. "If I didn't, we'd never see each other," she says with a laugh.

It's difficult even for Ray to pin down what led him into this line of work. For 28 years he had a good job with an auto parts firm. He supplemented his income painting cars in his spare time.

About 11 years ago, he says friends who worked in funeral homes told him about the "first-call" business.

He gave it a try, availing himself on nights and weekends. His first trip was to a plane crash to recover the body of a pilot who had burned beyond recognition.

Ray discovered he had the constitution to handle such trauma. "It doesn't bother me because I realize there is nothing I can do for that person."

Almost two years ago, Ray quit his auto parts job to pursue "first-call" full time. Oddly enough, being bombarded by death has given the man perspective.

"I pick up so many people who are younger than me, well, it makes you think," he says. "You just don't want to waste a minute."

Bonded, licensed psychic friend can lift city curse

The first sorceress member of the Spokane Area Chamber of Commerce says she can lift the Gypsy curse hanging over our heads before we all turn into frogs.

For just $7,500, Susan Johnson vows to end a decade of bad vibes that began after Spokane police raided a Gypsy leader's home in 1986 and seized $2 million in cash and jewels. Angry Gypsies responded by conjuring up a 50-megaton curse that they plopped on the city.

"You should see results within 24 hours of paying me," says Johnson, 44, a South Side resident who claims to have been a wizard in some of her past lives.

I found Johnson's name in the new members section of the May issue of *Your Chamber in Action* newsletter. The woman's otherworldly occupation leaped off the page like a flying monkey.

Calling herself the "Sorceress of Help," she specializes in the "psychic uncursing and protection business." I'm not a superstitious guy, but that sounds like the medicine Spokane needs.

We've been afflicted with spellbinding misfortune that is far too lengthy to chronicle other than a few memorable lowlights:

• The fire storm. The ice storm. The worst outbreak of crater-sized potholes since the bombing of London.

• Embarrassment struck City Hall when Mayor Jack Geraghty was found in contempt for failing to make support payments to his estranged wife.

• Two words: Dexter Amend.

What's next on the Lilac City's hoodoo horizon – flesh-eating locusts?

I say we pony up the $7,500 and take our chances. Besides, Johnson offers a 30-day money back guarantee, plus a 100-year warranty.

Try to buy a new car with those terms.

Paying $280 to join the Chamber, Johnson says she also registered with the Better Business Bureau. "I want to lessen the fear that would keep people from trusting me," she says. "I know how many people view psychics."

Johnson is a sorceress for the high-tech '90s.

In the upstairs office of her modest home, a Ouija board and crystal ball share a desk with a computer and fax machine. A framed Chamber of Commerce membership certificate hangs on a wall.

She's developed a special blend of incense and incantation to remove even the most stubborn curses. She will also de-haunt a house for 10 percent of the home's value.

Most of us would rather live with a ghost than shell out that kind of money, but Johnson's fee for removing the Gypsy curse strikes me as a bargain.

A still-unresolved civil rights lawsuit the Gypsies have waged against Spokane for the last 10 years has nicked taxpayers for an untold bundle in legal costs. Without giving an exact figure, city attorney Jim Sloane confirmed the bill is way more than $7,500.

Probably another quarter-million of our money was recently flushed down the privy by the U. S. attorney's office. On Friday, bonehead Feds failed to convict snarling Gypsy activist Jimmy Marks and his witless cronies for allegedly intimidating relatives who are witnesses for the city in the aforementioned civil rights suit.

We must end this Gypsy curse before it breaks us, but our leaders don't have the smarts to call on the Sorceress of Help.

"I absolutely have no comment on this," says City Manager Bill Pupo, between strangled laughter. "But if you're on the street corner soliciting donations, I may drop off a quarter."

Pupo could be right. Perhaps we need to start a grass-roots fund drive and raise Johnson's fee ourselves.

Is anyone out there willing to open a trust account? If everyone gave a quarter, we could get this done. Any extra money will go straight to the Mayor's Alimony Fund.

Imagine what a wonderful life we will all live in an uncursed Spokane:

The Davenport Hotel will reopen. The potholes will fill. Downtown will become a thriving retail mecca. Area grass burners will spontaneously combust. Bloomsday will move to another city . . .

Who knows? With no curse hanging over our heads, I may start growing hair.

Heroes

Chapter Five

Stand-in soldier saluted: Man went to Vietnam in friend's place

He dodged bullets during the Vietnam War in place of a frightened pal who hid out back home.

It always sounded wild, but Paul Mahar never wavered from his incredible story that I first wrote about in 1988.

Today, the U. S. Army believes him.

"I earned my gray hair over this, that's for sure," says Mahar, a 46-year-old Coeur d'Alene man.

Although not endorsing the deception, a military panel ruled last month this stand-in soldier served his country with honor and distinction for 406 days in 1966 and 1967.

"In fact, considering (Mahar's) lack of formal preparation, his performance as an infantryman in combat was extraordinary," wrote the military brass.

It took the army two years to reach the conclusion that Paul Mahar served in Vietnam as Frank Clouse, Jr. I knew Mahar wasn't lying in 1988, after a brief telephone call to Clouse, the friend who stayed home.

"If he said he did (it), then he did it," said the New Jersey man. "I have no other comment."

The reaction was typical of Clouse, says Mahar.

"He was always afraid, weaseling his way out of things as kids," says Mahar. "It's almost an ostrich thing, keeping his head buried in the sand."

It began in the fall of 1966, when Mahar says he and Clouse were just "two nutty kids" growing up together in New Jersey.

After high school Mahar was declared ineligible for the draft because of a steel pin in his arm. The pin was there thanks to Clouse, who Mahar says accidentally broke his arm while the two were wrestling on a street corner.

Clouse was drafted, did his basic training and was ordered to Vietnam as a combat infantryman.

He was scared beyond belief. On leave after boot camp, Clouse went absent without leave for six weeks. Mahar decided to help pull his agitated buddy out of the fire.

The idea was for Mahar to pose as his best friend and use the bum arm to win Clouse a medical discharge.

The two teenagers falsified the height and weight descriptions on a form. Mahar cut his hair, put on the uniform and headed to Fort Dix, New Jersey, where he told officers he had lost his military ID card.

Sympathy, however, was in short supply in those bloody days. Clouse's AWOL status ruined the plan, says Mahar. "The Army didn't want to hear anything I had to say."

Mahar was told to choose between jail and Vietnam. That's how an untrained kid became a member of the 2nd Battalion, 27th Infantry.

His debut as a soldier was an understandable embarrassment, but the possibility of dying is a terrific motivator. Mahar learned fast and eventually was promoted to sergeant.

His proudest moment came on January 14, 1967, when he helped save a fellow soldier from drowning in the Saigon River.

A small boat capsized in the swift, deep current. Mahar and his platoon leader dived in and pulled the struggling man to safety.

The Army Commendation Medal was awarded – in Clouse's name, of course.

"In a way, because I was so terrible at first, I had to prove myself to the others," explains Mahar. "I couldn't just be somebody in the back."

Wanting overdue recognition for his service, Mahar asked the Army to investigate his claim in 1991. Hand-writing samples and dental records convinced a five-member board of review.

An Army spokesman said he had never seen such an unusual case. Because of the statute of limitations, it's unlikely either man will be prosecuted.

Soon Mahar will have the documentation due a soldier: a military file, an honorable discharge, citations . . . .

"I didn't do Frank any favors," says Mahar, an unemployed wood worker who recently finished a book on the ID switch. "Living with this over the years must have been hell for him."

Returning from Vietnam in December 1967, Mahar gave Clouse everything connected to his military service.

The war that divided a nation did the same for Mahar and Clouse. It turned one into a hero, the other into something else. They never again would be friends.

Mahar, however, has no regrets.

"I belonged over there, in Vietnam," he says. "It's hard to describe the bonding of men at war. It's a major feeling of the human spirit."

Spokane boy's years of suffering did a world of good

The name Bruce Bryer doesn't mean much to Spokane right now, but just wait. History is about to give this remarkable person his due.

He died on December 26, 1983, after 17 years of a life filled with too much pain and too many trips to the doctor. But if there is any justice left in this world, Bruce Bryer will be remembered as one of our greatest heroes: a sickly boy whose legacy helped cure the deadliest form of muscular dystrophy and untold thousands of lives.

A sufferer of Duchenne muscular dystrophy, an almost exclusively male disease, Bruce submitted tissue and blood samples that led to a remarkable discovery in 1987. Scientists found that the basic defect in muscles affected by the disease is the lack of a protein called dystrophin.

Researchers announced that they have reached another milestone in understanding the role dystrophin plays in Duchenne, which has afflicted between 20,000 and 50,000 American boys.

"The cure could be happening right now or in six months; they're that close," said Arlen Calhoun of Spokane's office of the Muscular Dystrophy Association. "The saddest part is that Bruce died never knowing that they had isolated the gene. But because of him, the course of history has been changed."

Bruce's contribution to medical science has already been trumpeted in a medical journal as one of the most spectacular discoveries of the decade. *The Wall Street Journal* compared it to the invention of polio vaccine. Last February's edition of *Reader's Digest* headlined Bruce as "One Boy in a Million." Scientists say other cures for neuromuscular diseases such as cystic fibrosis and multiple sclerosis could come as a result of the Duchenne breakthrough.

But it all began in Spokane on the shakiest of foundations. On November 21, 1966, Bruce came into the world at Sacred Heart Medical Center, and everybody knew something was terribly wrong.

Unwanted by his mother, Bruce was immediately put up for adoption. The infant's head was too large. Doctors suspected brain damage and more.

Laurene and Robert Dixon, veteran foster parents, agreed to care for Bruce although they were continually warned that the frail child would probably not live long.

"The first few years were really bad, he was such a sick child," said Laurene. "But we've loved all the children and Bruce was no different. You can't keep a child an hour without getting attached."

Were it not for the nourishing environment provided by the Dixons, who can say what would have happened to Bruce? The Dixons' unconditional love for children is known statewide. Governor Booth Gardner gave the couple an award commemorating their 47 years as foster parents caring for some 450 children.

"You could never prove it scientifically," wrote Stephen Hall in *Hippocrates* magazine, "but it's nice to think that all that affection helped to keep Bruce Bryer alive long enough for doctors to discover his secret."

Bruce's medical problems were enormous.

He had chronic granulomatous, a rare inherited disease that keeps the body's immune system from fighting infection. He had McLeod blood type, which causes anemia and makes a transfusion a potentially fatal procedure. He had retinitis pigmentosa, an eye disorder that invariably leads to blindness.

And he had Duchenne muscular dystrophy, which over time devours the muscle cells and confines its victims to a wheelchair and a short life that requires constant care.

Yet despite all of his difficulties, Bruce Bryer lived a happy life. He always had a smile and joke to tell. He was the MDA's national poster child when he was 8 and always expressed the desire to help others.

It was that last characteristic, said Laurene, that kept Bruce going to the University of Washington Medical Center, where he allowed researchers to explore his unusual condition. His combination of genetic problems made him the perfect candidate for study.

"Bruce had four abnormalities," immunologist Hans Ochs told *In Health* magazine, "and the only link was that all were inheritable."

Unfortunately, Bruce would never enjoy the results of his generosity. On Christmas night 1983, a car ran a red light and Robert Dixon swerved his van to avoid a collision. Bruce, a passenger in the van, slipped out of his wheelchair.

He appeared to be unhurt, but the Dixons knew only too well how fragile their foster son's condition was. "I think it was the trauma of the accident that was just too much for him," said Laurene. "We took him to the hospital and about an hour later he started having difficulty breathing. We just lost him."

Long before he died, Bruce had made sure that his eyes would go to researchers to help find a cure for retinitis pigmentosa.

"The way we feel about it, the Lord just decided it was Bruce's time," said Laurene. "He was a very special child."

Age takes no toll on Belle

Cystoscope. Resectoscope. Syringe. Catheter . . .

In operating rooms at Sacred Heart Medical Center, Belle McGuire is like the center who snaps into action at a quarterback's command.

She is a certified surgical technician in the Spokane hospital's urology department. The job is high stress and rocket-paced. Incompetence or confusion can't be tolerated.

Doctors describe Belle as the best at what she does, a tireless perfectionist who arrives at 6:20 a.m., five days a week. Year in. Year out.

It's easy to forget that Belle McGuire is 80 years old.

"If we ever get to cloning humans, here's one we should clone," says Dr. Chad Baxter, a pediatric surgeon who worked with Belle from 1963 until he retired in 1987.

"I don't know of anybody working in surgery at that age at any hospital. At any time. Anywhere."

Belle is a rarity in a world where retirement at 65 is so often the rule. At Sacred Heart, there is no magic day when an employee suddenly becomes too old to keep. Though a few other post-retirement age people work at the hospital, Belle is a one-of-a-kind wonder.

"She's in better shape than people half her age," says urologist Dr. Michael Henneberry, who works with her whenever he can. "There's no reason for her not to work."

Belle takes part in as many as five surgeries a day. She preps patients, mixes dyes and watches over the equipment like a mother hen. A zealot for cleanliness, she personally sterilizes every instrument.

During operations, her deft, practiced hands make sure the right tool reaches the surgeon's fingertips at precisely the right moment.

"Keeping your mind occupied keeps a person young," says Belle, who is off work, but still wearing blue surgical "scrubs" when I visit her at Sacred Heart.

Belle is small and trim. She moves with loose-jointed ease and really doesn't look that much different than the way I remember her.

I've known Belle all my life or roughly about half of hers. The McGuires' tidy white house was a few doors away from where I grew up in a working-class South Hill neighborhood.

My mother tells me that at age 6, I announced I would never live with Belle and her husband, Earl. The house, I said, was "too antiseptic."

Belle was reared on a cattle ranch where staying clean took determination. Every night, she scrubbed away the grime by bathing in a wash tub.

Life was hard. She rose at dawn to milk cows and then rode a horse nine miles to school.

During Prohibition, bootleggers running whiskey from Canada to Spokane paid Belle's father to bunk at his ranch 18 miles west of Republic, Washington. When they left, Belle would herd cattle over the dirt roads, obscuring the tracks of the rumrunners' caravan.

She is a woman from a bygone era, a time when the work ethic, not leisure, was the dominant force in American culture. Belle managed a gas station, cooked in a restaurant, cleaned houses and spent years lugging cases of beer in a Spokane brewery.

In the late 1950s, she went to work at Sacred Heart as a nurse's helper for 50 cents an hour. She was trained to assist surgery and eventually became a fixture in the urology department. Since her husband's death in 1978, Belle has lived with daughter, JoAnn, and son-in-law, Don Bearden.

"You have to be on the ball to work with her," explains Ann Baker, a Sacred Heart clinician. "You get in the way, you get run over."

How long can she continue? As long as she passes regular physicals and does her job, the hospital doesn't care if she's 105.

"Let's be honest. I don't think about my age, but naturally I can't go on forever," says Belle. "Lord willing, I'll stay here a bit longer. When you love your job, it doesn't seem like work."

[Update: Belle finally retired in 1997 at age 82.]

In this family kids come first

They don't give medals for what Ed and Kathryn Parry have done, and that's a shame. This Spokane couple deserve some kind of award or at least a paid vacation.

Next time you're balancing your checkbook and feel sorry for yourself, consider this: The Parrys just put their 12th and final kid through college.

Mary Elizabeth Parry, 22, will graduate in the spring from Gonzaga University with a degree in business administration.

"I think the people at the college are probably sorry we don't have any more kids," says Ed with a chuckle.

No kidding. Having the Parry kids around must have seemed like an automatic endowment program.

The good Jesuits at Gonzaga hit the jackpot by getting to educate 11 Parrys. The University of Idaho got one Parry – John, who graduated with a degree in electrical engineering in 1982.

When I heard about this family, I called Ed to congratulate him. He did his best to go through the lineup.

Let's see, I've got four engineers, two CPAs, a bookkeeper, one has a master's in French, two business school grads. Wait a minute. I'm leaving somebody out. Let me think again."

Who could blame him for being perplexed? Even by today's high educational standards, the Parrys' accomplishment is extraordinary.

In Spokane County roughly half the adult population has ever started college and only 21 percent has finished with a bachelor's degree.

But in the Parry household, studying hard was a part of the daily regimen.

"It's something we always told the kids, that homework came first," says Kathryn. "They learned early on that school was their career."

How much it cost is one mystery Ed doesn't want solved. "I don't even want to begin to calculate it."

It's not hard to use your imagination. GU's annual tuition is $13,000, not including books or food.

But that's only part of it. The Parrys, who are Catholics, also sent all of their kids to parochial schools. At one point, Ed says, they had four at the university, four at Gonzaga Prep and four at St. Al's grammar school.

A ton of tuition.

"We kept wondering if they were going to give us a free one, but they never did," he says.

Ed is an attorney and no doubt makes a comfortable income. Even so, paying this kind of educational tab takes organization and discipline.

Raising eight girls and four boys is not recommended for the weak-willed either.

The Parrys live in a big yellow house on the South Hill. A selling point when they bought the place was a cavernous bathroom with four sinks, two toilets and a walk-in shower with three shower heads.

The older kids were expected to help out. Each year, the senior in high school was responsible for driving the others to school in the Parrys' old red station wagon.

"They called it the 'Parry school bus,'" says Kathryn. "We ought to have it enshrined."

Dinners, she says, always were entertaining. "We thought it was important for them to learn how to run a household. We rotated chores. Everyone helped out."

Kathryn and Ed can't fully explain why they decided to have such a huge family. Each came from families of only three children. "We just like kids," he says.

The Parrys met in the second grade in Los Angeles, but it wasn't love at first sight. Ed moved away and then returned as an eighth grader. He was "a very gentlemanly boy," recalls Kathryn, not as "rough-and-tumble as the others."

During World War II, Ed and Kathryn worked as assistant air-raid wardens, walking the streets to make sure houses were dark in case any Japanese bombers flew over.

Somewhere during their times together, they fell in love and decided to raise one whale of a family of well-educated kids.

"I don't want a medal," says Kathryn. "I just wish more parents understood the importance of their children – that they come first."

He fought death with courage, wisecracks

Mark Busse, 18, didn't want the typical chin-dragging-in-the-dirt funeral.

No sappy crying, he told his parents as he neared the end. No sissy flowers.

If not, "I'll have to come punch your lights out," he added in his trademark way of using a wisecrack to take the sting out of a bad moment.

What Mark wanted was for everyone to be filled with joyous memories.

Memories of a young man who idolized basketball star Michael Jordan. Memories of a once-energetic kid who reacted with cocky optimism and a mischievous half-grin after life dealt him a lousy hand.

Mark's battle with lung cancer made international headlines in 1993 after his Reardan High School pals shaved their heads in a show of support.

He died at his home west of Spokane in the early hours of a September morning in 1995. True to form, Mark fought death as if it were game seven of an NBA championship.

His ravaged lungs laboring for each breath, he turned to his sister, Jill, 20.

"You think I'm getting better? I think I am," Mark said, pausing a moment to add, "It could happen."

Twenty minutes later he was gone.

"Nothing kept him down," said his mother, Bonnie, a teacher at Spokane's Salk Middle School. "He loved life. He did the most he could. He didn't want to die."

Although in the final stage of a terminal disease, Mark ignored the pain and tried to cram a lifetime into his last summer.

He played in Spokane's Hoopfest basketball tournament. He water-skied. He drag-raced the jet-black '68 Camaro given him by the Wishing Star Foundation.

Mark commemorated his 18th birthday with his first trip to a casino. He began his senior year and, though barely able to stand, attended a football game a week before he died.

"I don't think we'll ever know what he really went through," said Bonnie Long, Reardan High's athletic director who was Mark's confidant at school.

"He never griped about his cancer. His philosophy was, 'Suck it up and do it.'"

That tenacious spirit won him legions of fans.

Consider that more than 800 people attended his memorial Thursday in Reardan, a farm town with a population of just 525.

The service was held not in a chapel, but appropriately on the school's old basketball court where Mark worked on his jump shot and warred against rival schools.

Despite his wishes, there was a flower or two and more than a few tears as Mark's loved ones bid him a deeply moving farewell.

"A soul like that will always live on," said Abayomi "A.J." Adejokun, a family friend. "He was like a beautiful rose walking by."

Calling Mark his hero, Tim Busse, 24, offered a raw glimpse of the daily turmoil his younger brother quietly endured. "I'd hear him puking his guts out in the bathroom," he said.

"The toilet would flush. The door would open and there'd be Mark, a little pale, but with this look of determination on his face. He'd say, 'C'mon, Bud, let's go play some ball.'"

Mark's courage was fueled by a gang of amazing friends who never deserted him.

Diagnosed with a rare, inoperable cancer in the fall of 1993, Mark began chemotherapy that made his hair fall out. He worried about going to school bald.

He had little to fear. Mark and five of his closest buddies gathered at a house one Sunday night and took turns shaving each other's head.

"I really appreciate this," Mark said at the time. "When I told my friends they didn't have to do this, Josh (Jenkin) said, 'Shut up. I'm first.'"

The Mr. Clean look quickly caught on. Soon the halls of Reardan High were bobbing with smooth, round symbols of support.

Mark's story broke in this column and was quickly carried all over the world. The Busses were flooded with calls. Mark was asked to appear on TV talk shows, but he declined, saying the media needed to "get a life."

The Friday before he died, Mark called his gang together one last time.

"The room was full," said Mark's father, Larry, an East Valley School District administrator. "He joked, said goodbye and then asked everybody to come shake his hand."

They did, "but nobody would leave."

Mark looked at his weeping pals. He realized it was time to take the sting out of yet another bad moment.

"Aw, don't be such a wuss," he scolded them, flashing that half-grin. "If you're not gonna leave, sit down. Let's watch some TV."

Quadriplegic an inspiration to all she meets

Fifteen years ago, a wheelchair-bound Appellate Court judge visited the bedside of a paralyzed Spokane teenager he'd read about in the newspaper.

He urged the girl to get out of bed and get on with life. She could achieve great things, he said, if she'd only try.

Ben McInturff never realized how seriously Holly Caudill would take his words.

On June 15, 1995, McInturff came out of retirement to help Caudill make a bit of history. The former judge will take part in the swearing-in ceremony as Caudill becomes what is believed to be the nation's first female quadriplegic attorney.

Caudill, 32, passed the bar in May. U.S. Attorney General Janet Reno added a Spokane staff position to hire Caudill as a full-time assistant U.S. Attorney.

"Most girls dream about wedding gowns and vows," says Caudill. "My dream has also included tailored suits, courtrooms and independence."

This is a woman who can't scratch her nose. She can't pick up a telephone or brush her teeth. The most routine chores of life – everything – must be done for her.

It's been that way since a car wreck snapped her neck like a twig. Yet Caudill stubbornly defies her debilitating condition.

"She's a miracle girl," adds McInturff, who knows all about overcoming physical disabilities. The former judge lost use of his legs and left arm to polio. He was the first wheelchair graduate at Gonzaga University's School of Law.

Caudill, he says, is something else. "I don't know of anyone who has gone through all she has and accomplished so much."

Finding enough superlatives to describe Caudill is difficult, but I'll put it this way: She is, without exception, my hero.

In 20 years of journalism I've never encountered a more soul-stirring example of the human spirit than this charming, determined woman.

Caudill's severely retarded brother died when she was four. Her mother killed herself when Caudill was 10.

At 13, she was a cute, athletic girl whose life forever changed on April 23, 1977.

It happened during a ride home with her best friend's brother. He lost control and rolled his van 125 feet down a north Spokane hill.

What little settlement there was didn't begin to cover Caudill's astronomical medical bills.

It was a hopeless case until Caudill decided to rise above the depression and despair. After that, there was no stopping her.

She was a Lilac Festival princess for Gonzaga Prep. She earned a license to sell real estate. She graduated from Spokane Community College and Gonzaga University.

Then she got it into her head to try Gonzaga's Law School. It took five grueling years, but she earned her diploma in 1993.

None of this could have happened were it not for a legion of devoted fans who supported Caudill at every point.

The Jesuits at Gonzaga gave her full scholarships. Spokane attorney Pat Sullivan has been a rock, raising money and opening doors. Attorney Mike Keyes tutored Caudill for the bar exams.

At the U.S. Attorney's office, Deborah Hargreaves spent countless hours of her own time customizing a computer for Caudill to use in her legal work.

But this is no charity case. People are drawn to Caudill because she is a vibrant, articulate and intelligent woman who wants nothing more than a shot at being productive.

Jim Connelly, Spokane's U.S. Attorney, saw her potential and took a chance. It was a gutsy move, hiring Caudill as a paralegal and petitioning Reno to put her on staff. "We're not just carrying her," explains Connelly. "We treat her just like we do everybody else."

As usual, Caudill hasn't stopped dreaming big dreams. There is an autobiography in the works. She plans a second career giving inspirational speeches.

"What I've achieved as far as the law goes is wonderful," says the miracle girl. "But the big accomplishment is all the friends I've found along the way."

Neo-Nutsies and Other Wackos

Chapter Six

Task force chips away at cornerstone of civil rights

Only halfway through my clam chowder, and already I was sick to my stomach.

Not that there was anything suspect about the North Shore's chowder. It's quite good, actually.

No, what was making me queasy was the way things were developing during a lunchtime gathering of a usually high-minded group: The Kootenai County Task Force on Human Relations.

After listening to all the nattering and debate, though, I found myself facing the worst of all possible scenarios.

I was (gasp!) siding with Keith D. Gilbert.

Self-avowed racist, monger of hatred, venom and other assorted nastiness. Ex-con and all-around troublemaker. The man that I have referred to in past columns as both "cockroach" and "coprolite."

That Keith D. Gilbert.

Woe was me.

I felt like the turncoat Christian who, after buying a season's pass to the Colosseum, had decided at the last minute to cheer for the lions.

However, if I'm not mistaken, the task force was established in 1982 to promote and protect the sacredness of an individual's civil rights regardless of race, creed or politics. That lofty ideal is the organization's cornerstone, as well as the very essence of the anti-harassment legislation it fought so hard to see made into law.

Most task force supporters would heartily agree, I think, that civil rights should never fall prey to personal whim or the heat of the moment.

Yet, that's exactly what happened to Gilbert when he was booted out of the meeting in a rather mean-spirited, if not ironic, display I find impossible to overlook.

What occurred was justified by the majority vote. But when a premise is as trumped up as this one was, the differences between "majority" and "mob" rule become microscopic.

Gilbert's expulsion was orchestrated by our would-be attorney general, Kootenai County Prosecutor Glen Walker, and some other well-intentional souls who argued that the white supremacist's presence made a sham of the task force's noble intent.

Perhaps. But what they were really saying was:

"We don't like what you think or what you stand for, so get to the back of the bus."

Sounds familiar, eh?

With a show of hands sought by Chairman Bill Wassmuth, Gilbert was history, 14-9.

As he had earlier promised, the so-called Aryan warrior made good his exit.

"I'll leave if I'm asked to," he said. "But if you exclude me, you have provided a bigoted forum. Your trying to exclude me goes against everything you supposedly stand for."

To the task force's red-faced shame, Gilbert was absolutely right.

Walker once quipped to me about a dimwitted fellow Republican who surprised everyone by finally coming up with a cogent idea.

"Even the blind pig finds the acorn once in a while," Walker said.

It seems an appropriate time to use the prosecutor's own countrified gewgaw against him.

On this occasion, Keith Gilbert found the acorn.

The task force luncheon was billed as being open to "any concerned citizen." There is, as far as I know, no formalized rules of membership that could have been used to exclude non-members.

Even we scumbag journalists were allowed to stay.

With that sort of set up, I find it rather ludicrous – and probably unconstitutional, as well – for anyone to try to screen out Keith Gilbert, Mahatma Gandhi, or anyone else.

As Coeur d'Alene Chamber of Commerce Manager Sandy Emerson put it: "Until there is a problem, I have no problem with having the press or any citizen attend these meetings."

Afterwards, Emerson said he almost walked out with Gilbert.

Not that the two have anything in common.

It's just that Emerson has an understanding of what a democratic way of life is all about.

Democracy, you see, cuts both ways. It takes risks. Sets an example. It is long-suffering. Gracious. Attributes the Kootenai County Task Force on Human Relations could apparently use a little brushing up on.

John Birchers discover Masons behind every bush

It's a little after 7:30 p.m. and we've already been led through the flag salute by a gangly red-haired guy with a dark suit and an overbite.

The tension inside the Gonzaga University classroom is building, and I can't tell you how excited I am to be attending my first John Birch Society meeting.

That's right, the John Birch Society.

You're probably thinking, "What's Clark doing with a bunch of right-wing coconuts like that?"

Or maybe you're thinking, "I always knew Clark was a right-wing coconut."

Who cares what you think.

The point is that many people are unaware of how the Birchers have mellowed and become more representative of mainstream politics over the years.

Sure, back in the 1960s they took quite a drubbing for advocating some pretty flipped out ideas.

They tried to impeach Chief Justice Earl Warren, and John Birch founder Robert Welch called President Eisenhower a traitor. Birchers also wanted to pull out of the United Nations, and a few, I've heard, thought that American currency should be changed from the worthless pot metal it is to Necco candies.

The response to these wild ravings by left-wing, pinko media czars like me was to basically point our fingers at the John Birch Society and – in a dignified manner, mind you – yell: "Nyah, Nyah, Nyah. Look at the crazies!!!"

Try as they would to ignore this subtle attack, over the years it had a chilling effect. John Birch membership plummeted.

Finally, a decision was made to temper many of their radical views.

No longer would John Birch members be allowed to see Communists hiding behind every rock.

Nowadays, the rocks are crawling with evil Masons.

"A liberal once asked me why I was always finding conspirators behind every bush," says Ralph Epperson, an Arizona Bircher who has stepped in front of the podium and is about to present the audience with some of his reasonable and moderate views.

"I told him, 'That's because liberals like you are always putting bushes in front of conspirators.'"

We all chuckle knowingly at that.

A man to my right drops his pen, no doubt as a clever ruse to check under his chair for one of those conspirators. You never can be too sure.

There are at least 80 in attendance, a fact that, if you're a Bircher, is very encouraging. If you're not a Bircher, however, you may feel the urge to dial 911 and tell the guys in the white coats to bring their butterfly nets.

Epperson is the author of *The Unseen Hand*, a book pregnant with, shall we say, strange notions. He is an espouser of something he calls the conspiratorial view of history.

That is to say that history has not been shaped by sheer coincidence or accident. Only a left-wing fool would think that.

No, the events of the past have all been produced by the careful design of insidious secret societies like the *Illuminati* and, more recently, the Masons.

"By saying this, I do not infer that all Masons in America have knowledge of this conspiracy," says Epperson. "The majority are not Illuminated Masons."

It is these Illuminated characters causing all the problems like the French Revolution, World Wars I and II and even the Civil War.

Oh, yeah.

Epperson says it was a bunch of European bankers (Illuminated, of course) who got the North and South shooting at each other.

These vile guys had one of their secret meetings that probably went something like this:

"OK. This month's Illuminated secret meeting is hereby called to order. Any new business?"

"Yes, Mr. Chairman."

"The Chair recognizes secret member Harry."

"Thank you, Mr. Chairman. As you fellas know, the secret society biz has been a little slow lately, and I was thinking maybe, what say we all sneak over to America and stir up a civil war?"

"The Chair sees that as a good idea. All in favor say aye. All opposed? The ayes have it. America will have a civil war. Now, next Tuesday's potluck has changed to Thursday. Is that good for you guys?"

Epperson says this kind of horror has been going on unchecked for centuries.

The big problem is that these secret societies tend to meet in secret so nobody knows about them. If these groups would do a little better job of advertising, something could be done about them.

Of course, if they did that, they wouldn't be secret any more, and Epperson wouldn't have anything to give speeches about.

Anyway, some other important things Epperson has discovered are worth noting.

One is that the famous bank robber Jesse James was in cahoots with John Wilkes Booth in the plot to kill Lincoln. They were both members of the same secret club, you see.

After the assassination, a Booth look-alike was killed in the barn shootout and the real Booth was ordered to drink poison by James.

Epperson says that President Franklin Roosevelt – a 32nd degree Mason, wouldn't you know – helped stage World Wars I and II because he wanted to be president of a ONE WORLD GOVERNMENT.

Thank God for Epperson and the John Birch Society, which remains vigilant in exposing these foul conspiracies that, well, seem to be just about everywhere.

I'd love to write more and warn you good readers about how the Shriners were behind the eruption of Mount St. Helens, but I'm running a little late. There's this certain meeting I have to attend and the blood oath I signed says I better be there on time.

Or else!

Doggone gag has neo-Nazi teary-eyed

Richard Butler has ridiculed the Holocaust, burned crosses in his back yard and denounced non-whites as mongrels. His sermons have inspired killers, bombers and thieves.

But he's not completely cold.

Yes, there are still some things left in this world that will bring even a neo-Nazi like Butler to tears.

"The dog, I dunno," says a choked-up Butler, Hayden Lake's notorious Aryan Nations leader. "I guess that's the first time I cried in a long time.

"I really loved that dog."

Of course, not everybody will share Butler's grief. Some, once they hear what happened to the racist's pooch, may be apt to even express a giggle or two.

Either way, this is one shaggy dog story that is all true.

Central to our saga is Bon, Butler's new German shepherd. (You gotta figure anyone who considers Hitler's birthday a holiday isn't going to buy himself a French poodle.) Butler says he bought Bon in California for $500.

The dog was meant to sire champions.

But that was before Bon, who had the required racially pure blood of any Aryan warrior, decided to harass some porcupines that had waddled onto the North Idaho compound.

Bon learned an important lesson. Although porcupines may be a slow and inferior species, they have some superior quills, which were soon painfully buried in Bon's tender muzzle.

A trip to the vet was arranged, and it was there that things got quite interesting.

Somewhere in the broad interior of Kootenai County there lurks an individual who wishes Richard Butler considerable ill. That criteria, of course, narrows the suspect list to about 60,000 or the current population of Kootenai County, whichever is larger.

But this person is also a fair-to-middling Richard Butler impersonator. Or at least convincing enough to bamboozle the receptionist at the Prairie Animal Hospital near Hayden Lake.

After Butler's dog had been admitted as a patient, the impersonator phoned the clinic and said something like: "This is Dick Butler again. As long as you have the dog in there, why don't you go ahead and have it neutered."

Not long after that it was "snip,snip" and Bon voyage to doggie manhood.

"We still have him," laments Butler of his castrated dog. "Of course, he's no good for anything now."

Obviously, a eunuch German shepherd doesn't quite fit the machismo image of the Aryan brotherhood. Nor will it breed much of a master race.

Butler figures it was either "somebody who knew we had brought it in" or perhaps even an insider at the hospital who had Bon turned into Bonnie.

However, Dr. David Tester, the veterinarian who performed the, uh, delicate surgical alterations, says he has no idea who called. Such a mistake, he says, is practically unavoidable. "The only way you can is to have people sign for everything you do and do everything in person."

Whoever it was, Butler says he can't believe anybody would stoop so low. To do such a thing "was something more than I could cope with."

He's not the only one in Kootenai County having difficulty coping.

"Oh, wow, oh, wow," chuckled Sheriff Merf Stalder upon hearing the story. "I can't help but laugh. I wonder who recognized him? I can understand him being upset. But it is a pretty ingenious effort by somebody."

Larry Broadbent, Stalder's undersheriff, says he, too, feels sorry for the dog, but adds that Butler has brought on his own problems.

"He's the one who has contributed to his own demise," says Broadbent. "Oh, dear. That is comical."

After the operation, a horrified Butler retrieved his dog and began contemplating what to do. Aryans tend to be law-suit-happy, but Butler decided against litigation. Last year, after all, wasn't a very good one if you were Richard Butler.

The Aryan chieftain was charged with sedition, saw the arrest and prosecution of some of his most faithful followers, and had open-heart surgery to boot. In separate incidents, thieves made off with the Aryan Nations signs outside the compound and broke into his home, stealing fancy silver- and gold-inlaid rifles and pistols.

With all that on his mind, Butler filed an insurance claim and took $700 for Bon's losses.

"We actually wanted him to litigate," says an insurance adjuster who preferred not to be identified. "We would have lost the case to anyone else, but I didn't think there was any way Richard Butler could win a lawsuit in Coeur d'Alene.

"But the doctor kept saying 'Please pay it. Make it go away.' So we settled."

So Butler took his money. "I guess you have to take your lickings," he says. As for Bon, the diminished dog, he's living a happy, albeit less rambunctious, life on the compound.

It's a peaceful existence that Butler compares to the eunuchs of old who oversaw Arabian harems. "You know," says Butler, "when they were castrated they were very docile. They didn't give (anyone) any trouble."

Come to think of it, those are attributes a lot of us wished Butler possessed.

Little-known Nazi made large impact

It's said that the good die young, which is why I think Hal Hunt made it to 95.

The old cigar-chomping Nazi apparently gave up waiting for the archangel Michael to swoop down from heaven and set the world straight for his beloved white race. Hunt died February 8, 1988, in the Seaview Convalescent Hospital in Eureka, California, miles away from the white wonderland he envisioned for North Idaho.

Four years ago, however, Hunt was very much alive when he invited me inside his rustic Hayden Lake print shop. It was there he told me all about the blacks and Jews that Hunt had devoted a lifetime to hating.

But that's not why Hunt agreed to see me. Mainly he wanted to set the record straight about his role as one of North Idaho's founding fathers. Hunt was more than a little miffed by all the media attention that Aryan Nations leader Richard Butler had been getting.

If there was a true leader of the North Idaho white identity movement, the old man said, it was he, Hal Hunt, not Richard Butler.

"Butler hasn't got any more Identity in him than my tan cat out there," snapped Hunt, pointing an aged finger.

Yet even in death Hunt has once again been upstaged. On trial for sedition in Arkansas, Butler is still getting the headlines. All Hunt could manage was a short obituary in the newspaper of Redding, California, where his daughter still lives.

That's unfair. Because Harold W. "Hal" Hunt does deserve his place in history. If anyone is to blame for North Idaho's soiled image as a hangout for Nazis, it is Hunt.

Hunt and Butler, both followers of the Reverend Wesley Swift, founder of the white Identity movement, arrived in Hayden Lake at about the same time in 1973. But the choice of North Idaho as a white supremacist stronghold was due mainly to Hunt's bigoted newspaper, the *National Chronicle*, which served as a network for kooks.

"I had a lot of subscribers up here," said Hunt. "They wrote me letters and told me about the area, that it was still a place where the white man dominated."

Butler, who lived in Lancaster, California, was also a *National Chronicle* reader who had heard of North Idaho's virtues. Hunt had been publishing racist newspapers since 1928, when he became enamored with the Ku Klux Klan and started printing its literature.

Nobody paid much attention to Hunt until 1963, when, through his newspaper, he started spreading a rumor that United Nations troops were preparing to take over the United States. "All would be under Russian and Zionist Jew generals," warned Hunt. "In the meantime, lay in a supply of guns and grenades."

As absurd as it now sounds, the rumor fooled Representative James Utt, R-California, who inserted it into the *Congressional Record*. Utt, by the way, was a member of the John Birch Society. Others were fooled, and letters by the hundreds poured into legislative offices from frightened citizens.

Hunt received his moment of fame when CBS newsman Roger Mudd tracked down the rumor to the racist's cluttered print shop in Burney, California. "There on Main Street – well, almost Main Street," reported Mudd in a documentary, "the *Shasta County Chronicle* is published once a week and mailed all over the country."

So taken with the national television exposure was Hunt that he immediately changed the name of his paper to the *National Chronicle*. His circulation, he said swelled from 1,000 to more than 3,000. He became a cause célèbre in racist circles.

In Idaho, Hunt continued printing his vile diatribes. He helped underwrite the movement. Even before Butler created his Church of Jesus Christ Christian, he and Hunt organized a North Idaho chapter of the Posse Comitatus, a right-wing vigilante group with racist overtones. In 1976, Butler and Hunt were charged (and later acquitted) with assaulting one of their former followers.

"They were quite close," said Hunt's daughter-in-law, Gail Hunt, adding that Butler even performed Hunt's marriage service.

(Family members estimate Hunt was married eight times; some of his wives were wealthy widows whose fortunes ended up subsidizing racism.)

Shortly after that, however, the two men had a falling out over some money Hunt claimed Butler owed him. "We don't have much to do with each other," sniffed Hunt in 1984. "He does his thing and I do mine."

Largely through the violence and crimes of his followers, Butler's notoriety spread. Hunt stayed in the shadows, quietly printing his newspaper and writing stories that endorsed Hitler's treatment of the Jews and advocated shipping blacks off to Africa.

His views were never shared by family members.

"None of us ever agreed with any of it," said Gail Hunt. "It was just something we could never accept. He really put all of his kids through the wringer. His beliefs estranged him from his parents and everyone in his family."

Hal Hunt died a broken man. Over the years, family members say, Hunt's racist confederates bilked him out of all of his property and bank accounts. He signed away the title to his house and, in 1986, was forced to auction off his vintage printing equipment.

"When he finally figured out that the paper was gone, he just gave up," said his daughter, Dale Thompson. "He quit eating and just went downhill."

Though few will mourn Hunt's passing, it would be a mistake to forget the role he played.

Let's hope Aryan Nations goes to the dogs

(Sung to the tune, "The Teddy Bear's Picnic")
If you drive out to the Idaho woods,
You'd better be white as snow.
If you drive out to the Idaho woods,
Be careful where you go.
There's crosses burning bright and hot,
There's Hitler heiling, guns are cocked.
Today's the day the Aryans hold their ha-ate fest.

People today give swastikas such a bum rap, Jeff Dissell tells me, pointing to the Nazi symbol around his arm.

The red in the band, he explains with great reverence, actually represents the blood of Christ. White is for the Savior's purity. And the black . . . .

Stupid me. All this time I thought swastikas stood for that sawed-off paper hanger named Hitler and the systematic slaughter of 6 million Jews.

You know, I have to pinch myself sometimes to make sure what I'm seeing is really happening.

That sums up my day at the racists. I have the unholy feeling I'm surrounded by vampires and the sun is sinking fast.

Here I am, standing in the North Idaho woods with a melonhead who's garbed like he's ready to start the Fourth Reich: shiny jackboots, a black German field cap, blue shirt, bright Aryan patches and, oh, those misunderstood swastikas.

How many snake-eyes must the hand of fate roll before a person cashes in enough mental chips to join Richard Butler at his seedy white supremacist headquarters north of Hayden Lake? Butler says at least 100 of the faithful will be on hand for this weekend's "Aryan World Congress" – aka Loserville. They have come to hear the speeches and to feel that singular glow that can come only from a flaming cross at night.

"This is Mecca," states Jeremy, a 19-year-old skinhead who hails from Oklahoma (the Big Bang State).

Breaking with normal teen fashion, Jeremy sports the black-shirted Gestapo look once made popular by goons who hung der Fuhrer's enemies on meat hooks.

Yes, the Butler compound is a goose-stepping vunderland populated by a vast cast of caricatures.

There's the 16-year-old kid at the guard shack with a mutant four-pronged ice ax strapped to his waist. The last time anyone saw something that lethal, it was sticking out of Leon Trotsky's head.

Reporter: "Er, what do you call that kind of a weapon?"

Kid: "Oh, just some fun."

Who says neo-Nazis don't know how to party?

There are Hans und Fritz, Butler's German shepherds who guard the property. It figures an old racist like Butler wouldn't have any black Labs roaming the Aryan acreage.

There is the young woman in the black bonnet who assails the public school system for abandoning academics to teach American youth "how to cornrow hair and how to raise a homo in a homo world."

There is the aptly named Gerald Gruidl (rhymes with strudel) who looks at us gawking race-traitor reporters and quips, "Now we know what the lions, tigers and monkeys feel like."

I bet you do, Herr Gruidl. Especially der monkeys.

Only Colonel Klink is missing from this menagerie.

At 78, Butler is facing the nacht music. He knows he soon must choose a successor to lead his Aryan warriors into the next century.

Will it be Gruidl? Or Louis Beam? Or John Miller?

And will these contenders wrestle over Butler's power like snarling jackals after road kill?

For now, Butler isn't saying who is man enough to fill his jackboots when he joins Adolf and Eva in that great bunker in the beyond.

Personally, I'm pulling for Hans und Fritz.

Road name could send a message

I'd love to hear North Idaho's Nazi king, Richard Butler, giving these directions to his Aryan Nations hideaway:

"Well, (gulp) after you get to Garwood, head south on (gasp) Martin Luther King, Jr. (choke) Drive."

Hey, maybe it could happen. The area's top racist-busters want to rename Rimrock Road – the rural lane bordering Butler's headquarters – after America's slain civil rights leader.

What better way to commemorate the 50th anniversary of the Nuremburg Trials than to tweak our own Hitler-loving hairballs?

Renaming Rimrock is the brainchild of North Idaho College instructor Tony Stewart.

The longtime human rights advocate says he's thought of attempting such a name change for several years. He sees it as a tribute to King as well as a message to Butler and the neo-Gestapo goons who follow him.

Stewart finally brought his idea up for discussion after a recent meeting of the Kootenai County Task Force on Human Relations.

All the atta-boys bolstered Stewart. He says he probably will put his proposal up for formal vote at the next meeting.

"I'm willing to get out there and get behind it," says Task Force president Linda Payne. "It would really be a great thing."

Of course, a Task Force endorsement won't necessarily mean Stewart's plan will happen. Renaming a public road is a bumpy proposition. There always are people who don't take easily to change in any form.

Toss in a controversial name like Martin Luther King, and there's guaranteed to be plenty of heartburn.

"With the politics around here, it may be easier to rename the road (after the late black comedian) Redd Foxx," says Dick Panabaker, chairman of the Kootenai County Commission.

To approve a new road name, Panabaker says, a simple majority of property owners along a road must agree to the change.

A woman at the Kootenai County planning office says it's far tougher than that. According to her, renaming a road takes 100 percent approval of all affected property owners.

Either way, it's a safe bet that an old racist like Butler, 77, won't jump at a chance to live on Martin Luther King, Jr. Drive.

A couple of his dim-bulb thugs were seen passing out "Abolish the King Holiday" propaganda outside a meeting for schoolchildren.

Panabaker says he's no racist, although he's no fan of Martin Luther King, either. He told me a story about how upset he was when he discovered Seattle had renamed Rainier Way after King.

To his credit, Panabaker says Butler once branded him as a "disgrace to my race." That happened when Panabaker was Hayden mayor and refused to let Butler hold a skinhead meeting at city hall.

Being a fair-minded muckraker, I telephoned the Aryan compound to get Butler's reaction to Stewart's road name proposal.

"Yeah," says the Aryan receptionist, snickering at me in disbelief. "Thanks for your call." Click.

Giving the Nazi a second chance, I dialed the Idaho number again and repeated my spiel. "No, really," I explained. "They really want to rename it Martin Luther . . ."

"Yeah," repeated the same receptionist, still snickering. "Sure." Click.

Richard Butler is a cancer who has done incalculable harm to North Idaho.

The worm-ridden gospel he has spewed for the last 20 years has inspired killers, bombers and thieves. Like a pile of festering road-kill, Butler has attracted swarms of social outcasts who have contaminated our area with their hateful filth.

Changing Rimrock Road to Martin Luther King, Jr. Drive may be a long shot, but it's a spectacular idea.

This is the perfect, non-violent way to honor one great man and show an old scorpion exactly what we think of his poisonous ways.

Characters

Chapter Seven

Shoeshine meant chance to let his character rub off

I hope James Jones died thinking of fresh worms and a fat bass pulling on the end of his line.

That's not such an unhappy ending for an old shoeshine fisherman.

James' frail heart gave out July 17, 1995, just three days after his 89th birthday. He had no social status, power or wealth, but was a beloved fixture in this city. He will be greatly missed.

For more than half a century, this sweet-spirited, tiny man shined the shoes of Spokane's well-heeled gents.

Customers sat high on his battle-scarred stand while Jimmy applied the wax and popped the cloth and clicked the wood brushes together like oversized castanets.

Two bucks bought a shine. The conversation was free and invariably got around to James' true love – fishing.

He claimed to know where catfish lurked in the Spokane River. When I once told him how I hated the taste of perch, he rattled off a recipe guaranteed to change my mind.

James spent the last 14 years at the Lincoln Building barbershop. There he became pals with judges, lawyers and company presidents.

It wasn't a case of a bunch of fair-skinned big shots trying to patronize a humble black man. People were drawn to Jimmy because of the strength of his character.

"James thought of everyone as the same," says Betty Brown, who hired James at the barbershop and later adopted him as her surrogate grandfather.

"He was color blind. No matter what they did or who they were, they were all just folks to him."

James loved his work. After he had previously suffered a near-fatal heart attack, the thought of getting back to his shoeshine stand probably kept him alive.

"He didn't ask much from the world or anybody," says Jackie Stephens, president of an environmental services firm. "He was a giver."

U.S. District Judge Frem Nielsen is another fan. "Here was this humble person who took all the travails life had to offer and handled them with dignity."

James was a devout, church-going Christian. Maybe he knew his time was near.

On the day he died, James stepped outside the Lincoln Building. In his hand was a bouquet of helium balloons given him as a birthday present.

One by one, James released the balloons and watched as they drifted to the heavens. "They looked like little marbles," he told Brown when he went back inside.

A Spokane Transit Authority van was to pick James up in front of the bank building.

When James didn't show for the appointment, the van driver says he poked his head in the barbershop. James may have been in the bathroom. The driver left, assuming the shoeshine man found another way home.

Brown never saw the driver. If he did stop by, she says, he should have asked where his passenger was.

James later went outside to wait for his ride. He was easily confused after his heart attack and often got his bus times mixed up.

The STA van was long gone, of course. Without telling Brown, James started walking home.

An 89-year-old man with a bum ticker obviously had no business trying to hoof it on such a scorcher of a day.

But James was going fishing the next day with Brown and some friends. All he'd been talking about was getting to his yard and digging some worms.

Jimmy died on the sidewalk in front of the Paulsen Building, where he began his career as a Spokane shoeshine man in 1942.

A witness saw him raise his arms. Then he collapsed in slow motion, as if a pair of unseen hands laid him softly down.

The only identification on him was his fishing license, tucked in a pocket.

At the barbershop, the familiar shoeshine stand is now a shrine. There are flowers and photographs, but the sign Betty Brown propped on the seat is as good an epitaph as you could write for James Jones.

Just two words: "Gone fishing."

Topless maids give customers gleaming eyes

The letters at the T&A Housecleaning Service sure don't stand for Tide and Ajax.

As further proof that Spokane is no longer the drowsy, Leave-it-to-Beaver city it once was, a topless maid business opened the other day.

"The telephone has been ringing off the hook," says Naomi Leong, the 24-year-old entrepreneur who dreamed up this titillating venture.

"I thought conservative Spokane was ready for something like this."

Maybe so, Naomi, but it's a safe bet the Chamber of Commerce won't feature your new business in its next newsletter.

Moralists will naturally bristle at the notion of half-nekkid young women being paid to scrub Formica. Naomi, however, swears there is nothing kinkier going on than a lot of soap suds and elbow grease.

"This is a legitimate cleaning service," she adds. "I even went out and bought a Kenmore vacuum."

That certainly gives new meaning to those "softer side of Sears" commercials.

As part of my continuing commitment to expose the latest developments in the Naked City, I conducted a journalist debriefing with Naomi and her assistant, Tiffani, during one of their weekend cleaning missions.

Their assignment was to tidy up a modest home on the North Side. Derrick, the 27-year-old homeowner, was there to watch. His wife wasn't.

Before firing up the Kenmore, Naomi and Tiffani changed from street clothes into their cleaning attire: thong bikini bottoms, frilly aprons and lace chokers.

"You know, if you two would fix breakfast I'd be in heaven," said Derrick, who wore a very lopsided, goofy grin on his face.

"Sorry," says Naomi, heading into the kitchen to mop the floor. "We don't do breakfasts."

As you might expect, semi-nude housecleaners don't work for free. Naomi charges 80 bucks for an hour or $50 for a half-hour.

So far, her customers have ranged from a 75-year-old seasoned citizen to two Gonzaga University students.

The good Jesuits at Gonzaga will be rattling their rosary beads when they hear about that.

"Aw, there's nothing wrong with this," says Naomi. "Not only is it entertaining, but you also get a clean house."

Tell it to your mom.

Naomi says her mother, Avra, takes a dim view of topless housecleaning. "She thinks it's degrading to women," says Naomi. "My stepfather, however, is fascinated."

Naomi says she's always had a wild streak in her, but apparently she is not short on brain power.

She claims she made the dean's list and will soon graduate from Eastern Washington University with a psychology degree.

Naomi showed me her letter of acceptance into an EWU master's program next fall.

The exotic housecleaning idea, she says, came as a way to make a few bucks on the side. "I take the European view of nudity," she says. "Everybody's got 'em, so what's the big deal?"

Before embarking on this, Naomi says she checked with a lawyer on legalities and how to incorporate her unusual business.

Naomi, a dark-haired woman with a dancer's body, says customers may look, but not touch.

For safety's sake, she always works with a partner, carries pepper spray and has a bouncer sit in her van in view of the client's house.

Naomi's ad in some Spokane shoppers produced a flood of interest. Most inquiries were people wondering if the whole thing is a joke.

Another call was from a bachelor who tried to hire Naomi & Co. to mow his lawn au natural. "Sorry," she told him. "We don't do landscaping."

Then there was the guy with an idea that's probably a bit ahead of its time for Spokane. He told Naomi he was looking for women to start a topless espresso stand.

I know, you could call it "Star-buck Naked."

Interplanetary prospector digs local auditor

They laughed at Thomas Jefferson when he bought the Louisiana territories from Napoleon.

They laughed at William Seward when he got the Ruskies to unload Alaska.

They laughed at Thomas P. Budnick when he staked out Martian mineral rights for his very own.

Of course, everyone's still laughing at Budnick. That is, everyone except the Spokane County Auditor's Office, where the Massachusetts social worker's weird astronomical mining claims are routinely filed and placed on the public record.

"I love Spokane," said Budnick, 39, who believes he's the first to take into outer space the American historical concept of Manifest Destiny.

"I love the people of Washington. You're the only ones who have filed my papers, who haven't ridiculed me or called me a crackpot."

According to Budnick, every auditor's office he tried save Spokane's, scoffed at his submissions and refused to do business with him.

"They all laughed at me," he said. "I tried every place in my own state. Then I moved on to New York and Indiana and Iowa and Illinois and Idaho and California . . .

"They don't realize that the nation that fails to expand eventually collapses. So we'd better get clicking in outer space or we'll collapse, too."

In 1981, Budnick – who works for the Massachusetts Department of Public Welfare in Holyoke – discovered how open-minded Spokane's County Auditor William Donahue and his staff were.

"We like his money," chuckled Donahue, noting that his office brought in $1.5 million in revenue last year, some $100 of it from Budnick. "We'll take anything anybody wants to file as long as there's a title and a name on it."

That policy, says the auditor, is based on an opinion that came out of the prosecuting attorney's office years ago.

"We were told that the quickest way to end up in court was to refuse something," Donahue said. "Ever since then we've had a pretty open door and, over the years, we've filed some weird things."

Mary Freese knows the truth of that.

In the last 15 years she's worked in the office, Freese has seen a stampede of goofballs who are convinced that filing something with the county – no matter how bizarre – somehow legitimizes or protects their document legally.

But all a person gets for a filing fee ($5 for the first page and a buck for every one after that) is knowing that the item has been placed on a log open to public inspection. This primarily benefits those wanting to record real estate transactions.

"I'll tell you, the world is full of strange people," Freese said. "But if they wanna file it, we'll take it."

Freese recalls the time an elderly woman filed a letter that told her she had won a prize in the *Reader's Digest* sweepstakes. And the time a man filed a prayer because he didn't want anyone to steal it.

Then there was the guy who filed what Freese called a rambling four-page document on how everyone was out to get him.

"He used to come in here and file things all the time," she said. "The trouble was that every time he came in, he used a different name. He was a doctor once. Then he was a lawyer. He used so many names I couldn't keep track of him and had a lot of difficulty locating items when he wanted to look at them again.

"One time I couldn't find a particular item, but that didn't seem to bother him. He just smiled and said, 'It's all right, the president has a copy.'"

But when all is said and done, Freese has to admit that if Budnick isn't on top, he's high on her list of favorite eccentrics.

It's not every day you get a guy who wants to sew up, as Budnick notes on one claim, "all minerals, and unlimited air rights to the planets, asteroids and stars."

"He even sends us Christmas cards," Freese said.

Why not? Nobody else takes the man seriously.

"I was afraid you'd say his name," groused Budnick's boss, public welfare Director Donald Pijar. "I don't know why he does these strange things."

"I've heard about him staking some mineral claims in odd places, but this is the first time I've heard about Mars. So I think maybe it's best not to say anything more about it."

Budnick is used to abuse. All of his co-workers, he said, regard him as a nutcase and make plenty of nasty remarks around the office.

It isn't the first time. While growing up, he said, he was a favorite target of mean-spirited louts who constantly rhymed his name with sputnik.

"I suffered through that for 10 or 12 years of my life," he said, although admitting that being called sputnik may have helped him keep an open mind regarding space exploration.

Like great visionaries before him, Thomas P. Budnick will have to endure countless slings and arrows before he finds his proper place in the solar system.

"Once you leave Earth's heavy gravity, getting to Mars is a piece of cake," he said. "You see, space is just a super highway waiting to be traveled. And when that happens, these claims will eventually be worth billions."

Not that Budnick wants to hog it all. He has filed a number of claims on behalf of the survivors of late American heroes such as Samantha Smith and Christa McAuliffe.

You will all be pleased to note that an eighth of one Martian claim has been donated exclusively to the residents of Washington state.

In other words, we're all going to be filthy rich – thanks to Budnick.

And who knows, if the Spokane County Auditor's Office keeps accepting his paperwork, our children's children may someday be able to tune their telescopes on the red planet and make out the William E. Donahue Memorial Mars Gravel Pit.

Navy's "mad" scientist turns out to have both genius, guts

Back in college, Jim was always the one with the wild ideas.

From the 10th floor of Pearce Hall, one of Eastern Washington University's silo dormitories, he would spend hours tossing paper airplanes out a window.

Some of the more ecology-minded students considered it littering. Jim claimed it was science.

After each flight Jim would calculate the distance. Then, he would reshape the wings and try again, keeping track of the progress on a rumpled scratch pad.

Once he sent his designs to an aeronautical engineer. Another time Jim made an appointment with a physicist to discuss whether heating an airplane's wings would enhance performance.

All of us loved Jim. But how could you not laugh at someone whose thoughts seemed as scattered as a blast of buckshot?

As it turned out, we were too busy having food fights to appreciate genius.

Last month, the Ferris High School graduate took command of a U.S. Navy tactical electronic warfare squadron in Key West, Florida. He now has 500 people to lead and an airplane with his name stenciled right under the window: Commander James R. Powell.

"It's no big deal," says Jim with a laugh.

Yeah, right.

Jim replaced Commander Bruce Nottke in a ceremony held at the Boca Chica airfield. He accepted the pin signifying his first command and kissed his wife, Barb.

"It's something to see your husband up there and to hear him say, 'I relieve you, sir,'" she told me.

Jim's modesty doesn't fool his wife or his friends. We know just how big a deal this really is.

It wasn't long ago that Jim's Navy future appeared to be washed up. The odds were long that he'd ever walk again, let alone fly.

In July 1986, Jim nearly died when the EA6B Prowler airplane he was navigating had to ditch during maneuvers off the coast of Australia.

Something went wrong when the plane was catapulted off the nuclear aircraft carrier *Enterprise*. As it cleared the flight deck, the Prowler went into a pitch. The pilot lost control and hit the ejection button.

Jim popped out first. Unlike his three crewmates, who safely landed in the water, Jim was blown back onto the deck.

His landing wasn't graceful. He shattered his elbow and crushed both ankles, one heel and his pelvis. He broke fingers and eventually lost his gall bladder.

"I've thought back a few times about lying in the hospital and wondering what I was going to do," Jim recalls.

What he didn't do was take the easy way out. The Navy offered him a sweet deal with monthly tax-free benefits. All he had to do was sign the medical discharge papers and quit.

Jim refused.

"There was this chief petty officer who kept saying, 'Sir, you'll be making money on this.' It made me mad. I said, 'Hey, look at my face. I'm not signing it.'"

Jim almost didn't have a choice. Had the Navy conducted its usual six-month medical review, he would have been history. "He wasn't even walking after six months," adds Barb.

Fortunately, some of Jim's commanding officers saw his drive. A few rules were bent and Jim stayed in. He pushed himself. Eventually he became recertified for flying in any aircraft that doesn't have an ejector seat.

"The bottom line is my jump shot's back," says Jim, who has always loved a fierce game of basketball.

Actually the bottom line is that the Navy had sense enough to hold onto a winner.

The top secret radar-jamming device Jim invented for his master's thesis has become standard equipment on our planes. It worked so well during the 1986 raid on Libya, that no U.S. planes were even scratched by enemy missiles.

Jim received a Naval excellence award in recognition of what probably started out as just another one of his wild ideas.

"He's like the mad scientist around here," says Lt. Greg Friesen, one of the men in Jim's squadron. "He's always working equations out on a piece of scratch paper on his desk. He's the guru."

Some things never change.

Gentle dropouts still marching to their own chords

They are fixtures in Spokane, as much a part of the local tapestry as the clock tower, Dick's Drive-in or those rusty iron runners in the park.

Their names – Michael and Barbara Karpack – probably won't ring many mental chimes. It's a safe bet, however, that anyone familiar with the downtown area has encountered this unmistakable duo a zillion times.

Michael, 54, is Spokane's premier street musician, a guitar-strumming hairy refugee from the hippy-dippy 1960s. This guy dropped out and stayed out. Waaay out.

He's a skinny, sun-baked dude who performs in a trademark black leather jacket and tie-dyed T-shirts. A headband does little to contain the gray jungle spewing from his face and head in a wild nimbus.

True, Michael's virtuosity consists of two chords. But he flails at them with such cosmic abandon that it's hard to resist feeding spare change into the guitar case yawning hungrily near his moccasin-clad feet.

The amusing lyrics he invents on the spot add to the package: Jesus loves you, yes, I know. Specially when you rock and rooolll . . . .

"I call my music gutter rock," says Michael, a gregarious charmer who speaks in quick atomic bursts. "Man, when you're standing on a street corner, like, you ain't got the time to do a pretty song."

Barbara, Michael's wife, never strays far behind him. She has close-cropped hair and downcast, furtive eyes. She doesn't speak much to strangers.

Barbara's uncle, Darrell Jones, says she grew up in Spokane and was bright and articulate. She suffered brain damage from a drug reaction before she met Michael.

To her husband, Barbara is the sun and the moon. "She's symbolic, man," he adds. "She's the greatest person. She's me as a woman."

Jones, social workers and police officers who know the street scene say that despite his offbeat ways, Michael is a gentle spirit who does a fine job caring for Barbara.

He fell in love with her shortly after arriving in Spokane 15 years ago. "She was the only one who liked me," says Michael, who dutifully keeps his wife clean and fed.

Michael was born in New Jersey, studied acting in New York City and says he was once a professional dog trainer. Fate and drifting eventually carried him to Spokane.

For the last several years, Michael and Barbara have lived in a tent in the weedy fields near the courthouse.

They pay a dollar apiece to shower at the YWCA. They eat at McDonald's. They brave the winters and get by on her monthly $600 disability check. The money Michael makes performing is a bonus. Sometimes they splurge and spend a warm night in a motel.

"He actually saves the state a lot of money," says Major Bambino, a Washington State Patrol trooper who befriended the Karpacks. "If he wasn't taking care of her, she'd be in an institution."

A moment later, Bambino adds, "If I won the lottery, I wouldn't hesitate to give him $50,000, but he'd probably still keep the same lifestyle."

The Karpacks used to rent a cabin in Peaceful Valley. They have stayed in a few apartments, but Bob Peeler of the Spokane Neighborhood Action Program says it is difficult to find renters who will accept them.

"I'm not complaining, man," says Michael. "Being outside is a lot of fun. It's like playing hooky from school."

Not always. Exposed as they are, the Karpacks are ripped off regularly. Last month, in fact, two street thugs attacked Michael and Barbara as they hiked across the Maple Street Bridge one night.

One of these sub-humans cracked Barbara over the head with a rock. She needed eight stitches. His accomplice snatched Michael's guitar and smashed it to pieces on the road.

Michael is anything but stupid. He realizes his appearance and the way he and Barbara live are open invitations to getting hassled.

Take, for example, the Karpacks' ill-fated bus ride to New Orleans last year. Michael thought performing in such an illustrious city would lift his street musicianship to new heights.

Instead, he got roughed up by cops for loitering and was hauled off to jail. While Michael was cooling his heels, Barbara panicked and inexplicably threw his guitar and their backpacks into a trash bin.

Michael was only too glad to return to friendlier faces in good old Spokane.

"I'm on stage wherever I go," he says cheerfully. "I like my life, yes, I do. My life is all I got."

Hassonland perfect place for escapism

One small step out a window. One giant attraction for the Spokane County Courthouse: Hassonland.

It hasn't reached theme park magnitude yet. But quirky County Commissioner Steve Hasson's first-floor office is attracting hundreds of curious pilgrims.

Their destination is the south window Hasson leaped out of in 1992. He then led a pack of quote-hungry reporters on a bizarre footrace through city streets.

As yet, there are no Hassonland postcards or T-shirts. Instead, gawkers commemorate their visits by signing their names and the date on the wall.

Some can't resist leaving a few choice words of wisdom:

"You're no Jack Kennedy," reads one dig.

"Turncoat" is a message from a Democrat probably sore about Hasson's recent switch to the Republican Party.

"Keep truckin'," reads the note from Hasson's mother.

"Steve, stay on the main floor," writes Cathy Ramm, probably worried about any future window leaps.

"Berlin – China – Hasson. All are walls of distinction," was left by John Maxwell.

U.S. Representative George Nethercutt's signature is among the notables, along with judges, journalists, business leaders and the new sheriff.

It's the old "Kilroy was here" syndrome, explains Hasson. "People want to see where it all happened and then leave their mark."

Spokane union leader Bill Keenan was first to sign in December 1992.

Keenan popped in to see the famed window. Hasson invited him to take a test jump. Keenan declined, opting to sign his name instead.

"At least I'm No. 1 at something," says Keenan, chuckling at the strange trend he began.

Some 700 others have followed Keenan's lead. Hasson's office now looks more like a cast on a teenager's broken leg than a place to conduct serious county business.

Graffiti cover the windowsill and all of one wall and are beginning to sprawl like suburban blight through the rest of the room.

Hasson says he has counted the autographs himself. That should silence critics who don't think the commissioner does enough important things with his time.

But is writing on walls a proper way to treat taxpayer property?

"It's purely decorative, not unlike buying art or painting the room," says Superior Court Judge James Murphy, whose name adorns the wall.

"I imagine if Steve moves on to something else, the county painters will be in there in a minute."

Superior Court Judge Michael Donohue, who is writing a history of Spokane, says Hasson's offbeat antics and glib humor will leave him remembered long after he is gone.

Hasson fits in well with other Washington loony luminaries, says Donohue, such as a former secretary of state who once campaigned wearing a loincloth and leading a goat down the middle of Seattle.

Hasson is "an interesting man," says the judge. "There's more there than meets the eye."

Maybe so. But his goofiness – such as endorsing the cornbread at Sam's Pit, an all-night hangout for dopers and hookers – has infuriated many who don't want their elected officials clowning around.

Hasson's great window escape was a classic. It happened November 19, 1992, shortly after he learned he had defeated Jack Hebner by 253 votes.

Locked in his office, the commissioner ducked out the window rather than face reporters waiting in the hall. A photographer heard the window open. Soon the chase was on.

Many people wanted their votes back. One TV anchorman wondered if Hasson was "a few fries short of a Happy Meal."

Hasson says he isn't crazy. It's just the way things work in Hassonland.

"Somebody like me comes this way only so often," says the Cornbread Commissioner. "You just have to make the best of it."

School Daze

Chapter Eight

Special schoolteacher changed the life of a young goof-off

It was 1963. I was 12 years old and headed for big, big trouble.

Then a lanky athlete with a crew cut and a kind heart came along.

His name was Don Kolb. He was my seventh-grade teacher and he changed my life.

I've thought about him a lot over the years, but especially Tuesday morning as I delivered the commencement address at my son Ben's graduation from Franklin Elementary School.

It didn't quite have the pomp of Harvard, but I couldn't have been any prouder.

Twenty-seven years earlier, I had sat in the same brick gymnasium and scratched and fidgeted my way through a similar ceremony.

That time I was lucky to be there.

High up on the west wall you can still make out my last name. A few days before graduation, I got into the gym, climbed to the top of the chin-up bars and scratched out a legacy in chalk.

The dour old principal, weary of my smart-aleck ways, wanted to suspend me. Kolb interceded. He got the sentence reduced to cleaning the entire gym, which I did.

Except for my name.

For some unexplained reason, Don Kolb always saw the best in me.

It wasn't easy. Before he came along, I had earned a reputation as an incorrigible goof-off, a poor student and a playground bully, fighting one kid after another.

My parents were worried. My teachers sent me to the office and mailed home nasty notes.

At one point, I was called to the school district offices for an IQ test and evaluation. When my scores came back in the high ranges, the district people gave up and sent me back with a few bewildered looks.

Then Kolb showed up.

He was just 24. Franklin was only his second year of teaching.

Yet in my mind, he exemplifies the high calling of education.

Don Kolb was a teacher not because he wanted his summers off and good benefits. Kolb was a teacher because he wanted to change the world a kid at a time.

To him, teaching was even more important than baseball.

In 1957, Kolb, a pitcher and outfielder, played on North Central High's undefeated team. At Eastern Washington University (it was called a college in those days), he was All-Evergreen Conference, led the league in hits and was named MVP his junior year and most inspirational player two years in a row.

When he graduated, the Yankees came calling.

They offered him $10,000 to sign and play in one of their minor-league franchises. That would be pocket change to a Don Mattingly, but it wasn't bad money back then.

But Kolb turned down the Yanks.

His mission was not a ballfield, but a classroom.

Many of today's teachers would have chalked up my attitude problems to poor self-esteem. Kolb was more concerned about my sense of remorse.

He set standards. He took the time to show me there were consequences for my actions. He wasn't mean-spirited. He cared.

Good self-esteem, he taught, is an outgrowth of good performance. It's not the other way around.

Because of this young ex-ballplayer, I began to use my wits instead of fists.

"Doug," he told me over lunch the other day with a wink, "any time I can see a kid like you stay out of Walla Walla, it makes me feel 20 feet tall."

After spending seven years teaching in School District 81, Kolb was hired by Community Colleges of Spokane, where he has risen to the position of vice president.

I'm proud of his success, but in a way it's too bad. Public school classrooms are desperately short of Don Kolbs.

That fact makes it hard to sympathize with the Washington Education Association's constant whining for bigger paychecks.

Let's be honest. For those who do the minimum, teaching is an excellent deal.

The contract requires teachers to work only 190 days a year. They get 10 weeks off for summer, 10 days for Christmas and five days for spring break. They get paid sick leave and medical, dental and vision insurance for all family members. They go to work at 8:45 a.m. and aren't required to stay past 3:45 p.m.

The pay scale varies some, but according to Spokane School District 81, the average salary is $35,000 a year.

But the Don Kolbs are never satisfied with doing the minimum. To them teaching is a way of life. They could get $100,000 a year and still be underpaid.

I told the Franklin graduates about Don Kolb. I even wore a Yankees jersey in his honor.

He never played for the Yanks, but my seventh-grade teacher was a major leaguer all the same.

Teachers take heed: Intolerance will not be tolerated

It was 1965 and I had sinned against truth, decency and the American way.

I had dared wear a yellow sweat shirt to high school, which was acceptable, except for the black Playboy Bunny logo on the front, which was not.

One of the school's enforcers – a big guy who played army on weekends and was thus heavy into discipline – took offense.

The teacher grabbed my shirt and performed a military maneuver, slamming my frail freshman body so hard against a row of steel lockers that the wind exited my lungs like a rip in the Goodyear blimp.

"Woooomph!"

Then he pointed a knobby finger about a centimeter from my nose and said the following few words that were acid-etched into my brain cells:

"Don't you ever let me see you wearing that disgusting thing to school again, or I'll have you and the sweat shirt expelled."

I learned my lesson. My back hurt all day from the imprint a combination lock had left. I ditched the sweat shirt, fearing the consequences a second encounter might have on my permanent teeth.

But those were the Dark Ages, weren't they?

Twenty-five years later, the educational system has learned plenty from it's silly attacks on Playboy sweat shirts, peace symbols, long hair, shaved heads, Afros, beads, holey jeans, short skirts, headbands, no socks, funny shoes.

Oh yeah?

As a few educated fools in nearby Reardan have demonstrated, 1989 can still be the Stone Age when it comes to civil rights, good manners and common sense.

Case in point is what happened the other day to Nick Both, a 14-year-old eighth grader who attends Reardan Elementary School.

Nick was kicked out of science, math and P.E. and made an example of.

He didn't bring a gun to school or slug a teacher. His crime was that he wore a little green stud in his left ear.

"What this is all about is we're trying to reserve this community's norms," science teacher Brian McCall told a *Spokesman-Review* reporter.

No Brian, what this is all about is plain, old-fashioned intolerance.

"Oh, gawd," laughed Jerry Sheehan, legislative director for the Seattle chapter of the American Civil Liberties Union, when he heard about the earring incident. "Does that mean Bruce Springsteen would not be allowed to perform, were he to volunteer to do an anti-drug concert for the Reardan school?"

"Is this kind of thing just getting to Reardan?"

If only it were true.

But ignorance can't be Reardan Elementary's excuse. It would defy belief to assume these teachers had their heads buried during the last quarter-century of civil rights litigation.

It was 1966, in fact, when 13-year-old Seattle honor student Tom Poll was suspended for having hair that touched his eyebrows. The school rules governing hair length were found to be illegal by a King County Superior Court judge.

Reardan's earring crackdown sounds awfully similar to what happened to Poll. It's not the only current example of intolerance in the school system, either.

Kathleen Taylor, executive director of the Washington ACLU, cities a number of affronts to personal freedom:

• The Mukilteo School District administration has banned Los Angeles Raiders T-shirts because it believes the shirts are associated with violent youth gangs.

• Seattle's Highline School District is considering adopting a dress code to ban any clothing it deems gang-associated.

"What's next?" writes Taylor. "Are gang members going to start wearing Seahawk sweat shirts? Or will they start rolling up their pant cuffs?"

Have the witch hunts started again? I doubt it.

Educators who pursue such discriminatory paths will learn the hard way that they are treading on some pretty well-established case law. Whether it's over hair length, earrings or Raiders shirts, they're going to end up in court.

And when it's all over, who knows? Nick Both might be able to junk his little green stud and buy himself a whole bunch of new earrings.

With diamonds.

"Feel free to put our phone number in your article (206-624-2184)," said Sheehan with a chuckle. "I fell very confident in saying that issues of this sort have already been addressed.

"The school district has no business telling this student or that family how that student can clothe himself or what jewelry he can wear."

Rural school has top crop of children

A sure sign you're becoming a big shot is being asked to deliver the commencement address at a major center of learning.

Having accepted just such an honor, I drove to a crowded Grange hall stuck in the lush alfalfa fields northeast of Spokane.

There, I tried to inspire the members of the 99th graduating seventh-grade class of Orchard Prairie School.

All seven of them.

Gabrielle McClintock, Tiffany Miner, Eric Pederson, Alisha Pedey, Kjirstin Strandy, Kyle Stussi and Jiorgia Trobaugh.

Because of lack of space at Orchard Prairie, school events are held a few blocks away in Central Grange 831.

The graduation was a wonderful evening that harkened back to a bygone era, when education was an abiding community concern.

After each graduate entered arm-in-arm with a parent, a student opened the ceremony with prayer.

The American flag was unfurled and rolled back up by kindergartner Carl Cutler, a fourth-generation Orchard Prairie student.

The graduates gave a skit. Diplomas were handed out.

A kindergarten student didn't show up to accept her perfect attendance award. The audience roared with good-hearted amusement.

"Everyone turns out for these things whether they have kids in school or not," Melodie Miner told me before graduation began.

"I grew up here and my dad gave me my diploma. Tonight I'll give a diploma to my daughter, Tiffany."

This may sound like an *Andy Griffith Show* episode, but Orchard Prairie School is one of the area's best-kept educational secrets.

Tucked behind Bigelow Gulch Road, the white country schoolhouse is home to 65 students (grades K-7) and four teachers.

Orchard Prairie is five miles away from the NorthTown Mall. Yet the school is decades removed from the serious problems larger institutions wrestle with daily.

Students are well-groomed and respectful. Drugs aren't a problem. The last weapon brought to school was probably a slingshot.

And the setting couldn't be more idyllic.

The original 1894 building, with its tall bell tower, belongs on a postcard. A newer, three-classroom structure was added near the old one in 1971.

The playground behind the school is grassy and wide with a panoramic view of Mount Spokane.

To prepare for next year's centennial, students have put their artistic impressions of Orchard Prairie School on ceramic tiles. The tiles will be arranged into a large mural and mounted on a wall behind glass.

In the tradition of the one-room schoolhouses of yore, grade levels at Orchard Prairie are combined. Teachers trade classes with one another. Older students are encouraged to help younger classmates.

Does this homespun education work?

According to one standardized test, Orchard Prairie sixth-graders work at the 10th grade level.

At a recent high school graduation, three out of five valedictorians were former Orchard Prairie students.

State educators "don't count our test scores because they say we're not statistically representative," says Bob McMillian, Orchard Prairie's superintendent.

"Well, that's the advantage we have here. Our kids are not statistics."

McMillan is a plain-speaking guy who grows alfalfa on the side and runs the state's smallest school district (5.5 square miles) out of the basement in his home.

"We don't have any administrative space in the school," he explains. "The secretary works out of a desk in the hall."

"But three of our teachers have master's degrees and our kids, oh, they are really something."

They certainly are. Not knowing all this, I chose "pursuing excellence" as the topic of my first graduation speech.

I'm afraid I was preaching to the choir. Pursuing excellence is what this tiny school is all about.

"The teachers here really stress academics," says Debbie Stussi, whose son, Kyle, was one of the graduates. "When they go on, they are well prepared. They aren't afraid to write a report. They know how to do research."

Stussi grins, "I don't envy teachers at bigger schools. We have the best system right here."

BOOBs: *The group that bans offensive books*

The trouble with teaching children to read is the next thing you know they're walking into libraries and going to schools.

We all know what the trouble is with libraries and schools: Dirty books. Violent books. Racist books. Evil books.

Books like *Moby Dick*. How a book with such a filthy title is allowed to remain on the shelves is way beyond me.

Fortunately for Spokane, more and more of us right-thinking adults are standing up for decency and the American Way.

Sandra Armstrong complained to Spokane school officials that the 1938 classic *The Five Chinese Brothers* was too violent. The following month, *Halloween ABC*, an award-winning poetry book, was challenged by an unnamed parent as the work of the devil.

To Kill a Mockingbird may have won the Pulitzer Prize in 1960, but it took a courageous student who didn't want her name made public to expose this book for its demeaning portrayal of blacks.

Along those same racial lines, Pamela Fuller complained that the prestigious Coretta Scott King Illustrator Award book *Tar Beach* was a stereotype because it showed blacks eating watermelon and chicken.

Get a load of the lame excuse *Tar Beach* author Faith Ringgold came up with. The black woman says her book is an autobiography. She claims she really *did* grow up eating watermelon and chicken.

175

Hallelujah, brothers and sisters. Soon all rancid books will be purged from the shelves like Democrats from the House of Representatives.

What we enlightened people need to do is to organize. We can hold secret meetings and wear hoods and call our group something catchy such as "Ban Overly Offensive Books."

Yeah, I like the sound of that.

We BOOBs can then elect a worthy leader, someone who is absolutely above reproach – probably me – to compile an ultimate list of books we want outta here.

In fact, here's a sample:

• *Slugs*, a childrens' poetry book by David Greenberg. The pictures are cute, but the books says you can put slugs in a blender and eat them for breakfast. Disgusting!

• *The Billy Goats Gruff*, a Norwegian fairy tale. A terrible story about a troll who wants to eat the goats. Too violent!

• *Romeo and Juliet*, by William Shakespeare. Teenagers in love. Too sexually suggestive!

• *Working*, by Studs Terkel. One of the profiles is of a hooker. Glamorizes prostitution!

• *Deenie*, by Judy Blume. One passage has a teacher answering questions about masturbation. Morally unfit! Who does this Judy Blume think she is, Joycelyn Elders?

• *The Shining*, by Stephen King. A family takes care of a haunted hotel. Vulgar language!

• *As I Lay Dying*, by William Faulkner. Story of how family members react to their mother's death. Obscene!

• *The Wizard of Oz*, by Frank Baum. Teaches that courage, compassion and intelligence are personally developed and not God-given. Heresy!

• *The Clan of the Cave Bear*, by Jean Auel. Book includes a rape scene. Shocking and lewd!

• *The Big Sky*, by A. B. Guthrie. Uses the Lord's name in vain throughout the book. Blasphemy!

Well, that's good for starters.

The beauty is I didn't have to go to the library to compile this list. These are all actual attempts to ban books.

This shows the nation is already filled with lots of people who qualify as BOOBs. So let's get going. To the dumpster with nasty books.

You know, I just had another great thought about what I'd like to do to you censors. I'd get a paddle and *??!!&$!!??*.

Editor: Clark's last remark was considered inappropriate for a family newspaper.

Cola giants fill teen minds with tiny bubbles

Like a United Nations' peacekeeper in Bosnia, I recently toured one of Spokane's war-torn high school campuses to assess a carbonated conflict.

Signs of change at North Central were easy to spot: Sprite. Mr. Pibb. Diet Coke.

In a bitter bidding battle and market test, Coca-Cola clobbered arch-enemy Pepsi for sole rights to dispense its fizzy wares from strategically placed vending machines in District 81 secondary schools.

School board members burned up 90 minutes at a recent meeting ratifying the change – far more time than they usually spend on an educational matter.

As a result, students returned to school after Christmas break to discover Pepsi products had evaporated like Bob Dole's presidential bid.

As with politics or religion, soft drink superiority is one of those inflammatory issues that brook little middle ground.

"Pepsi is gross," says avid Coke fan Sara Earnest, 17. "It sugar-coats your teeth."

177

"Coke burns your teeth," counters Duner White, 16, who moments later inexplicably blurts out that Mountain Dew, a popular Pepsi drink, "lowers your sperm count, man!"

I was afraid to ask Duner how he goes about substantiating his odd claim, however, kids aren't the only ones arguing the cola wars.

Pepsi pooh-bahs, who lost the school contract after holding it eight years, have popped their tops. They suggest, and not too subtly, that their cola rivals may have rigged results that showed Coke vastly outselling Pepsi in a three-month comparison at four Spokane schools.

"In my mind it was a sham," grumbles Spokane Pepsi General Manager Don Bradley, who is upset that Coke controlled the test data.

"Basically, we whumped 'em," offers Coke's Jim Davis, who takes offense at Pepsi's accusations of skulduggery. "That's what it all boils down to."

Corporate soda jerks sound petty until you remember they are involved in a very serious business where billions in global sales are at stake.

Yet profit is the last concern when it comes to landing a contract with a school district.

To seal the deal, Coke agreed to give the Associated Student Body a whopping 67 percent cut of the gross on every ounce sold. As a bonus, Coca-Cola gave each high school $1,000 plus $250 apiece to each middle school.

Don't think this is about generosity. All the giveaways and sponsorships are "designed to get the next generation of Pepsi drinkers," concedes Bradley.

Pepsi, by the way, has cornered the soft drink market at Spokane's new Arena as well as the Spokane Indians ball park. It also leads Coke in overall area sales. Hmm. Think there's a connection?

Cola kingpins know that soft drinks are as much pop culture as pop. Getting hooked on the "Right One" or the "Real

Thing" is one of those peculiar American conversion experiences – like deciding whether you favor Elvis over the Beatles or Chevy over Ford.

Most of us take the sip of faith when we are young.

Let me make a confession. I'm a Diet Coke-aholic. I swill the stuff like tap water – sometimes four or five cans during and after dinner.

I wouldn't switch to insipid Diet Pepsi if Bradley gave me a lifetime supply.

But there's no accounting for bad taste. For reasons I cannot comprehend, Pete Lewis, Shaw Middle School's affable principal, guzzles more Diet Pepsi than humanly possible.

This man doesn't need a cup holder in his car so much as an IV line. The school district's Pepsi betrayal will not change the principal's beverage preference one whit.

For his recent birthday, generous Shaw staffers left enough fresh Diet Pepsi cans on Pete's desk to rebuild the giant pyramid.

"From a health standpoint," says Lewis of his titanic cola intake, "it's not something you'd be proud of."

I asked Lewis if he somehow had managed to consume all of his birthday gifts yet. Pete paused. "Actually," he adds sheepishly, "I'm working on my Christmas supply."

On the Road

Chapter Nine

Desperado, Wild West died together

Harry Tracy had outwitted the law for two full months and had gunned down seven men when the small posse tracked him to a farm 15 miles southwest of Davenport.

It was August 6, 1902, and one of the baddest badmen to ever ride the range was about to have his final showdown.

"It was a day much like today at about this hour when the events began to unfold," says Jim Dullenty with theatrical glee. "That was when an era ended and it ended right here."

We are standing, Dullenty and I, on the very site of Tracy's last gun battle. Dullenty, who owns a bookstore in Hamilton, Montana, is on a tour to sell his newly released book – *Harry Tracy: The Last Desperado*.

But you can tell by the look in the author's eyes that his subject represents a good deal more to him than the ringing of a cash register.

It is here, Dullenty proposes, that Tracy and the Wild West took their last gasp together. Automobiles would soon replace horses and phones, and better law enforcement would put mounted gunslingers like Tracy out of business.

Tracy was unaware of all that when he saw the posse coming. He grabbed his 30.30 rifle, jumped into the barn and steeled himself for business as usual.

As Dullenty writes:

A moment later he bolted from the door with his Winchester in hand. At first, the barn shielded him from the posse, but as soon as he passed it, he ran for the haystack some distance from the barn. The five Creston posse members opened fire and Tracy returned fire on the run.

The haystack was at the edge of a wheat field and from it Tracy ran through the wheat a considerable distance to a large rock, as big as a haystack, in the middle of the field.... Just before Tracy reached the big rock, he fell forward. He had been hit! He grabbed his right leg and it was obvious to the posse he had been seriously wounded.

Today, this part of Lincoln County remains virtually unchanged from what it was 87 years ago. The large, rectangular piece of basalt Tracy had been running for is still there, a fitting tombstone.

"Tracy Rock is one of the most important outlaw artifacts left in the West," say Dullenty. "That's because Tracy's criminal career covered a lot of territory and included a lot of shootouts."

If you use your imagination, you can almost smell the smoke from the posse member's carbines. Or hear the desperate last shot, when Tracy, bleeding to death from two severe leg wounds, put his revolver to his head and squeezed the trigger one last time.

Dullenty has spent a good part of the past 17 years researching what began as a simple assignment when he was a reporter for *The Spokane Daily Chronicle*.

"For some reason or another, I was sent out to do a story on Tracy and found there was very little reliable information," he says. "But being the good reporter I was, I was paid to write a story so I wrote a story."

After Dullenty left the *Chronicle* in 1975, he landed a number of journalism jobs, including editor of several magazines with Old West themes. Wherever he went, the Tracy story continued to nag at him.

"I always wondered why somebody hadn't done something reliable on Tracy's past. After a while, I decided to do it myself."

What Dullenty uncovered was a classic tale of a good boy gone bad. Dullenty learned Tracy's real name was Harry Severns and traced his roots back to Pittsville, Wisconsin, where he as born in 1874 into a prominent, respected family. Tracy's grandfather had even served the community as justice of the peace.

For some unknown reason – Dullenty figures it may have boiled down to a quest for excitement – Harry Severns took the Tracy sobriquet and headed west in 1895 to pursue a life of crime and bloodshed.

Although he was arrested several times, no prison would ever hold him for long. On June 9, 1902, Tracy made his last and most famous escape, this time from the Oregon State Penitentiary. He and his partner, David Merrill, killed three guards in the process and eventually made it to Washington, where three more men were gunned down. Tracy also is credited with killing Merrill over some unknown dispute.

As Tracy made his way east, the Spokane newspapers carried regular apocalyptic reports of his progress. People read every word and were terrified like never before.

"They locked their doors and hid under their beds," says Dullenty. "They could see the menace approaching, that at any moment, this fiend from hell would appear."

Over the years, the Tracy saga became the inspiration of dime novels, countless articles, silent films and even the 1982 movie, *The Last Desperado*, starring Bruce Dern.

Walt Kik, 80, says he grew up in Davenport hearing the story told over and over by his dad. "It was legendary," he says with a chuckle. "My Dad made it sound like he was so close to it, if he hadn't done the right thing he'd have been shot."

Karen Cole, who owns the Tracy site with her husband, Everette, says it's been fun caretaking such a historic spot. "Gosh, we've entertained movie stars, producers and bus tours."

She winks. "But I'm still waiting for Robert Redford. That's when I'll know we really have something here."

185

Shake, rattle and head for the hills

SOMEWHERE AROUND WILBUR, WASHINGTON – There I was, teetering on a slippery slope, staring into the poisonous fangs of death.

Rattlesnakes. Everywhere.

Yegads! The loose basalt rocks in front of me were crawling with blunt-headed, dark-striped snakes. One venomous bite could land me in a hospital. Or give me the nickname "Stubby."

The hills were alive with the sound of rattling. No wonder my neck hairs were doing a snake dance of their own.

A few feet ahead was a sight far weirder than the damnable snakes:

Two grown men, gleefully pulling the writhing critters off the rocks the way happy fishermen haul lunkers out of a hot trout hole.

There's one vital difference between catching fish and catching rattlesnakes. People who troll for rattlers pray there won't be any biting.

"This is more fun than golf and *waaay* better for your heart," says Roger Jensen, a 58-year-old wheat farmer whose dad taught him how to hunt rattlers when he was 21.

Every year about this time, Jensen and his pal, Don Ashenbrenner, carry on this bizarre tradition.

Ashenbrenner, 41, a sergeant with the Coeur d'Alene Police Department, supposedly turns the snake skins into hat bands and belt buckles for his friends.

That's their cover story. I suspect, however, that these characters do this more for the adrenaline rush than for arts and crafts.

They let me take a serpent safari so long as I swore an oath not to reveal the whereabouts of any of their treasured rattlesnake hunting grounds.

"A lot of people would love to know where these dens are," Jensen told me. Oh, yeah. I'll bet the line would stretch longer than tone-deaf hayseeds at a Garth Brooks ticket window.

To most sane people, the notion of getting up close and personal with rattlesnakes is scarier than walking into a biker bar and yelling "Harleys suck!"

"You guys are sick, sick, sick," says Jensen's wife, Bonnie, who refuses to accompany her hubby on his snake hunts.

"But I thought you wanted us to do more things together," says a snickering Roger.

Bonnie is also mayor of this small town 65 miles west of Spokane, so she probably has her own creepy crawlies to contend with down at City Hall.

Neither Jensen nor Ashenbrenner has ever been bit, which strikes me as somewhat amazing.

They don't wear gloves. They catch the critters with 3-foot tongs. The flaw in the ointment is that some rattlers are longer than the tongs.

A few years ago, Jensen's heart got a marathon workout. He grabbed onto a tail. The irate snake turned and shimmied up the tongs, stopping about three inches shy of Jensen's bare hands.

"You know you've got a big snake when that happens," he says.

Some of the snake dens – places where rattlesnakes congregate like Teamsters to keep warm during the winter – are located precariously on the sides of mountains.

Translation: If the snakes don't kill you, the fall just might.

One year Jensen took a tumble down a rocky slope. He couldn't stop rolling until he hit bottom. Fortunately, he walked away with only bruises to his body and pride.

The snakes aren't so lucky. Once nabbed, Jensen and Ashenbrenner use their tongs to quickly pinch the heads off.

It's a grisly sight: gap-jawed rattlesnake heads littering the ground, their decapitated bodies still undulating despite death.

At the rocky den we climbed to, Jensen and Ashenbrenner killed and bagged a dozen snakes. Probably 40 more slipped away.

Reptile rights supporters won't like this, but hunting rattlesnakes is perfectly legal.

According to a Washington Fish and Wildlife spokesman, the snakes aren't classified or protected. So it's always open season.

That suits the rattlesnake hunters just fine.

"I don't like those people," says Ashenbrenner of the animal rights crowd. "I hunt and fish and hunt snakes and eat steaks. I'm an outdoorsman."

Thousands will take bite out of bull

ROCK CREEK, MONTANA – The truck driver rolled his 18 wheels all the way from Ohio. The bikers straddled their Harleys from southern Idaho and the Washington coast. A group of Japanese tourists is rumored to be on its way in a rented bus.

By the time I get to Nardstock we are several hundred strong. Soon, thousands of pilgrims will join me in this weedy field 20 miles east of Missoula.

We are here to celebrate three days of peace, love and deep-fried bull testicles.

"Colonel Sanders went to his grave without my recipe," says Rod Lincoln, who for 13 years has hosted the strangest picnic on the planet at his Rock Creek Lodge.

Lincoln's specialty is a legend of the West, a dish made famous by waste-not, want-not cowpokes who weren't too picky about what they called grub.

Rocky Mountain Oysters. Montana Tendergroin.

Whatever the moniker, we are talking about slicing bull testicles into thin patties that are soaked in brine, marinated in beer, dipped in a batter and finally fried two minutes in hot grease.

The result is golden brown fillets I guarantee will never be featured in a McDonald's value meal.

"You can't write about 'em if you don't try 'em," says Lincoln, 51, sliding a steaming platter under my nose.

The things a serious journalist must do for a story.

I hold my nose. I close my eyes. Mmm. Cheeewy.

The taste is, well, hard to discern.

Veal? Chicken? It really all depends on how well you can flush from your mind the image of what you have willingly stuck in your mouth.

The Donner Party, I suspect, had similar culinary obstacles to hurdle.

"It bothered me, but I had to give 'em a try," says Dorothy Marty, 68, who came here as part of an RV caravan from the Seattle area.

"It makes you want to put your legs together," adds Stan Thompson, 56, of Missoula.

"If you have to come this far, you sure as hell don't want to eat chicken," says Randy Holloway, 45, an Idaho Falls computer programmer in black leather biker clothing.

The crowd couldn't be more diverse. There are lawyers, doctors, retirees and ne'er-do-wells with only one thing in common – a taste for testes.

They consumed 3,600 pounds of oysters last year, so Lincoln upped his supply to 2 tons for the 1994 go-'round.

Even a Clinton Cabinet member knows that quality bull nards don't grow on trees. Because of a limited supply of beefy victims, Lincoln buys what he can from cattle ranchers all year long.

"I've got them stored in every freezer of every acquaintance of mine all over the valley," he says. "Even so, we'll probably run out."

Nobody's more shocked by the raging success of this annual lunacy than Lincoln, a latter-day P. T. Barnum who once taught junior high in Greenacres.

He quit educating America's youth and bought the Rock Creek Lodge, a sprawling clapboard tavern in the middle of nowhere.

In 1981, maybe out of boredom, he dreamed up the first Testicle Festival. A few dozen brave souls showed up. By the fifth year there were hundreds.

Last year saw 7,000 visitors. Front page coverage on the *Chicago Tribune* and stories in CNN and in magazines such as *Self* and *Harper's* have made this a national event.

People from 44 states, four Canadian provinces and several foreign countries have paid $3 for a platter of oysters. (Five bucks gets you side dishes of bread and beans along with the main attraction.)

For some, however, the festive atmosphere is plenty.

"I will not. I will not. I just won't do it," says Patty Anderson, a Spokane woman who is enjoying her third festival *sans* glands. "I bring my own food. I just can't handle those things."

Consuming Rocky Mountain Oysters is apparently helped by copious amounts of cold beer. Fourteen hundred cases of cold beer, to be precise.

Like Woodstock, the vast majority of these festivalgoers party in a state of befogged bliss. Amazingly, the festival is nearly fracas-free.

"These things make you *reeeal* mellow," slurs a sloshed, hairy biker.

Only in America can a businessman strike the mother lode with bull testicles. One needs wander no farther than the

Rock Creek Lodge gift shop to understand the method to Lincoln's madness.

Hats, toothpick holders, T-shirts, bandannas, mugs, key chains, golf balls, playing cards, pennants, aprons, bumper stickers . . . every gimmicky item imaginable bearing the Testicle Festival logo is for sale.

For one health care professional, wearing an official T-shirt is as close as she wants to get to a Rocky Mountain Oyster. "I have people in my family who eat those things," says the woman. "No thank you very much."

Town tradition goads residents into donations

Just because we wear shoes and live in a big city doesn't mean we can't learn something from our cousins out there in the bumpkin patch.

Which is why Spokane residents should follow Omak's example and adopt our own version of Goat Day.

No, you don't need to change the batteries in your hearing aid. I said Goat Day.

On Friday, March 29, 1996, Omakians will again celebrate their grand tradition of sending live goats to friends and enemies.

Most communities would probably keep something like this chained up in the attic like a drooling, half-wit uncle.

Not Omak. Representatives of this fine city (population 6,000), located about 160 miles northwest of Spokane, proudly mailed out Goat Day press releases for the world to see.

For 10 bucks, the Chamber of Commerce will deliver a pygmy goat to "the business/person of your choice." Or you can buy "goat insurance against delivery anywhere in Omak" for $25.

This unique fund-raiser started about a dozen years ago as an April Fool's tribute. It usually adds $1,500 to the chamber coffers.

It's not known, however, if the goats have any say in this.

Considering Omak's twisted history with animals, I'll wager they don't.

Omak, after all, is home of the Omak Stampede. In that annual summer event, unsuspecting horses are ridden off a cliff.

"It's what Omak is made of," says Chamber of Commerce worker Lynell Wiegand. "It's our future. It's our past."

Lynell's future is to be part of the goat delivery crew. They are "so cute and cuddly, and they'll probably ruin your carpets," she adds.

As a professional journalist, I felt obliged to check out this Goat Day business. So I called the Cedars Inn coffee shop, which is technically in Okanogan (population 1,500), but the two towns are within tobacco-splatting distance of each other.

"Goat Day is wonderful," says Bob Liff, 66. "I think it should continue."

Bob once sent a goat to his friend, Donna, at her office. "It was a helluva surprise," says Bob, a retired diesel shop owner.

What was Donna's reaction?

"She's not my friend anymore," adds Bob, chortling.

Half of Omak apparently thinks Goat Day is *ba-a-a-a-d* news. A woman attorney is reportedly still steamed at another lawyer who sent a goat to her office. Insurance agent Jack Miller says nobody better send him a goat.

"My goat insurance is a .357 magnum."

"That's why we do it," explains Bob. More chortling. "To make the other half mad."

Tedi Brian, my second coffee shop interview, says some people would welcome an IRS audit more than a surprise visit from a goat. "Someone sent one to my father-in-law, who owns a restaurant, and he threw a fit," she says. "I mean, you're doing your job and in walks a goat."

We big-city sophisticates could use something like Goat Day, but why mess around with harmless critters?

What Spokane needs is a Spike Day.

On Spike Day, citizens could send Spike – the fang-happy Spokane Police dog – to community leaders who have disgraced their office.

Spike, as you may recall, chomped a cigarette-smoking transient. In a separate incident, he attacked two citizens who were singing the Beatles song "Martha, My Dear."

Homophobic County Coroner Dexter Amend should be the next hors d'oeuvre on the Spike gravy train.

Secretary: "Uh, Dr. Amend, there's someone here to see you."

Amend: "Yes, show him . . . Hey, who let that thing in . . . Down boy. Nice doggie. Get thee behind me, ye cursed beast of Sodom. *Aaaaarrrrgggghhhhh*!!"

Maybe we'd better call this Good-bye You Old Goat Day.

Kids

Chapter Ten

Love for grandparents made sacrifice "no big deal"

John Alling's 2.4 grade point average in high school didn't exactly qualify him for Harvard. His 5-15 wrestling record didn't turn his living room mantle into a trophy shrine.

But make no mistake, John Alling is anything but average. In fact, this 18-year-old is as fine and extraordinary a representative of the Class of '88 as you'll ever hear about.

That's because of a courageous decision John made as a junior at Post Falls High School. It was during Thanksgiving break in 1986 that he decided to sacrifice a few of his own dreams for the love of his grandparents, Phil and Freddie Gardner.

The Gardners live in Creston, Washington, where they both suffer from Alzheimer's disease.

"Ever since I can remember," said John, "my grandparents have played an important part of my life. They were the type of people that, when I needed them, were always there for me."

So when the state of the Gardners' health got family members talking about finding a nursing home, John took the toughest stand of his life. "I thought, 'no way,'" he said. "I decided to give up a few things and go help them out."

So John dropped out of Post Falls High and moved in with the couple he had idolized as a youth. He also entered the tiny high school in Creston, where he and the nine other members of his class graduated last Sunday.

"Actually it's Creston-Wilbur High School," said John with a good-natured chuckle. "We don't have enough players

197

for sports, so we have to go down to Wilbur to recruit for teams."

He added, "There's no theater in town, but we do have a drive-in. Not the kind you watch movies at, but the kind where you eat."

At an age where most teenagers struggle with basic responsibilities, John kept a careful watch over his grandparents, tending to their needs without getting in the way. Above all, he wanted the Gardners to maintain whatever dignity and independence they could.

Ask John, though, and he'll claim it was no big deal, that all he was doing was lending a helping hand.

John's mother, Judy, knows different. She knows the real story about the awesome job her son took on.

"He's grown up a lot in the last two years," she said. "He has his moments like any kid. But he's also a strong young man."

Judy, an instructor at the Kootenai Family YMCA in Coeur d'Alene, said it wasn't easy to let her son move to Creston. It's one thing, she said, to allow a child to venture to a far-away school or some other enriching experience.

"But to send our 16-year-old to take care of two Alzheimer's patients was the hardest thing my husband and I have ever done. I don't think there is a more devastating disease on earth than Alzheimer's."

Alzheimer's usually results in the gradual death of a victim's brain cells. As the cells die off, so goes a person's memory and, in the disease's later stages, even the simplest decision-making skills seem to evaporate.

Said Judy, "I've watched John follow his grandma around the house, actually putting food in her mouth. He would come home from school to fix them lunch. His grades suffered terribly for it."

"Taking care of an Alzheimer's patient is hard. Yet he's willingly done things many adults would balk at."

According to John, it was his own memories of his grandparents that motivated him. How his grandfather taught him fly fishing and was there when he got his tonsils out. How his grandmother would pitch baseballs to him in the back yard.

"I remember when I was about 5 or 6, when my grandpa took me elk hunting for the first time," recalled John. "We were sitting in his pickup when he saw a herd of elk coming. Grandpa had shot plenty of deer before but he had never shot an elk. He was pretty excited.

As the elk lumbered closer, old Phil readied his rifle. But young John had brought his weapon along, too. Just before the crucial moment, John crawled over his grandfather's shoulder and began banging loudly away on his toy gun while the surprised herd vanished.

"He never even got mad," said John, laughing hard. "But he did love to tell that story."

Nowadays, though, his 86-year-old grandfather finds the stories harder and harder to tell. "He'll look at pictures and ask me where they were taken," said John. "And this was a guy who used to be able to rattle off from memory anyone's phone number in the county."

The disease has been worse for Freddie. Despite John's help, the 84-year-old woman has had to be placed in a nursing home. That, he said, has led to a significant decline for Phil.

John realizes the time he has spent so close to his grandparents is nearing an end. In the fall, he will enter North Idaho College in Coeur d'Alene.

For the summer, however, he will stay in Creston and work as a lifeguard.

"That'll give grandpa another three months out of a nursing home," he said. "I figure he'll appreciate even that much quality time."

Pulling the trigger on a young life

She should be outside scuffling her feet through leaves on a lovely fall day like today.

Or maybe she should be in her bedroom, moving to the urban rhythms of her favorite rap group and taping more Reebok and Nike logos to the walls.

She should be somewhere, reveling in the boundless glory that goes with being a 13-year-old kid.

She should not be hooked to machines in a hospital. The last place a vivacious, pretty teenager like Erin Rockstrom should be is in the intensive care pediatrics unit of Spokane's Deaconess Medical Center.

Yet she is. Accidentally shot in the head by a 14-year-old middle school classmate on September 5, 1993, what remains of Erin's life drags by in Room 202.

Minute by minute. Hour by hour . . .

Erin Rockstrom is in a vegetative state. She is unable to make purposeful movements. She doesn't respond to commands.

Nourishment trickles along a tube inserted into her stomach. Although she breathes on her own, a tracheotomy tube runs into her throat to keep her air intake constant and her lungs clear.

IV lines drip medication and antibiotics into her veins. Splints keep her hands and feet from curling.

There is brain activity still going on, but no one knows if Erin is aware of the nurses as they come and go. No one can say if she hears the stories her mother, Debbie, reads to her by the hour.

No one knows if Erin will ever be Erin again.

"I just want her back, to wake up," says Debbie, fighting back tears. "I know she'll never be the same."

If it hadn't been for a handgun – taken from a father's drawer by a visiting teenager – Debbie may never have learned of her daughter's all-night escapade.

Erin, says the mother, was supposed to be spending the night with her best friend. Instead, the girl tagged along with some other Glover Middle School classmates to a party at the home of a boy whose parents were out of town.

What followed is a senseless tragedy that can never be explained:

A boy who shouldn't have had a gun did; a second boy who should have known better picked it up.

The revolver went off. The party was over.

"I've never had a gun in my house; I've always been afraid of guns," says Debbie. "Erin had to be so naive. I can't imagine her staying in a place where there was a gun."

Erin was sitting on the floor when she was hit.

The .22-caliber bullet pierce her right cheek, traveled through her brain and lodged in the brain stem. Because of the bullet's delicate location, surgeons have decided not to try to remove it.

In Room 202, Debbie maintains a vigil at Erin's bedside, stroking her hair, whispering in her ear and waiting for the slightest sign of progress.

Teddy bears, get well cards, flowers and balloons line a wall. If only Erin could appreciate them.

"Your emotions go up and down," says the 35-year-old woman. "At times you just get overwhelmed. Sometimes you don't know what day it is."

Since her divorce seven years ago, Debbie says she has tried her best to raise Erin and her 11-year-old sister, Robyn. Debbie is an attendant counselor at Lakeland Village, a treatment center for the mentally handicapped.

Trying to earn a college degree, Debbie has worked the 3-11 p.m. shift for the last year. She feels sad for not having enough time to always be there for her kids.

"She's a good mother," says Debbie's closest friend, Jeannie Gaffney. "She's the strongest person I know. She was working hard to go to school so that she could make a better life for her children."

That life has unraveled with a blast of gunfire.

Robyn doesn't like to see her mother cry, so she tries to cheer her up. But at night, says Debbie, "I'll go into her room and find wadded up Kleenex and know she's been crying alone."

A lot of families have been shedding tears of late.

In less than two months, three area teenagers have been cut down by senseless shootings.

Cedric Willis, 17, died after he accidentally shot himself. Erin was shot a month later. Mae Marsura, 13, died when she put a rifle to her head on a dare and pulled the trigger.

April Croy, Erin's primary care nurse, was on duty when an ambulance brought in Mae. The nurse took one look and knew that nothing could be done.

With children of her own, she says it's impossible to see young lives ruined and not to be deeply affected.

"I've never had insomnia in my life, but now I can't sleep," says April. "I can hardly stand the thought of children having their heads blown off."

Assault charge filled with fizz, no substance

Anah Clark will get her day in court next month for a felony assault on her teacher.

The Spokane girl didn't carry a gun or a switchblade to class. She didn't use her fists.

This 11-year-old's weapon of destruction was far more insidious – Efferdent.

You heard me, Efferdent. The same fizzy stuff Granny puts in the water glass beside her bed to clean her false teeth.

The sixth-grader pulled off her Big Crime March 25, 1992, at St. Aloysius, a Catholic school at East 611 Mission.

While her teacher, Virginia Roth, was out of the classroom, the girl dared plop an Efferdent tablet into the woman's bottle of drinking water.

Anah brought the tablet from home. (Aha, premeditation!)

Some of her classmates giggled when she told them what she intended to do. (Yegads, criminal complicity!)

Roth returned. She took a swig.

The crime would not go unsolved. You let a kid get away with planting an Efferdent in a water bottle, next thing you know there'll be Ex-Lax in the aquifer.

After three hours of inquisition, Principal Tom Ward finally convinced Anah to confess.

She was suspended. Her mother later enrolled her at another school to avoid expulsion.

But that wasn't near enough punishment. Oh, no.

The cops were called in. An investigation was launched. Roth decided to press charges and got her wish.

Second-degree criminal assault carries a possible sentence of eight to 12 weeks in juvenile detention. Anah has been given a public defender and a court date has been set.

Efferdent.

"It was right around April's Fools Day and I think she thought it was going to make her the big popular person in class," says Anah's mother, Lettie.

"This is a nice girl. She takes violin lessons. She plays baseball . . . ."

She's Lizzie Borden as far as the law is concerned.

Sure, county Prosecutor Don Brockett may whine all the time about being understaffed and overworked, but he's got enough tax-paid lawyers to work over a sixth-grade prankster.

Thank God he wasn't around when I was in grade school. I'd be doing life without parole for the stuff I pulled.

No question what Anah did was ill considered. And few would argue that the girl doesn't deserve some punishment.

But second-degree felony assault?

Come on.

Teacher Roth decided to file charges because Anah and her parents didn't see what happened as being in the same league as the Lindbergh kidnapping.

"I'm not doing it (filing charges) for a pound of flesh," she says. "I'm doing it to get her help."

Roth says the Efferdent water gave her first-degree burns from her throat to her stomach. This, according to the police reports, required four trips to the doctor over the period of a month. Based on this, the detective investigating the case agreed charges should be filed.

Top Warner Lambert researchers, however, say their Efferdent wouldn't harm a hamster: "The product has been shown to be essentially non-toxic and non-irritating, the latter through studies of human oral soft tissues and hamster cheek pouches."

Speaking of crimes, Mr. Brockett, where were your troops when these unholy hamster experiments were being performed?

"I think it's shocking that the Spokane County Prosecutor's Office would choose to use its resources in this way," says Dennis Clayton, whose two children got their schooling at St. Al's.

Clayton, who is also an attorney, was asked to look into the case by angry parents who thought Anah was getting the shaft. He speaks fondly of the school and wonders why a solution more in the spirit of Christian charity couldn't have been reached.

The man has asked Catholic leaders to intercede and pursue this through a venue other than the criminal justice system. Nobody, he adds, has had guts enough to do anything but stand back and watch.

"I think this also says something really serious about the principal at St. Al's."

And it's not as if Anah hasn't learned a lesson.

"It probably hurt (Mrs. Roth's) feelings because someone in her own class had done this to her," says Anah. "I will never do something this stupid again, because it hurt someone."

Tooth Fairy cares even after magic is gone

"Fairy tales can come true, it can happen to you, if you're young at heart."

— From the song "Young at Heart," by Carolyn Leigh

Once upon a time there was a sweet, 8-year-old girl who believed with all her heart in the power of magic.

So strong was her faith that when one of her baby teeth wriggled out of her mouth, as baby teeth so often do, she taped it to a small piece of paper and wrote a letter to the Tooth Fairy.

And you know what?

The Tooth Fairy wrote her back!

But nearly three years have passed since that day the postman brought Emily Haxton such an inexplicable reply. Her father, Jim, called me recently to tell me that his daughter has wised up to the ways of the world.

Emily is now a precocious fifth-grader at Colbert Elementary School. She turns 11 next month and is learning to play the piano.

At night she lies awake reading Nancy Drew mysteries, using a flashlight to illuminate the pages. She thinks her parents don't know.

Emily believes more in the power of Paula Abdul than she does in magic.

So today, my friend, the truth can be told. I was the Tooth Fairy who wrote you on March 7, 1990.

In a way, what happened was plenty magical. I was eating lunch at Big Frank's Deli in the Paulsen Building one afternoon when the owner, John Klapp, handed me a folded scrap of paper.

"Somebody must've dropped this in here," he said. "I dunno, it might make a story."

I unfolded the paper and began to read:

Dear Toothfairy,

Here is my tooth. I am sorry my room is a mess. I was sick today. I like you.

You are my friend. Love, Emily.

The simple words were a magic carpet that flew me back to my own world of childlike trust, when the Easter Bunny and Santa and the Tooth Fairy were as real as the president.

Intrigued, I carried the letter back to the office, hoping the mystery would be solved. The next morning, the telephone rang with the answer.

"You've got my daughter's tooth."

It was Jim Haxton. He explained that Emily's letter had fallen out of his pocket while he as eating at Big Frank's. He wondered if he could drop by the newsroom and get it back.

There was a better way . . .

I sat down at a typewriter and tried to think like a mythical being:

Dear Emily,

Our Lost and Found Department here at Tooth Fairy Headquarters has given me your sweet letter and tooth, which was apparently misplaced the other day.

It was a very nice letter and I can see by our records that you are indeed my friend. That's why I am sending your tooth back with a little surprise.

We in the Tooth Fairy business never like to see a job go undone or a child without a smile.

Someday you will stop believing in me, but that's all part of grow-ing up. Just know that for now, I remain your good friend.

Yours with Love and Magic,

T. Fairy.

P.S. Don't worry about your room. You wouldn't believe some of the messes I've seen over the last thousand years. Besides, when you're not feeling well, it's easy to let things get a little cluttered.

I dropped a dollar into the envelope and mailed it away.

"It was great," says Emily's mom, Gail. "She was so thrilled to think that the Tooth Fairy would write her."

Last week Emily lost another tooth. She didn't compose any letters this time. But she wasn't quite ready to give up the ritual. She went to her parents and told them straight out: "You know, some of my friends are getting five bucks for molars."

That seemed a little steep. But her parents agreed to play along with what might be Emily's last grasp at magic.

The girl was reading in bed when the Tooth Fairy arrived. Jim Haxton, pretending to be a sleepwalker, entered his daugh-ter's room with his arms outstretched. He laid a dollar on the table.

Remaining in his trance, he turned to leave the room like some slow-walking.

Emily looked up from her book and smiled at the Tooth Fairy. "Thanks Dad," she said.

Synchronized swimmers sink snide remarks

Today's misadventure finds Moby Doug gasping and floun-dering like a harpooned manatee in the chlorinated waters of the Shadle Park High pool.

He is surrounded by a jeering gang of inhumanly fit teenage girls who hoot with great glee at Moby Doug's love handles.

At the water's edge is a woman who possesses all the sensitive feminine charm of Marge Schott.

Her name is Ann Murphy. She is the head coach of the Spokane Silver Mermaids, a synchronized swimming club founded in 1954.

Murphy is trying very hard to drown Moby Doug.

She orders him to swim 50 yards. Then another 25 yards underwater. She makes Moby Doug tread water for about a lunar cycle and then commands him to perform an unnatural act she calls a "split-crash."

This, Murphy explains, is a classic synchro move where the swimmer suspends herself gracefully upside down underwater, sticks her legs in the air and then does the splits with each toe touching the water.

"The hips should be well out of the water," barks the coach into a microphone.

Moby Doug's hips have the buoyancy of a bridge abutment. His split-crash looks more like a fatal highway accident.

The *Titanic* going under was a prettier sight.

All the flailing makes Moby Doug's heart flutter and chug as if he has suddenly traded tickers with Boris Yeltsin.

What, Moby Doug wonders aloud, would happen should cardiac arrest occur in the pool?

"Our girls have had lifeguard training," snaps the unsympathetic Murphy.

Moby Doug is learning a valuable lesson. The polar ice caps will probably melt before he writes any more nasty things about synchronized swimming.

That's how he got into this unholy stew.

During a recent column on pro foosball champ Laurette Gunther, he made a seemingly innocuous remark.

"If the Olympics have room for silly pursuits like synchronized swimming, can gold medal foosball be far off?"

That word "silly" scalded the Silver Mermaids, three of whom stormed into the newspaper last week to read an official dare:

"Whereas synchronized swimmers have the endurance of long-distance swimmers, the agility and strength of gymnasts and the grace and poise of dancers . . .

"The athletes seek to challenge you to join us in the water for a workout and demonstration."

So Sunday night, Moby Doug leaves his family to go take his lumps.

Four times a week, the 34 rock-hard girls swim 1,000 to 2,000 yards. They learn to hold their breath for a minute at a time while practicing complicated, precise naval maneuvers.

Kicking their legs in a weird egg-beater motion, they can keep their upper bodies well above the water line for up to five minutes.

The girls roar with laughter when Moby Doug shows up wearing swim fins, a snorkel and mask.

"You can't wear that stuff!" they holler.

What sweet little angels, these synchronized swimmers.

Somehow, Moby Doug survives the humiliating evening. In appreciation, the Silver Mermaids present him with an autographed stadium cushion.

This is an extremely appropriate gift, considering how thoroughly the Silver Mermaids have kicked Moby Doug's ample butt.

"So-o Mr. Clark," says 15-year-old Mead High sophomore Beth Moore in the sing-songy sneer of victory, "do you still think synchronized swimming is silly?"

"Only when I do it," says Moby Doug, dripping a watery trail as he slinks to the locker room.

It could have been worse, Moby Doug tries to tell himself. He could have hacked off the local karate club.

State foster-care system failed boy for the last time

Most dogs are treated better than Shawn Segle was.

Life for the 13-year-old boy had been one letdown after another. Family turmoil and neglect had been compounded by years spent in and out of court-ordered care.

In the last 15 months, Shawn had bounced through seven foster homes and six different schools.

On August 10, 1986, at about 12:30 a.m., the system failed the boy for the last time.

In the basement of an East Wenatchee foster home, Shawn was shot in the back at point-blank range with a .22 caliber, semi-automatic Browning handgun.

The bullet sliced through his upper spine and caused massive internal bleeding. Paramedics arrived within minutes, but to no avail.

The boy was pronounced dead at 12:57 a.m. in the emergency room of Wenatchee's Central Washington Hospital.

Those who knew Shawn describe him as a likable kid who could steal his way into your heart with one wide-eyed, innocent stare.

He was sandy haired and slightly built, and he exuded – one social worker says – the typical, all-American, Huck Finn kind of look.

But hidden beneath the ready grins and exterior charm was a darker reality.

That grim tale is chronicled in a 4-inch pile of documents and reports kept in Spokane's dreary Child Protective Service offices.

The confidential file on Shawn Segle's life and times won't get any thicker.

Shawn's funeral was Friday, but it will be some time before his story is laid to rest.

Douglas County's prosecutor has filed manslaughter charges against 16-year-old Fred McKinnis, who has admitted pulling the trigger.

The circumstances surrounding the death have also sent a shock wave through the state Department of Social and Health

Services. In fact, the shooting has prompted administrators to reevaluate the state's entire foster care program.

"It's a classic case of the right hand not knowing what the left hand was doing," said Barb Paccerelli, area manager for Region I of Children and Family Services.

"At least that's what I would go after if I was going to sue anybody."

Here are the facts:

In late June, Shawn was placed in the home of Helen Mattern – a woman in her 70s who has provided disturbed kids with foster care ever since the death of her husband, Red, 15 years ago.

The elderly woman has a good heart and a good record of dealing with some pretty tough customers. Case workers hoped that with Mattern Shawn would receive the help he so desperately needed.

On July 30, however, Mattern agreed to take in McKinnis on a private contract negotiated by probation officer Bruce Voy. McKinnis had stayed in the home before as a foster child, but was out on probation stemming from two 1985 burglary convictions.

"We had no idea Fred was even there," said Paccerelli. "The first we heard about it was after the shooting."

Mattern says that, until the shooting, Fred and Shawn were good for each other.

"They wrassled and played together just like brothers," she said. "Fred thought the world of Shawn and Shawn thought the world of Fred."

Some details on what happened are still a bit out of focus.

Mattern believes McKinnis' latest story, which is that the shooting was not deliberate, but the result of some dangerous horseplay.

"Fred knew it was loaded and was trying to secure the safety when it went off," said Voy. "He's maintaining it was purely an accident."

211

Shortly after the shooting, however, McKinnis – who dialed 911 for help – told authorities Shawn had committed suicide.

An autopsy performed by Douglas County Coroner Dr. Robert Bonifaci revealed the impossibility of that statement. McKinnis was questioned again and admitted to his role in the tragedy.

Mattern, who was asleep at the time, said she always kept the basement of her home locked and off-limits to foster children. Those rooms, she said, were used occasionally by her son and contained his stereo equipment and other personal belongings, including firearms.

"After I went to sleep, they came in and got the key to the door," the woman said. "I don't know. I'm about ready to give (foster care) up."

The state may make that choice for her.

Paccerelli is unsure whether a foster child will ever be placed in Mattern's house again.

"Our licensing requirements do not permit her to take private placements," she said.

"We wouldn't have placed Fred with Shawn anyway. Our purpose was to give Shawn individual attention in a setting without – I don't know how to say it – any excitement."

Paccerelli describes her department as heartbroken over Shawn.

"It was still a sad case even before this tragic shooting. We need to look better at what we do.

"Sure, we don't have funds or the staff, but, darn it, that's not a good enough excuse."

One solution, Paccerelli feels, is to place juveniles with criminal backgrounds in specialized homes where foster parents are professionally trained and paid high enough wages to eliminate the need of outside work.

As it stands now, the standard payment is $268 a month for letting a Shawn live in your home.

"Many times you're gonna get what you pay for," said Mary Ann Murphy, who directs the Youth Help Association, a private and non-profit social service agency that provides counseling for foster parents.

Murphy would give the state's foster care program only a C grade.

"And the care for a child should be an A," she said. "When you don't adequately care for a child, you'll feel the repercussions for a long, long time."

Hard Luck

Chapter Eleven

Bullets shatter idyllic setting, feeling of safety

It is one of those Kodak moments claustrophobic Californians dream about.

Clean skies. Pine trees. Cold beer . . .

Four family members relax around a front-yard picnic table, swatting mosquitoes and swapping yarns in the waning light of a glorious July day.

Spokane's Tom and Jan Stanley often visit this rustic homestead between Hamilton and Darby, Montana, to see Jan's sister, Marlene Porter, and her husband, Don.

The rugged setting, 45 miles south of Missoula, seems as removed from the horrors of a drive-by shooting as a fast-running trout stream from a rush-hour freeway.

But the sound of a slowing car followed by the sudden pop-pop-popping of rifle fire forever shattered the serenity for these people.

"My first thought was that kids were setting off firecrackers. Then I felt something hit my right side hard and I dropped to the ground," recalls Tom. "The next thing I heard was Marlene yell, 'I've been hit.' I looked up and saw blood literally squirting from her face."

A pharmacist at the 29th Avenue Safeway store, Tom is a familiar face to South Hill shoppers. The Stanleys invited me to their Spokane Valley home the other day to recount the worst moment in their lives and how the aftermath may bankrupt their relatives.

July 27, 1996, marks the one-year anniversary of the senseless attack that outraged much of Montana.

Two brutes are in prison. Marlene spent five weeks in intensive care. The bullet hit her dead center in the chin, shattered her jaw and clipped the left carotid artery in her neck.

Her progress has been agonizing. After surgeons wired her ruined jaw together, she spent six months sipping nourishment through a straw.

The tragedy continues. The $25,000 maximum the Porters received from Montana's victim's fund covered less than half of Marlene's medical bills.

Uninsured and barely getting by before the shooting, the couple still owes $32,000. Tom says the Porters could lose the home Don's grandfather built.

Once a vibrant, energetic woman, Marlene is profoundly changed. "I can't work. I don't trust anybody. I don't really care to be in social situations," she says in a telephone interview. "I know I'll never have the life back that I had. But to just live a normal, simple existence – when do I get to do that?"

It was nearly dusk when a car drove north past the Porter residence on U.S. Highway 93. From the back seat, Clyde Allen Johnson, 27, aimed a semiautomatic .22 rifle out a rear window.

Ravalli County's first drive-by shooting "is as vicious as anything you see anywhere," says Prosecutor George Corn, adding there was no connection between Johnson and the Porters or Stanleys.

Johnson, who was out of jail awaiting a rape trial, squeezed the trigger as if he were at an amusement park shooting gallery. Ten bullets sprayed into the area where the two couples sat some 75 yards away.

A mile down the road it was Kenneth Weinreber's turn. The 27-year-old, whose wife was driving, fired a .270 rifle at a pickup occupied by a Hamilton resident. The man wasn't hit. Both Weinreber and Johnson were arrested within hours.

It could have been far worse. The bullet hitting Tom was slowed by a double ricochet. It left only a fist-sized bruise.

A paramedic arrived quickly, considering the remote location. Even so, says Jan Stanley, "When you're holding your sister's head in your lap while she's bleeding to death, 15 minutes seems like forever."

A judge sentenced Johnson, who pleaded guilty, to 100 years in prison. The first 20 are to be served without the possibility of parole.

The extreme sentence combined wounding Marlene with the 1994 rape conviction. Weinreber got 20 years for his crime.

No sentence could be too long for these punks who turned the innocence of a glorious July day into a bloody nightmare.

"They stole something," says Jan. "My whole family grew up in Montana. I guess we thought we were insulated. The truth is that you aren't safe no matter where you are."

Justice was never served for murdered girls

Two little girls snatched during a walk to the candy store.

One found dead hours later, her body hidden under a pile of smoldering pine needles. The other still missing.

A prime suspect fingered by police.

What happened to Nikki Wood, 11, and Rebecca West, 12, on October 23, 1991, outraged this city like few crimes do.

It was the catalyst for a new police substation, dedicated as a memoriam to the two young victims.

It sparked renewed interest in Block Watch programs, helping make the girls' crime-ridden West Central neighborhood a safer place to live.

This ghastly case also brought out the usual bottom feeders: vote-seeking politicians from the City Council to former House Speaker Tom Foley. They rode in parades and speechified, vowing never to forget what happened to Nikki and Rebecca.

Nearly 3½ years later, the hot air has blown away. Spokane's attention has turned to other atrocities. Other victims.

Few recall that justice has never been served for these girls. The case against Michael W. Tarbert – a drug addict who is serving a rape conviction in the state pen – has gone nowhere.

The files have grown mold in the county prosecutor's office since October 28, 1992, when Sheriff's Detective Jim Hansen sent them there to ask that Tarbert be charged with two counts of first-degree murder.

"It was obvious in my mind that nothing was going to get done," says a frustrated Hansen. "I've got my own ideas what happened, but I'm not going to bad-mouth anybody."

He's too polite to lay blame for the stalled case on Don Brockett's dismal last hurrah as county prosecutor.

Brockett, who mercifully retired, spent the waning days of his career waging unsuccessful judicial campaigns and sniping at imagined political enemies, rather than concentrating on dirtbags like Tarbert.

"The last several years Brockett got more difficult to work with," agrees Hansen.

Adding to the prosecutorial confusion was the December 1993 retirement of Clark Colwell, Brockett's chief criminal deputy and right-hand man.

"I think about that case often," says Colwell, who adds that at the time he left he didn't consider the investigation ready for filing.

It's true that evidence against Tarbert is largely circumstantial.

Bloodhounds tracked his scent from a cabin he once lived in to the spot where Nikki's burned body was found. Tarbert was a friend of Wood's mother. The more police questioned the man about the girls, the more he changed his tale.

But it's also true that Hansen's handiwork won't age for the better like a fine cabernet.

One witness has died. Other witnesses were in the sixth grade at the time. Hansen worries that their memories will get shakier as the years go by.

"To let this sit is a travesty," says the detective.

The last hope that Nikki and Rebecca will be avenged rests with Jim Sweetser, Spokane County's new prosecutor.

Sweetser talks the talk. He vows to examine the file soon. He says he trusts Hansen's judgment.

The evidence may not be air-tight. But should the murder of two girls be shelved because some overcautious lawyer doesn't think the case has a high enough win factor in court?

"Sometimes you have to take a risk," Sweetser says, and "let a jury have the option to decide."

Preach it, Jim. There are people who still care about what happened to two Spokane kids who thought they could walk safely to the store for a bag of candy.

"I'm beyond mourning for my daughter, she's in a better place," says Dan Wood, Nikki's father. "But I tell you, I'm still mad as hell."

[1998 Update: The case is still in limbo. No charges have been filed against anyone.]

Needle points one man's life down hard road

We had more in common than our first name.

We both stand over 6 feet, are 38 years old and graduated from a Spokane high school in 1969.

But the ensuing 20 years had taken us down different paths.

On Monday morning, this Doug unrolled his sleeve and shot $90 worth of brown heroin into a vein. That was business as usual. What was different was that after his fix, he came downtown to see me, to talk about the frustrating addiction that had consumed the better part of his life.

"Every day starts off the same," he said. "You wake up in the morning and you're like the Tin Man, you know, with no oil in your joints. You ache and creak like you're all full of rust. So you go into the bathroom and do what you have to do so you can function during the day."

He showed me the fresh, scabbed track in his arm. He didn't have to call attention to his eyes. His constricted pupils, a side-effect of the heroin, stood out like two tiny periods on a sheet of blank paper.

For two decades, Doug's life has been inseparably tied to drugs.

The process began innocently. After graduating from high school, he was in a car wreck that did some major damage to his back.

He was in the hospital 30 days. Doctors helped ease Doug's pain with Demerol. When he got used to that, they gave him morphine. After that, Dilaudid.

Each new drug packed a little more wallop. But there were strings attached. By the time he left the hospital, he was hooked.

"You can't blame the doctors," said Doug. "I was in serious pain. But you add that to an addictive personality and this is what can happen."

Doug doesn't fit the junkie stereotype, the down-and-out bum who nods off on street corners and will steal your tape deck to get his next fix. Doug is an articulate guy who in the past has run his own business and owned his own home and rental property.

"In a lot of ways, I'm just like you," he said. "I mow my lawn on the weekend and pay my taxes. I've always been resourceful."

That resourcefulness led him to a sympathetic doctor in the early 1970s. The man was also a user and he kept Doug supplied with legal pharmaceuticals for years.

Then the doctor was busted. There would be no more easy prescriptions, so Doug took his business to the street.

"I didn't want to use a needle," he said. "But with the dope-fiend's rationale, I said, 'Well, here's a better way of administering the drugs.'"

Doug's habit grew to a $150-a-day bill for heroin. He can purchase the drug, he said, within 20 minutes from practically any location in Spokane.

When he can, he gets a friend who has cancer to share his morphine. "I know that sounds terrible," he said, looking embarrassed. "But that's what I do."

As the years went by, you could say that Doug wasn't using the drugs so much as the drugs began using him.

"I sold the rental house, I lost my home, I lost my vehicles, I quit my business, I lost everything," said Doug, who is now living with a friend. "That monkey on your back doesn't care if you're right-wing, left-wing, black, white, brown or indifferent."

Doug said that was why he had come to talk to me.

"I read your stuff. I know you don't like snivelers or whiners. But I don't think I'm a whiner. If people don't hear what this is like, they'll never know."

He's no whiner. Doug even applauds the anti-drugs crusade that President Bush took into the nation's classrooms.

"I have to look in the mirror every morning and realize that I'm being controlled by this stuff," he said. "Kids especially need to hear that. It's something that needs to be brought into the curriculum just like the ABC's."

Doug's biggest desire right now is to kick his habit.

He's tried to get into Spokane's only methadone program, which provides a synthetic heroinlike drug to users, but the admissions process can take up to three weeks. "In three weeks," he said, "maybe I'm gonna lose my resolve."

Doug is smart enough to know the seductive hold that drugs have over him. He knows the courage to quit doesn't come that often. So Doug has decided to do it the hard way, to try and kick his habit all by himself.

A few days after our interview, I called him to see how he was doing.

The voice on the phone sounded sick as a dog. Going through heroin withdrawal can even be dangerous, but Doug said he knows what to expect. He's been through detoxification programs five times before.

"I'm sick all right," he said. "But I'm doing it, I'm doing it. Maybe by Friday I'll be back among the living and this time it will stick.

"Who knows? Maybe the misery I'm going through right now will have some meaning to someone else."

Ex-principal stole his own dignity, pride

The best-educated man in the Spokane County-City Jail marks his 111th day of confinement by polishing off *Eleni*, Nicholas Gage's non-fiction masterpiece about the Greek Civil War.

It's the 78th book the 50-year-old former high school principal has read since the January day when Spokane police officers placed him under arrest minutes after he robbed the South Hill branch of Washington Mutual Bank.

"You'd expect this kind of thing from a 5-year-old child, certainly not someone of my age and background," he says, eyes misting with emotion.

His hands rush to his face. He sobs silently.

"It was totally irrational. A devastating and destructive thing to do to people I had truly loved."

An uncomfortably long minute of silence passes before the owner of two master's degrees, the slightly built man who sits behind a wire-mesh screen, regains control. He lights his third cigarette of the interview. Finally, a wry smile appears at the suggestion that his life has taken on overtones of a Greek tragedy all its own.

Any way you slice it, James Verner Rogers is an unlikely felon.

Judge John A. Schultheis apparently agrees. The Superior Court jurist went beyond the guidelines stipulated in Washington's 1984 Sentencing Reform Act, choosing instead to award Rogers with an exceptionally lenient sentence: a year in jail, with work release privileges should he qualify. A standard first-degree robbery sentence would range from 31 to 41 months.

"Jimmy was a very dynamic, well-appreciated person when I knew him," said Richard Siegel, an administrative intern at New Providence High School in New Providence, New Jersey. "He was a person who realized the dynamics of getting students involved."

During the 1960s, a golden time for Rogers, his flare for teaching social studies and history coursed gained him national recognition. He helped organize and was spokesman for a conference of the Model United Nations program, where student representatives from all 50 states came together annually to emulate the U.N.'s procedures and protocol.

"My experience with him was extremely positive," said Walter McCarthy, who was principal at New Providence when Rogers taught there. "He was always heavily involved with students."

Every year for a decade, Rogers would chaperone his brightest students on a field trip to Washington, D.C. There he would lecture on the inner workings of government, introducing his charges to powerbrokers such as Vice President Hubert Humphrey and Chief Justice William O. Douglas.

Recounting these triumphs, Rogers' soft voice is no match for the jailhouse clatter and murmur that echoes about the drab, narrow visitation chamber of cinderblock walls and unpainted cement floors.

"I suppose you want to know where I went wrong," he says flatly. He pauses. His eyes focus on an unlit cigarette on the table in front of him.

It was 1968. Just south of Carlisle, Pennsylvania, Rogers fell asleep at the wheel and drifted across the median and into an oncoming car. When he woke up he was told he had killed three people – a mother and two children.

His wife, Judy, who was riding in the front seat with Rogers, was maimed. She lost an eye and would face years of plastic surgery and physical therapy.

"Instead of becoming a living memorial for those three people I killed, I kept everything inside. Oh, you can't imagine the feeling of desolation and despondence. The guilt."

The ensuing years were increasingly hard for Rogers. He took a job as an administrator at a high school in Dunellen, New Jersey, leaving in the late 1970s to become principal of Battery Creek High School in Beaufort, South Carolina.

Pressure building inside him, Rogers divorced his wife in 1980 and was fired from his job that same year because of personnel conflicts. He dropped out of sight after that, losing touch with his friends.

"It was the love of a lifetime," he says, running his delicate fingers through thinning brown hair. "You wouldn't believe what we had together. The joy . . ."

He made it as far as Tucson, Arizona. There, alone and in despair, he worked out an incredible plan to fly back to Spokane and make his bank-robbing debut.

On January 16, 1986, armed with two loaded pistols, Rogers drove a rented silver Dodge Omni to the bank at 14th and Lincoln.

Rogers handed a woman a note demanding cash. He pulled his coat to display the pistol in his belt. She coolly, calmly slipped exploding dye in the bag of money and checks.

"When I walked out, I said 'Well, you did it. Now what are you going to do?'"

He got his answer while making a getaway. As he pulled into the intersection, the electric triggered device went off.

Minutes later, James Rogers had a criminal record.

Family Life

Chapter Twelve

Naked race exposes a cover-up

My older brother Dave, a Richland minister, thinks we're headed to a Sunday morning radio interview.

Then I drove down a dirt road north of Spokane. Up ahead, on the left shoulder, stands a grinning naked man.

He waves at us. I wave back.

Dave wears a catatonic expression. He has taken a day away from the pulpit to visit me, and now his universe has tilted like a cheap pinball machine.

"What's wrong with THAT GUY?" he finally shouts in the voice of the demon-possessed.

Between howls of laughter, I begin to explain the evil trick I have played.

"Dave, we've had a slight change of plans."

Suddenly there is no need for words. We drive through the gates of the Kaniksu ranch at Deer Lake and find ourselves surrounded by a clothing-impaired legion: naked men, women and children of all ages, shapes and denominations.

Reality dawns on Dave, who again shouts, "You brought me to a NUDIST CAMP!"

Even better, brother. I have brought you to the ninth Bare Buns Fun Run – the world's first and largest annual three-mile streak.

Every year, the Kaniksu nudists graciously invite the public to join them in joyous celebration of Bunday – the last Sunday of July.

It's kind of a full-frontal Bloomsday.

"The only Bible verse that comes to mind is, 'Gird up your loins,'" mutters my befuddled brother.

Runners are free to encase their assets and liabilities in snowsuits and football helmets if they so desire. But only those who dare run bare earn the coveted "nude-finisher" T-shirt.

Believe it or not, says artist Grady Myers, designer of the Bare Buns logo, "nude-finisher shirts go for 75 bucks on the T-shirt black market."

Does it strike you as odd that a nudist camp would award naked runners articles of clothing?

The irony is lost here. Even on such a chilled, damp morning, at least a third of the 692 registered runners have doffed their duds.

"But why," moans my brother Dave, whose eyes soak in the skin scene, "why would people do this?"

There are a million stories in this naked city.

"The feeling of freedom to run without your clothes" brings Cheryle here.

Cheryle is a trim 36-year-old criminal justice worker from Spokane who stands out from her fleshy peers mainly because of a large, multi-colored parrot tattooed on her rump.

"It's a macaw," she explains, adding her hobby is raising exotic birds.

During our extensive and serious journalistic interview, I learn the tattoo cost Cheryle $110 and took "a very painful hour and a half" to install.

Walt Kik, who turns 84 today, says he's always been a young nudist at heart. "I never went through a mid-life crisis until I turned 80."

A tall Texan named Dallas runs the race wearing nothing but a black cowboy hat. I ask if the wind resistance on the hat slows him down.

"Not at the speed I travel at," drawls Dallas, 49.

A dare from her younger sister brought 53-year-old Eleanor all the way from South Korea, where she is principal of a small American school.

"Last year I jumped out of an airplane. This year I'm running naked. Who knows what's next?" she says.

This is a light-hearted bunch. Even the emergency services workers are bearing up.

"I have to stand over there by the nude finish line," says an ambulance driver, "so I can check on respiration and body color to make sure they're all right."

He grins. "Hey, somebody's gotta do the dirty work."

Besides my brother – who wonders how he's going to explain to his congregation that he was kidnapped by his little brother and taken to a nudist camp – the Bare Buns Fun Run is not for everyone.

Michael Holmes, a raw-running regular, is conspicuously absent at this year's nudefest.

Hmm. Could his current candidacy for the Spokane City Council have anything to do with this?

In an election year, "it just didn't seem like the right thing to do," Holmes conceded. "It would be like tempting fate."

Now isn't that just like politicians?

One day they have nothing to hide. The next day they're engaged in a cover-up.

Unexpected death spurs memories of childhood best friend

Rob lit the smoke bomb and I heaved it into the phone booth outside the Ranch Market on 17th and Ray.

Then we ran, two 13-year-olds flying through the muggy July night, up the dirt hill that divided the grocery store from

Fletcher's Pharmacy. Puke-green smoke billowed inside the booth below and we giggled until our sides hurt.

Then we heard the sirens.

"Oh, crud, Rob, somebody's called the cops."

Rob brushed back a strand of blond hair. If there was one thing Rob wouldn't tolerate it was messy hair.

"Aw, it's just a crummy smoke bomb," he said, fishing his trademark comb out of his back pocket and carefully adjusting his part.

A police cruiser screamed onto the scene. Rob and I sat on the hill, transfixed by the drama below.

A stocky policeman solved the crime, muttering as he kicked the spent smoke bomb out of the booth with his toe. His cop eyes scanned the area like radar, finally locking on two incredibly likely suspects.

We sat 100 yards away, frozen like deer caught in the high beams. My heart was doing the drum part to "Wipe Out."

Rob yelled, "Let's ditch," and we sprinted for the darkness of 18th Avenue. Halfway down the street, wheels closed in behind us. Brakes squealed. I put my hand up to surrender.

A familiar voice growled, "Get in, quick."

It was Rob's big brother, Steve. He'd been cruising up Ray in his Edsel and seen us run. The car had a V-8 and a push-button transmission and Steve tromped on the gas pedal and that's how Spokane's South Hill Smoke Bombers of 1964 avoided capture.

The events of that night never left me . . . . Maybe it was one of those pivotal childhood moments your brain crystallizes to keep it from decay.

Rob was my very best friend through grade school. We learned to play guitars together, and he was the only one I knew with a genuine bomb shelter in his back yard.

When the Reds started World War III, he promised me a spot in the shelter. Friends like that aren't easily found.

Rob was also the best looking kid I ever met. His madras shirts were wrinkle-free, and he came to school in slacks and wingtip shoes that he polished to a high gloss every night in his basement room.

He had a paper route, so I got a paper route. We slept over at each other's houses more times than I can count.

The night of our mad bombing was a sleep-over. We'd spread our sleeping bags in his back yard, then sneaked off to prowl the neighborhood when his parents went to bed.

By today's standards it was innocent fun: We climbed the Franklin School fire escape, set off the smoke bomb and then rode with his brother until things cooled off.

Back in his yard, we pricked our fingers with a pin and became blood brothers. Before we faded off to sleep, Rob swore he saw a UFO.

That was the last summer before we began to drift apart. After two years at Ferris High School, Rob transferred to Shadle when his family moved to the north side of town.

I saw him six or seven years ago when he was working in a bank. He still kept a mirror finish on his shoes and every hair was in place.

October 25, 1996, the newspaper he used to deliver printed his obituary.

I was a guest Wise Guy for KISC-FM radio when I saw it. While a song played, I glanced through *The Spokesman-Review* and joked to my host that a sure sign of age was when you began seeing the names of your friends in the obits.

Some joke. I looked closer and there it was: Rob Earsley, dead at 40.

Suddenly I didn't feel like such a wise guy. All I could think of was that warm night long ago, when death was as far away as the stars we slept under.

A call to Rob's mom, Barbara, filled in the years. She told me about Rob's personal pain, that he'd lost his job at the bank. That he'd begun to drink and there had been a divorce.

"He was too nice a guy to have had this happen," she said. "He went from doing well to just the bottom."

Rob died of pneumonia as he sat alone in his chair in front of the television. None of his friends or family even knew he had pneumonia. Rob kept a lot of things to himself.

"I'd like to think he's at peace now," Barbara told me.

So would I. Sleep well, blood brother.

Columnist relives haunting tale of the Halloween Tree

Halloween for me is a time of fear and trepidation.

Please understand. I've long outgrown the jitters of youth that accompany our most eerie holiday.

Those nameless, faceless dreads that shamble amongst withered cornstalks and October chill are sadly ineffectual against this disease called adulthood.

No, my goblins are real. My story is true, and it haunts me to this day.

Back when I was attempting the impossible – to learn journalism through classroom instruction – my professors, for lack of imagination, assigned their struggling students the job of producing an original Halloween photo.

Being young and ignorant, I took the teachers at their word and energetically set about to create the greatest Halloween photo of all time.

The "Halloween Tree."

I admit to borrowing the concept. It came from a Ray Bradbury story by the same title – a delightful fantasy about youngsters and spooks.

But the madness of rendering this great author's work into, as my teachers put it, "the medium of an 8-by-10-inch black and white glossy," was all mine.

236

The idea seemed simple enough.

Just carve up 50 or 60 smallish jack-o'-lanterns, hang them in an appropriately gnarled tree at sunset, light the suckers and then capture the entire phantasmagoria on Tri-X film.

Sounds crazy, huh?

At the time, though, the image of all those glowing, grimacing pumpkin faces, silhouetted against an autumn sky, seemed like a one-way ticket to an A-plus in Photojournalism 101.

A trip to the nearest greengrocer and the better part of a twenty found me inside my dumpy apartment surrounded by orange.

My ever faithful wife pitched in, only a trace of sarcasm in her voice. A flurry of cutting and scooping transformed the pumpkins into a roomful of toothy, sinister totems, which we carted out to our beat-up '69 Dodge Dart.

With the highest of hopes, we roared off into the unknown.

Twilight had begun to set in when I finally spotted a tree suitable enough. It wasn't the twisted, Tolkienesque tree of my fantasies, but it would do.

I'll be truthful. After three hours of driving around with a car filled with freshly gutted vegetables, the entire idea was beginning to grate on my nerves.

By then, however, things were quite beyond my control. I had become a small cog, an insignificant part of something large and dreadful.

Destiny would not be denied. The Halloween Tree would have the last laugh.

At this point, however, it should be noted how much traffic an otherwise deserted country road gets when a person attempts to hang pumpkins in a tree. If I were a liberal, I would suggest that a commission be formed and a fact-finding study be conducted on this topic.

I'm sure people who had never before been on that road, never even been to the same county, decided at that particular moment to drive by and gawk at the fool in the tree.

For some, gawking simply wasn't enough. These citizens slowed their vehicles and honked their horns. A few rolled down their windows and pointed while making rude, guffawing noises.

My ears burned as I heard a fat guy in a Ford use me as an object lesson to his kid, explaining to them why children shouldn't walk on deserted country roads alone after dark.

By then, even the forces of nature had turned on me. The wind had picked up and, because of it, half of my hollow companions sailed off their branches to a splattering doom below.

The candles inside the pumpkins I actually managed to hang wouldn't stay lit. I alternately whimpered and bellowed curses into the now gale-force tempest and rain.

Did I say rain?

Yes. It began to pour. And with the wind and the rain came a deep and sincere concern for my life.

"Fend for yourselves," I barked at the lousy, traitorous pumpkins.

Dark thoughts encompassed me while I held onto the brittle, wet branches like a sideshow contortionist.

In desperation, I shouted to my hysterical wife (hysterical with laughter, that is) to leave the car and bring me anything that would burn.

"It's an ugly world out here, Sherry!" I growled from my perch. "It's time you faced the music."

Laughing in waves that seemed to shake her lovely body like an attack of palsy, she managed to bring me a box of Kleenex, which I stuffed inside the pumpkins.

Then I brandished my Bic lighter like the Sword of Damocles and set the nearest jack-o'-lantern ablaze.

Then another. And another and . . .

Soon, all my reaming beauties were burning and glowing in ghoulish defiance of the rain-soaked night.

I sat back and enjoyed a moment of hard-earned satisfaction.

It was a mistake.

The horrible burning sensation I felt in my posterior region served as an excellent reminder of where I was – hovering precariously in a slippery Halloween Tree, just above a fire-breathing pumpkin.

"Aaaaaaarrrrrrrrggggghhhhh!!!"

Abandoning all respect for gravitational law, I let go – and crashed through the branches only to land on a mattress of slimey pumpkin goo.

Wild-eyed and dazed, I limped from the vegetable graveyard toward my wife, now reduced to sobs and howls, who offered me my camera.

It was too dark for conventional photography so I steadied the camera against the hood of my car. And as the Halloween Tree flickered its last, I tried desperately to salvage something from the horrific day.

Click. Click. Click . . .

It wasn't until later, when I was home drinking heavily, that I discovered I hadn't put film in the camera.

I am older now and supposedly wiser.

But every October I find my thoughts strangely pulled back to the Halloween Tree. The memory of that wretched event, those battered and leering pumpkins, still sends a cold, ectoplasmic shock wave down my spine as sure as any tale of evil by Poe or Lovecraft.

Yet, inexplicably, there lurks within me a masochistic urge to try it again, to give the world a Halloween Tree.

So far, thank God, my sanity has held.

Feeling the sadness when a life goes "on the road"

There were no headlines when he died, no front-page stories.

He never achieved any tangible form of greatness. He wasn't wealthy. He never ran for office or sat in a seat of power.

But although no history book will list his name with medical pioneers such as Barney Clark, Jack Burcham and Murray Haydon, my father spent a good part of his life engaged in his own valiant but ultimately unsuccessful struggle with his heart.

His name was Kenneth Ralph Clark. Five years ago, on July 26, 1981, the rusty old clock he had called a heart ran down in the intensive care unit of Spokane's Deaconess Hospital. He was 61.

I was there at the end, but I confess I haven't thought much about the event during the last few years. Repressed it, I guess.

Reading about the recent death of Jack Wilson, Spokane's first heart transplant recipient, brought all the memories cascading back.

It sounds corny to say this, but I think I know pretty much how Jack's widow, Kathy, feels. Anyone who has suffered through the final hours with a heart patient becomes familiar with a number of things – the cloying smell known only to hospitals, the interminable waiting, the false hopes that diminish with each fading heartbeat.

The seeming unreality of it all.

I've never felt so helpless, watching my father die. Earlier in the day, before his condition worsened and they moved him from the acute care ward to ICU, he spoke his last words to me.

"Well, Doug," he said, so frustrated by the way his lucidity was coming and going, "I guess the old man's on the road."

There was never any arguing with him. As always, my hard-headed father had assessed the situation with gin clarity.

And that was that.

I've never told my mother this, but I left his hospital room with tears in my eyes. I had to get out of that place before I put my fist through a wall or exploded.

I walked around town awhile and went to a movie. I couldn't even begin to tell you what the plot was. When my head cleared enough to go back, he had been moved and the doctors told us to go home and that they would call us if there were any changes.

I didn't like the sound of that. I figured it was a polite way for a man with M.D. after his name to say, "Look, the guy's gonna die and you can't do any good here so get of our hair and go home and save your strength. You're gonna need it when that dreaded phone call comes."

Sure enough, the phone rang.

In the middle of the night, my brother and my mother and I rushed down to say goodbye to the unconscious figure we knew as husband and father. The man who, indeed, was "on the road."

It took another hour or two for my dad to complete the journey. We filled up the time eulogizing him with comical recollections, which he would have enjoyed.

We talked about the time the furnace blew up in his face. My father, you see, had this habit of stripping down to his underwear, covering his bald head with a grimy painter's cap and then going into the basement to burn the week's accumulation of paper scraps in our old coal stoker.

One of his rules was absolutely no bottles or cans in the wastepaper baskets. But my mother, who had learned over the years to tune out many of my father's ravings, had violated this commandment with a bottle that contained a good inch of highly flammable permanent-wave solution.

He hadn't been in the basement long when the house rocked with a tremendous KA-THOOM!

I ran to the head of the stairs thinking my Old Man had been reduced to cinders. Peering through the billowing smoke, I watched as he emerged covered head-to-foot with coal soot. Amazingly, the hat had stayed on.

241

Never one to let compassion or sympathy ruin the chance for a good laugh, I covered my mouth with a hand and began to smirk.

"Which one are you," I asked sweetly, "Larry, Moe or Curly?"

My father, his beady eyes glaring like red-hot coals, pointed a finger of doom at me and rasped menacingly, "You laugh, Douglas, and by Gawd I'll kill you."

That was all it took. I howled until the tears flowed.

It was hard not to love the man.

He had plenty of faults, though. He had a hot temper and a pretty narrow way of looking at the world – a result, I suppose, of growing up fatherless in Chicago during the Great Depression.

It was sheer grit that got him out of there. He yanked away at his bootstraps, overcoming abject poverty, a lack of education and a bum ticker caused by a childhood bout with rheumatic fever.

Trouble was, he expected everybody else to be able to do the same.

Even so, I give him a lot of credit for making it out of Chicago. When he discovered Spokane he knew it was the place he wanted to settle in and raise a family.

So he built his own house and eventually became a certified life underwriter for New York Life Insurance Company. Then he died in the city he loved.

There were no headlines when that happened, just a brief obituary like most of us will get.

When you think of it, that's not such a bad way to go. I'm sure all the publicity has only added to the strain on Jack Wilson's friends and family.

My prayer is that they will find some comfort in this. At the very least, they should know that, headlines aside, a lot of us have stood in their shoes.

Give newlyweds anything but a piece of your mind

The lightning bolt struck on Sunday.

There she was, flesh of my flesh, looking sweet and innocent and sitting on my living-room couch with a nervous grin on her face.

"I wanted to tell you that I'm getting married Wednesday."

I sucked in a breath. The room did the "Minute Waltz" in half-time.

Kids, I mumbled to myself, whattaya gonna do with these crazy kids today? You clothe 'em and feed 'em and pay for their education and then, *Wham!*, the next second they're sneaking off behind your back and doing something stupid like getting married.

The fog lifted. I came to my senses.

This wasn't my kid sitting next to me. My daughter, last time I looked, was still 6 years old and preferring Pretty Ponies over braggadocio boys.

God be praised. I had years left to prepare for some nervy punk trying to steal away my Emily.

What I wasn't prepared for was that it would be my mother who would blind me with such a startling flash of news.

Talk about role reversals.

An overload of strange emotions pulsed through me like electric current.

This kind of thing wasn't supposed to happen. After all, I was reared in one of those endangered nuclear families that, defying the odds, remained intact to my father's death six years ago.

Mothers in their 60s from that kind of *Better Homes & Gardens* background don't go getting remarried.

What we sons expect of them is that they content themselves with the joys of widowhood and do grandmotherly things like baby-sit our kids, bake cutout cookies, join a pinochle club and . . .

243

And here she was upsetting my sense of order in the universe. As if she thought she had a life of her own. The nerve.

Fortunately, I held my tongue. Oh, I laughed a bit and secretly longed for a Valium the size of Vermont, but I didn't really say much of anything.

Don't credit me with keeping still. My wife says that's the way I am, that I rarely put words to my deepest feeling unless I'm sitting in front of a keyboard.

So here I am now, painfully working it through. I realize now how wrong it would have been to have reacted in the typical opinionated fashion most American newlyweds have to endure.

Everybody who received shabby treatment from meddling in-laws or know-it-all parents or angry children over the issue of choosing a mate, raise your hands.

Hah, I thought so.

How well I remember my own fire baptism. I was 20 and had the misfortune to steal the heart of an oldest daughter.

If that weren't bad enough, she had to be from the family of a prominent trial attorney who thought I was a bloody well out of order to rob his nest.

The cross-examination went on for days inside their South Hill home. This was no fair trial because the verdict was never in doubt. No way was I qualified to marry their wonderful baby girl.

Maybe if I were a doctor or lawyer. But an itinerant guitar player not yet finished with college was certainly not proper son-in-law material.

Back at my house, my father, an ominous fellow in his own right, threw in some left jabs, too. I was, he said, too irresponsible, too poor and too young to take on such an enormous obligation as holy matrimony.

In the end, however, Sherry and I did what we had planned all along to do. We married and, 15 years later, are still living happily ever after.

All the abuse and negative remarks accomplished was to leave wounds that never completely healed.

In contrast, the brightest memory of those rocky beginnings is that of my mother. She alone was supportive and caring enough to respect our decision and let go.

That's a tough thing to do, letting go. But it's time I followed her loving example.

Therefore I resolve:

To give her credit for knowing how best to live her life.

To give her advice only when asked.

To give her unconditional love, not love based on some preconceived idea of how grandmothers are supposed to act.

So good luck to you, Ma. Live a long life and don't waste your time worrying what others think.

And who knows? If I can act like an adult now, I just might not behead the horde of suitors who are sure to come scrambling after Emily.

"Cocooning" loses its charm after front porch invasion

All I wanted was a nice, quiet New Year's Eve, one spent with my loving family and not with a bunch of vulgar, drooling drunks.

How was I to know that airheads like columnist Ellen Goodman would officially declare "cocooning" (the new buzz word for staying home) as the latest thing for people my age?

But what Goodman doesn't know is that you can't run away from what makes New Year's Eve so special. Just when you think you have, it will come weaving up your street, stumbling up your porch steps and pounding on your front door.

Not even the Ultimate Home Defense Weapon will save you.

On New Year's Eve 1987, I stood with a zillion other semi-comatose Baby Boomers as we made our way down slow-moving lines at the local video market.

No more noisy parties – this New Year's would be a homespun affair. And for a time, my low-key celebration was all of that. Along with the movies there was a spirited game of Monopoly. There was even cherry pie and ice cream, and at midnight, we watched the ball float down in New York City and my kids, Benjamin and Emily, banged on the lids of soup pans and screamed.

I tossed a firecracker out the back door.

Whoop-de-doo.

Not long after that, the youngsters went to bed while my wife and a close friend and I stayed in the den to watch Jack Nicholson in that beloved family classic, *The Shining*.

But before the best part (when Jack attempts to dismember his wife and child with a fire ax), there came such a banging on my door.

It was 2 a.m. – and 1988 – and I opened the door on a most dreadful reality. If the Clarks wouldn't go to the party, the party would go to the Clarks.

There on my porch were a half-dozen sterling examples of American youth, including one Jason, a particularly obnoxious lout who made his namesake in the dreaded *Friday the 13th* movies look like a member of Job's Daughters.

"Call the cops," bellowed one of the strangers. "I gotta call the cops."

"The (bleep) you do!" countered Jason. "Let's just settle the whole (bleeping) thing right (bleeping) here!"

Jason, a belligerent drunk with the IQ of fungus, had a particular fondness for uttering what alarmed mothers the world over have dubbed: "The F-word." Adjective, verb, noun, dangling parimutuel . . . it made no difference to Jason. This lad could work that hummer into any sentence in the most surprisingly novel ways.

Believe me when I say the thrill of hearing such a vile utterance echoing down your neighborhood at 2 in the morning is quite heady. Only surpassing it is the knowledge that your startled and groggy neighbors will have no difficulty in identifying the Clark front porch as the source of their unusual wake-up call.

Through the racket, I pieced together what had happened. Two vehicles full of New Year's celebrants had bumped bumpers in front of my house. The occupants had quickly engaged in a heated dispute and somehow decided to take the issue up onto my porch, where there was better light.

Soon the commotion escalated into a first-rate brawl. Two combatants were rolling about my porch and walkway, flailing away at each other, marking the snow with flecks of blood. Jason kept busy yelling you-know-what, while another lad threatened him with a shortened ax handle. Then he took his turn on the ground.

My wife made several calls to the police, finally getting them to agree to dispatch a squad car no later than next July. After all, it was New Year's Eve and they were holster-deep in merrymakers.

Meanwhile, things were intensifying. Fearing for my picture windows, I decided to settle the matter with my Ultimate Home Defense Weapon.

It's a Winchester Model 12 riot gun, just like the ones you see in all the prison movies. I don't keep it loaded. I don't have to. I know from the movies that all it takes is one slide of the pump action; the unmistakable noise is enough to send any perpetrator begging to his knees.

Except, that is, for the brain dead.

I stood in my doorway and ordered Jason and the Jerk-o-nauts off my property. Then I slid the action just like Charles Bronson. It went "Chee-Chinkkkkk!!"

That caught Jason's attention all right. "Look," he roared, "the (bleeper's) gotta gun. Go ahead and (bleeping) shoot me with the (bleeper). Shoot me, shoot me. I dare ya."

Thoroughly disillusioned, I put the bleeper back in the closet and vowed never to trust Charles Bronson again. Eventually the freezing weather conditions sapped the spunk out of everyone but Jason, who kept yodeling The F-word louder than before.

Just when things were quieting down, the cops arrived. "I don't care what you do to them as long as Jason gets the electric chair," I told one of Spokane's finest. But he explained there was little he could do since he hadn't witnessed any of the violence.

I went back into the house.

Today I talked to Gordie, the guy who gave me my Ultimate Home Defense Weapon. I told him what had happened and how the thing didn't work. He wasn't listening. He had troubles of his own.

"I got up New Year's Day to find that some maggot had crashed his car through my fence."

Someone needs to tell Ellen Goodman that this cocooning business isn't all it's cracked up to be.

Fly People swarm into garage sale

The last of the Invasion of the Fly People was tapping away on the flimsy base of a $2 table lamp.

Tink, tink, tink.

"I don't think that's real brass," she groused as she continued to tap away.

"I might pay $2 if it was real brass, but this seems like a thinner, less expensive kind of metal to me."

I looked at the woman in disbelief.

"Well, gee," I said, varnishing my words with a couple coats of sarcasm, "if it were real brass, don't you suppose it just might be worth a bit more than two bucks?"

My wife, normally an affable and polite person, also had heard enough.

"And if it were solid gold," she added, "we probably WOULDN'T BE HERE."

Please excuse us. But after sitting around all Saturday on a hot, concrete slab selling junk, the entire Clark family was suffering from PTGSD.

Post Traumatic Garage Sale Disorder.

Not that there's anything wrong with garage sales. Actually, the garage sale – or tag sale as some people like to call it – can be a cathartic experience, much like giving your home an enema.

To prepare for our sale, we spent practically every night last week going through boxes in my mother's garage, boxes buried about the same time King Tut was laid to rest.

"Oh, look," said Mom. "There's the law book grandpa bought when he decided to write his own will."

Sweet old grandpa, who died in 1961, turned out to be more of a practical joker than a writer of wills. After all, he stuck us with his book and a box of his funny ties and all of his sweat-stained shirts . . . .

"Too bad grandpa didn't die intestate," I mused. "That way the state would have had to deal with all this crud."

And we could have avoided the Fly People. That's what I call those certain, pesky garage-saling addicts who make life miserable for sellers.

Don't get me wrong. Many customers are well mannered and friendly, honest folks who go to garage sales out of curiosity or to see if they can get a good price on a used thingamabob.

The Flies are those creeps who swarm and paw over your stuff with sheer profiteering in mind. They wear money belts and try to buy your stuff low so they can resell it at higher prices at their own, evil garage sales.

If you plan your garage sale for 10 a.m., the Flies will begin to descend at sunup. If you say an item is a dollar, they'll try to beat you down to 50 cents. If you finally wear out and offer to give it to them, they'll ask you to carry it to their car.

Sometimes your own dinner isn't even safe.

For instance, the first garage sale I ever held was supposed be on a Saturday. An hour after the ad in the Friday afternoon newspaper came out, two fat guys with overalls and what looked like limited genetic resources walked into our house without so much as a knock or a ring on a bell.

"We thought we'd come a bit early and see whatcha got," said fat guy No. 1, who then walked into our spare bedroom. My wife ran after him while I sat frozen with my mouth open.

Fat guy No. 2 waddled into our kitchen and began stirring our simmering spaghetti dinner. He held a spoon of it up to his elongated, encrusted nose hairs and took a deep whiff. "This 'ere smells purty good. Mebbe I'll buy some of it."

I have no patience with such people.

Put up a sign or run an ad announcing a garage sale and it's as if your right to privacy ceases to exist. The Flies don't care about you or your stuff. They don't realize that each garage sale item, no matter how trashy, is a family treasure, rich with significance and memory.

Such as what my mom called the baby buggy that bratty baby wouldn't sit in. As we dusted it off, she explained that she bought the buggy for me in 1951, but that I was always trying to crawl out of it.

"And now you've grown up into a very bratty man," she added.

I told my mother that, in light of this, there was no way she could part with such an heirloom. Why, it would be like selling her own son. She smiled and agreed that it was a very fine keepsake indeed.

Then a women in a red pickup asked if Mom would take 40 bucks for it.

"Sold!" she said.

I waved goodbye, a piece of my past heading north on Regal Street.

I love the place, but crime has us headed off course

To quote Jack Nicholson as the Joker in the first *Batman* movie: "This town needs an enema!"

Sorry, but I knew Spokane was in serious trouble even before some low-life purse snatcher mugged my dear mother.

The violence of the last 11 months – from Felicia Reese's murder in December 1994 to Tuesday's gang-related killing of a young North Side couple – has been a bloody reminder that we no longer live in "Leave it to Beaverland."

Nineteen bodies have piled up this year, tying the city's all-time murder total with two months to go. Violent crime has been proclaimed a "growth industry" by Spokane Police Chief Terry Mangan.

Youth gangs are a huge problem the mayor and council are desperately trying to solve.

Migrating to the Spokane Valley once was considered a peaceful alternative to living in the more crime-ridden city.

Think again. "We have more people coming (to the Valley) with the idea that this is an easy place to commit crime and get away with it," Spokane County sheriff's Sargeant Gary Smith told a reporter last month.

Drugs and more drugs – to nobody's surprise – are at the core of most of our social ills.

Don't misunderstand, I still love Spokane. This is, after all, the place I was born, grew up, schooled, married, had kids and settled down.

I'm fond of our parochial attitudes, our stubborn reluctance to change and especially our big-hearted residents who practically break their necks to help someone in trouble.

I wrote about two brutes who took a money jar collection for a baby's cancer fund. Within a few days, more than $5,000 in donations poured into a trust fund for the little girl's care.

A similar outpouring is going to Rob and Jill Schliebe, who lost their four sons in a terrible fire.

But what Spokane needs most of all is more cops, tougher judges, longer sentences and roomier prisons to keep the rats from overrunning the rest of us.

What happened to members of my family the other afternoon makes me wonder if we can win this war.

During the span of a few hours:

• I took my daughter to the Nordstrom cafeteria and encountered a profane lunatic who vowed to kill everyone in his sight. "I've got a .45 and I'll blow 'em all away," the middle-aged man screamed, peppering his speech with the F-word.

After several uncomfortable minutes, the man disappeared down the escalator, leaving a trail of violent vulgarities in his wake.

• My son left work to catch a bus home. He watched a street gangster viciously beat a wino a few feet from the new bus station's front doors.

The thug stomped the man's chest and kicked his head. "It went on about three minutes before any guards showed up to stop it," my son said. "I was a little scared somebody might pull a gun and start shooting."

• My mom was assaulted in the Lincoln Heights Shopping Center. "He wasn't gonna get my purse," she told me with defiance after the detective took photographs of her scrapes and bruises.

She was heading into the Payless Drug Store. An 18-year-old with a chubby, innocent face asked her for the time.

My mom's a sweetheart who is friendly to everyone. Getting attacked in broad daylight never crossed her mind.

The punk grabbed her purse and yanked. My mother toppled hard onto the pavement. She held on, though, hollering for help as this poor excuse for a human dragged her several feet.

He finally gave up and ran, maybe realizing the fish he'd hooked had way too much fight.

My mom is handling her attack well, wearing her battle scars with pride. We laugh about rigging her purse with explosives.

There is an edge to our humor. We both know how lucky she was.

I'm scared sick about where my city is headed.

What about that good old pioneer spirit?

Thanks to the nastiest ice storm in modern memory, my wife, Sherry's, much-talked-about idea of a dream way to spend an evening came to pass.

There we were, all four Clarks huddled in the living room around a crackling fire and glowing candles.

No power. No TV. No distractions.

Just the folksy way our forefathers and foremothers lived over a century ago.

Doug: "So, um, here we all are."

Sherry: "Yep, here we are."

Doug: "Awful quiet, isn't it?"

Sherry: "Very quiet."

Doug: "We could read a book, but the light's too dim."

Sherry: "It's very dim."

Doug (shrieking): "We're in hellll!"

Yes, I'm one of the bazillions betrayed by Reddy Kilowatt.

I live in a South Hill neighborhood where frozen tree limbs went down like Idaho Democratic candidates.

According to my useless electric clocks, my power frapped out Tuesday, November 19, 1996, at 12:33 p.m. As I write these words two days later, we are juiceless still.

Oh, sure, everyone talks about what swell romantic lives those mythical people of yore had – sitting merrily around the campfire singing "Jimmy Crack Corn," and swilling homemade barley wine and making quilts . . .

But let's be real.

What choice did those hardy saps have? They never heard THX or Dolby Digital sound at the neighborhood multiplex. There were no Walkmans. No VCRs. No Internet.

No Nintendo or Sega or Bose Wave radios.

We modern types are sensorially spoiled. We've seen, heard and felt way too much to ever really want to return to a monkish existence without Velcro or Cheetos.

As a result, we're pathetic survivors.

My dear mother grew up in a house with no central heating. She got dressed on goosebump mornings shivering behind the wood stove. My wife's parents had no plumbing in the farm house where she was born.

Not a lick of this rugged pioneer spirit was apparently passed down the genetic line.

Determined to up the level of light, I dug out our antique hurricane lamps and promptly doused my hands with stinky kerosene.

Cursing, I tried in vain to properly trim the wicks. This, however, is not a skill taught in public schools. Besides, getting your wick trimmed was something I thought sailors did on leave.

So in an act of complete foolishness, Sherry and I fired up the Camry and made a desperate dash for emergency provisions.

The Excell store at Ninth and Perry looked like a scene from one of Stephen King's end-of-the-world yarns.

"I can't believe they want a buck-29 for these little things," muttered a man who shambled past me clutching an arm-load of votive candles.

Undaunted by the horde, we elbowed our way past the bottled water and Pres-To-Logs to stock up on real necessities:

Skittles, licorice, Nutrageous bars, almond M & Ms, potato chips, clam dip and a box of Corn Pops. Fortunately, I had plenty of beer back home.

My biggest score came on the end of an aisle, where I managed to grab the last six D-sized batteries in the store.

We hurried home and put the batteries in my daughter Emily's boom box. We didn't give a wick about the emergency weather broadcasts, but wanted to catch *Frasier* on KHQ's FM channel.

You sure miss a lot of sight gags listening to TV without pictures. But when you're fighting for survival, well, you have to learn to make do with less.

Our family eventually grew weary from this overwhelming lack of stimulus and went to bed. We drifted off to the sounds of thick branches exploding to earth in an icy shower.

But we were confident in our slumber. Like Scarlett O'Hara, we knew that tomorrow would indeed be another day.

Plus, there'd be Corn Pops for breakfast.

Between those cold sheets . . . it's still cold

There's a cruel rumor being circulated that the next calamity to hit the Spokane area will be in the form of a sonic baby boom about nine months from now.

The theory suggests that those of us who plunged into the heart of darkness last week are enjoying more hanky panky than a John Wayne Bobbitt video.

I figure this rumor was concocted by smug people with power to burn.

I'm talking about people with VCRs and Christmas lights and blenders and stereos and electric nose-hair clippers. People who let the hot water run and don't have the slightest clue what life is like for us Morlocks down in the dark, deep freeze.

Well, let me set this whole sex issue straight.

As self-appointed spokesman for the juiceless families of Ice Storm '96, I can state with frigid authority that there is scant panky going on and all the hankies are being used for blankets.

Frostly, I mean firstly, it's difficult to generate the spark of romance when your body temperature is the same as a Swanson's frozen dinner.

Secondly, privacy is an elusive premium for those who live in a meat locker.

The Clark family, for example, spends the Arctic nights jammed together closer than a rugby scrum. Even our two cats and my dog, Elvis, have joined our biomass.

We're so thankful for our little pets.

Their bright loving eyes, their loyal presence, help ease the tension of even these hideous times.

The Clarks are comforted by the knowledge that should our icy misery affect the food supply, we can always eat our furry friends.

Lastly, there is the matter of, well, stamina.

I've slept so poorly the last seven days that I'm beginning to look like a *Night of the Living Dead* zombie.

I get out of bed more often than an old man with a swollen prostate. It's sleep an hour. Poke the fire. Doze another hour. Poke the fire. . .

This is definitely not the kind of poking that made Don Juan a famous lover.

"You're right. There's no sex when you're cold," said an editor from the sports side of the newspaper. "Power went off. It didn't happen. Three days later, power went on. It happened."

I have no idea why this man told me this, but it does prove my point.

Of course, there are exceptions to everything.

There are still some sights so titillating as to drive even a thoroughly powerless man into a lust-crazed froth.

I know. This happened to me Sunday while I was on yet another pathetic scavenger hunt for lamp oil.

There, on the corner of 29th and Regal, was the most gorgeous vision I've ever seen: A man selling – gasp – gas-powered generators.

Not just any generators. Oh, baby. Oh, baby. These sweethearts put out 5,000 watts of pure, unadulterated power. Enough power to light the house. Enough power to work the television.

Enough power, and I'm beginning to weep here, to start the furnace! I pulled into the parking lot, feeling testosterone surge through my chilled blood like supercharged antifreeze.

"How, um, how much?" I stammered through quivering lips.

"They're $895," he said, giving me the once over.

The man's steely eyes narrowed. He knew he was talking to a junky desperate for a fix.

"But, but, I don't have that much," I whimpered.

The dealer leered.

"We won't be here much longer," he taunted.

I drove back to my three-story igloo feeling as impotent as a Ross Perot supporter. Sex? Who can think about sex at a time like this?

All I want to do is curl up next to the fire, cover my body with hankies and beat my head in with a poker.

Critters

Chapter Thirteen

Employees at Bon worried about batrachian buddy

Billy Bob the Frog got himself busted and employees of The Bon are still hopping mad.

"It was awful," said Linda Porter, who had raised the pet from a tadpole. "We'd had Billy Bob for over a year. He had his birthday last month."

She said it was upsetting when two armed game officers converged on the store's stationery department during the late afternoon. They found Billy Bob blissfully frog-paddling about his tank. Then, while friends and loved ones looked on, the agents got the jump on Billy Bob and nailed him with a 232-12-017.

Suspicion of being an illegal amphibian, that is.

"We caught him green-handed," laughed Donna King, of the Washington Department of Game. "He didn't have a green card."

Worrywarts at the game department are saying that Billy Bob may look like Kermit, but, in fact, he is a yucky *xenopus laevis*.

(African Clawed Frog, to the rest of us.)

"Technically, he's more of a toad, but let's not get into that," said King, gasping for breath. "The truth is they're highly carnivorous. We're talking about the Frog Who Ate Spokane. I'm not kidding. They can't be stopped. They're considered an exotic and deleterious species."

And against the law, too.

Wildlife biologists fear that Billy Bob and others like him could find their way to, say, the Spokane River. Once there, they would throw parties and breed with wild and boisterous abandon, thereby upsetting the delicate ecosystem. For example: Fish eat tiny plant life, ducks eat fish, winos eat the ducks and Billy Bob gobbles up the winos like they were cheese curls.

"They're really voracious eaters," said King. "But they don't eat winos. They eat fish like crazy and they get real big. About as big as Ritzville."

King called back to report that the frogs were not quite as big as Ritzville, but that they do grow to a menacing four inches in length. Pity the underpaid game department officers who must risk their lives to capture such insidious beasts.

The African frogs, King said, were unwanted in Washington along with other undesirables of the Animal Kingdom such as: walking catfish, mongoose (or mongeese), grass carps, wild boars and Aryan Nations members.

Before the arrest, lonely consumers could order Billy Bobs of their own from a New York firm for $12.95 each. Department store chains like The Bon carry "Grow a Frog" order forms throughout the state. So do many card and specialty shops.

"They've been selling like hotcakes," said Jan Goss of the Card Farm at the Northtown Mall. "People love 'em."

No more. King said her department is bent on squashing the illegal frog market before our lakes and rivers and city councils are filled with the things.

"I can't believe that," said Mike O'Keefe of Three Rivers Amphibians of Farmingdale, New York.

"None of our frogs have criminal records.

"We sell clean-cut American frogs."

O'Keefe said Grow a Frogs are educational. They give youngsters a living example of all the development stages of a frog. No complaints have been registered, other than when a wayward tadpole gets accidentally flushed down the toilet.

"Basically, the calls we get are from people saying what a great time they had watching our frogs grow."

Not that Billy Bob's batrachian buddies always behave like princes.

Goss related the following ribbit-ing tale:

She was cleaning Georgia the Frog's tank the other day at her Card Farm outlet in the Seafirst Bank building. Before she knew it, the little bugger went on the lam.

"It got behind the counter and then fell 20 feet through an air vent," Goss said. "She's a real jumper. Georgia landed right on top of a bank teller, who screamed like bloody murder.

"The security guard rushed over to help the woman. She was crying. And then they found out it was a frog. We were in hysterics about it."

Georgia survived the fall, but had a human in her throat for a few days.

"They're tough all right," said King. "Once they get out you can never get rid of them. And we try to put fish out there for people to catch, not for frogs to eat."

Even so, Billy Bob's friends at The Bon want him back. They're afraid the game department will have him croaked without so much as a fair trial.

"He's being held for questioning," added King. "After that, I don't know."

One of the agents, she said, mentioned that Billy Bob might be put on display as a warning to people, to show them what evil African Clawed Frogs look like.

Bon employees hope Billy Bob is spared.

"He was kind of a trademark for the customers," said one. "Every morning, you'd walk by and look at him. He'd kind of jump up at you.

"You shouldn't kill anything that cute."

Pigeons upset pecking order at Courthouse

Comes now the honorable Judge William G. Luscher in a never-ending quest to rid said Spokane County Courthouse of a most low and pernicious villain, namely and to wit, pigeons.

"I'm looking out my window right now and, aside from the stream of (pigeon) crap running down the Public Safety Building, I see six pigeons, three of them that are on my window ledge," said an indignant Judge Luscher.

To achieve the jurist's goal of a pigeon-free Courthouse, county maintenance workers have taken it upon themselves to lure the birds into traps and even resort to attempted murder. Poisoned bait recently was placed in a coffee can lid on a Courthouse ledge, but Terry Hontz, who set the trap, says the pigeons weren't much interested.

"They wouldn't touch it," said Hontz. "That's probably because it was rodent bait. We kind of figured it was too big for them. At least that's my guess."

Hontz said he did find one corpus delicti recently, but figures the hapless pigeon probably died of old age rather than fowl play. "Somebody told me that if you put plaster of Paris out there, the pigeons would eat it and then their insides would slowly harden up."

As intriguing as making petrified pigeons sounds, Hontz is a bit reluctant to give it a whirl. "I've heard there are judges who like the pigeons and judges who don't and I don't want to be caught in the middle."

Smart man.

Without a doubt all the feathered furor has considerably upset the Courthouse pecking order.

"What's a courthouse without pigeons?" mused the equally honorable Judge John A. Schultheis, who wants this foolhardy pigicide stopped.

"Naw, they don't bother me at all," Judge Schultheis said. "In fact, we have some that we're quite close to. The birds are a lot more friendly than my staff."

Judge Schultheis was, of course, kidding about his help. A friendlier staff you couldn't find. They were only too happy to oblige a request for a peek at one of the popular pigeon hangouts, a fire escape outside Schultheis' chambers.

Nary a pigeon was in sight, however, which caused bailiff Kathy Williams to worry whether the poison had done its dirty work.

"The pigeons have been more like a tight-knit family to us," she said. "Sure there's some pigeon poop around, but what's a little pigeon poop?"

Pigeon poop, alas, is central to Judge Luscher's petition against the ill-mannered birds. The indelicate and unsightly messes they leave offend the Superior Court jurist right down to his robes.

"Yes, our problem is the filth," he said, "the tremendous filth and stench. In the summer, I can't even open my window.

"It's not that I don't like birds – I don't want that insinuation made; I do like birds. It's just the continuous filth."

And when it isn't the filth, it's the constant cooing. Judge Luscher doesn't like putting up with that, either.

A Courthouse worker close to the pigeons said she has spotted Judge Luscher pounding on his window to drive them away and making sarcastic cooing noises at them. Last summer, he suggested placing a large rubber snake on the ledge to frighten the mangy squatters off the county premises.

"The pigeons just drive him crazy," agreed Williams. "But it doesn't take much."

Steve Strawick, a court clerk, finds the pro-pigeon-purge position to be, well, petty. "We get plenty of stool pigeons in here so why can't we have some real ones of our own?"

As much as he would like to see his enemies fly the coop, Judge Luscher said he knew nothing of the recent poisoning attempts. Which is a good thing because introducing any poison into the general bird population is frowned upon by the Washington Department of Wildlife.

Pigeons – or rock doves as they're sometimes called – aren't a protected species. They originally were a domesticated critter that was let loose into the wild, which means they have no more rights than, say, a low-income resident of Sprague Avenue. The danger in offering controlled substances to pigeons is that other wildlife haven't learned to just say no.

"If, in fact, the indiscriminate use of poison would affect other non-target species, we would have to take a position on that," said Bruce Smith of the Department of Wildlife. "Basically, we'll have to make sure we don't have a bunch of tweeties falling off the ledge up there."

As strange as it seems, Judge Luscher's snake idea was closest to a non-violent final solution. However, said Smith, inflatable owls is hands-down a more effective way to get the job done.

But even if the pigeon extermination is conducted properly, Smith wondered what all the fuss is about.

"In the end," he said, "what's so bad about them?"

The Courthouse is hardly overrun with pigeons. Only a dozen or so of the critters make a home there. And the people who love them have grown fond of watching their eggs hatch every spring.

"We should show Judge Luscher Alfred Hitchcock's movie *The Birds*," sniffed one Courthouse worker. "Maybe then he'll know what a real problem is."

Harriet the fish wants your vote for farewell win

At the risk of appearing a tad too partisan this election year, I would like to make the following political announcement:

Stop whatever you're doing, hurry over to the Spokane Interstate Fair and vote Harriet the fish for People's Choice Award. That's "Tank 18" in the aquarium exhibit. Harriet the fish. Do it now! Thank you.

(Paid for by the committee to elect Harriet the fish.)

I know what you're thinking. You're thinking, "Clark has missed his morning dose of lithium. And what could be so all-fired important about voting for a fish, anyway?"

Actually, voting for Harriet the fish is every bit as important as voting for, say, a county commission candidate. Except that Harriet the fish is much more animated and would probably accomplish more in office.

Which is quite a trick, considering Harriet is dead.

Yes, poor Harriet passed away unexpectedly last May [1988], a victim of old age and the bloat. But her owners – Laura and Roger Poulin of Reardan – decided their beloved South American "Tiger Oscar Cichlid" (which translates into Looks Like a Big Perch) owed the public a last hurrah.

"We're hoping for one more win," said Laura. "After all, it would be such a nice way for the public to say goodbye to her.

"Such a fitting end."

It would be historic, too. Should Harriet win the People's Choice award, she probably would be first dead animal to out-poll live competitors. Think of it. This could open up a whole new category for deadstock.

As a faithful Spokane Interstate Fairgoer for more than 30 years, I must confess that cows and pigs, not to mention the ever-smelly and stupid chickens, have lost a bit of their charm.

But a pickled porker? Now that's worth a look-see.

And if it were handled with the dignity and grace that has been afforded Harriet, deadstock exhibits would even be easier on the nose.

"Roger always said that if anything ever happened to Harriet, we had to keep her," said Laura.

Norman Bates said the same about his mother.

"They had a relationship," said Laura. "So right after she passed away, he told me we had to get her stuffed."

The Poulins took Harriet to Spokane taxidermist John Lamers, who worked feverishly to get the fish spruced up in time for the fair. "He was very respectful," added Laura. "It was just like a funeral home only we didn't have to buy an expensive coffin."

Cynics might suggest that 150 bucks is a bit extravagant for an overgrown perch, too.

Harriet, however, is not your average fish.

Even in death, lying in state like some Russian leader, Harriet fairly radiates animal magnetism. The sign on the wooden plaque she is mounted on is simple. "In memory of Harriet, 1980-1988."

I became friends with Harriet on Saturday afternoon when I wobbled into the annex just off the main fair building. I had seriously overindulged myself on what my son, Benjamin, refers to as "Fair Fun."

This year's "Fair Fun" consisted of a double lambburger, immediately joined by a blimp-sized German sausage corn dog and a quarter-pound of fudge. The ensuing queasiness cut into an age-old fair tradition I have of signing up all my friends for Waterless Cookwear demonstrations, free aluminum siding consultations and home Tupperware parties.

I decided a tranquil visit with fish was in order. Fish are naturally relaxing and they would help take my mind off what was becoming an intense desire to rid myself of all that Fair Fun. What I never banked on was discovering a fish named

Harriet, a fish good humored enough to turn my bellyache into belly laughs.

Harriet hangs on an appropriate background of black. Above her two crosses and the words "Rest in Peace." There are flowers and a sympathy card from the Inland Empire Aquarium Society. It reads: Thinking of you with sympathy and sharing your sorrow in the loss of one who meant so much to you.

Harriet is surrounded by her past glories. There are two previous People's Choice awards, two fourth places, a second, a first and an impressive "Best of Show" for the big Northwest Council meet in Seattle.

This fish was no piker.

"She was a true champion," said Laura, beaming. "She was an exceptional female Oscar because of her bright orange color. But she had personality, too. Roger used to put his arm up on the tank and she would go right up and float by him.

"Sometimes she would nudge his finger. They were quite close."

Kind of gets to you, doesn't it?

Now Harriet is as dead as Ozzie Nelson. Gone to that great Pet Store in the sky. But if we all pull together and vote, Harriet will live on as a symbol for every pet fish that went belly up and was flushed away without ceremony or kind word.

"Harriet would have wanted it that way," said Laura. "And Roger, too. This has been a very somber time for both of us."

[Update: Harriet won!]

Cat-erwauling out with ol' DC on cat-afalque

DC the cat may have lost her ninth life to an electric garage door opener, but in the process, the departed feline may have achieved immortality at the Spokane County Courthouse.

269

That's because DC's rather grisly passing in September [1988] has become the stuff of which legends are made: the single event that has sparked what county officials are calling the strangest personnel grievance they have ever encounterd.

"Yeah, I've never seen anything like it," say County Treasurer Skip Chilberg of the case that will soon be heading into arbitration. "And I've been in public service a long, long time."

Chilberg, depending on how you view such things, is either the hero or the villain of this courthouse cat-tastrophe. It was he who denied Colleen Gilbert's request for a day of sick leave to mourn the ill-fated DC's passing.

"Look," argues Chilberg, "I could have called in the day after elections and said that I was sick because George Bush won. But did I have the right to take a day of sick leave?

"In all good conscience, you can't expect the public to pay for that kind of thing."

Besides, says Chilberg, if she wanted to take the day off she could have taken it out of her vacation time.

But Gilbert, a revenue compliance officer, is not at a loss for words when confronted by her boss's wit and logic.

"Sure, I was a little nauseated after the election, too," she admits. "But I wasn't as close to George Bush as I was to DC.

"George Bush didn't happen to live with me for 11 years, like DC."

DC, by the way, stands for "Darling Cat" or "Damn Cat," depending on Gilbert's mood at the time. Although, I suppose in this case "Dead Cat" works quite well, too.

But despite all the interoffice cat jokes that have come with Gilbert's unusual grievance, Chilberg swears there is a real issue here.

Honest.

"And that is," he says, "does an employer have the right to control sick leave?"

Therein lies the problem.

But before we address that, let us turn our attention to the day DC the cat went to that Great Litter Box in the Sky.

It was September 12, and Gilbert's husband flicked a switch that sent the electric garage door gliding smoothly downward. DC made a break for the fast-disappearing opening.

She didn't make it.

"The first thing my husband said was, 'I've killed her,'" says Gilbert, who, even today, gets choked up at DC's memory.

The next morning, Gilbert had a little burial service in her back yard and then went to work.

"I was a basket case all day," she says. "I knew I was unable to perform my job duties. So the next day I decided to stay home. I just couldn't get it together."

"I don't have children," Gilbert adds. "DC was kind of like my baby."

Gilbert phoned in sick. Eventually, however, Chilberg caught wind of the reason Gilbert was staying home.

"It became well known throughout the office," he says, "I asked her about it and, to her credit, she was quite honest. She was home grieving because of the demise of her cat."

Even though he denied her the sick day, Chilberg praises Gilbert as a wonderful worker. In fact, during her 10 years with the county, she has rarely used sick leave and practically has to be told to take her vacation time.

Skip Wright, the county's personnel director, agrees that Gilbert's work record has nothing to do with the refusal.

"It's almost a philosophical issue," he says. "After all, people can get upset about a lot of things that go on in their lives. I can have a terrible fight with my wife and the last thing I feel like is going to work. But that doesn't mean it's an appropriate use of sick leave.

"I don't know where you draw the line."

Bill Keenan – who represents the union Gilbert and other county workers belong to – would like to try.

Regardless of what prompted Gilbert to call in sick, he says, the county has no business making determinations of what causes somebody to be ill.

"That's what a doctor does," says Keenan. "And we're flabbergasted that the county would be willing to deny an honest worker like her a day of sick leave."

Keenan says he thinks the entire issue is a waste of time and money. The arbitration process, he says, could cost the county at least $1,000, not to mention the time attorneys spend researching the case and preparing their arguments.

Even so, arbitration is where all of this is headed. And in the meantime, Gilbert has tried to fill the emotional void by adding "Rum" and "Coke," two new Siamese kittens, to her household.

Not that DC could ever be forgotten.

"Just yesterday I finally washed the bedspread DC used to sleep on," says Gilbert with a sad catch in her voice.

"She was such a good cat."

Lust-crazed raccoons creating feelings of anger, envy

Love is in the air and it ain't the sound of music.

"You can't imagine the noise they make," says Judy Young of the two lust-crazed raccoons who have turned the Spokane Realtor's South Hill back yard into a bawdy bordello.

"It's worse than raking your fingers across a black board."

With Valentine's Day [1992] tomorrow it's humbling for us humans to note that we play a weak second fiddle when compared to the romantic symphony being performed in the animal kingdom.

If Judy's report is to be believed, not since Tarzan and Jane has there been such a tumbling in the treetops. The critters are – get this – doing the wild thing precariously perched 18 feet off the ground inside a big fir.

"They're big and they're beautiful," she says, "but they're louder than wildcats."

And as for their, ahem, staying power, Judy says they're going at it all day and all night.

"Every 20 minutes."

Gasp.

But as inspirational as this marathon mating appears, it has made for some strained relations between Judy and her nearest neighbor.

Actually the problem is a bit complicated. It began a few nights ago when the rambunctious raccoons provoked Judy's doggie visitors into an all-night yapping frenzy.

"They're not my dogs," Judy explains. "They're actually Italian dogs who have never seen raccoons before."

I told you this was complicated. The dogs, Tia, an African hound, and Grapa, a German shepherd, belong to Judy's daughter, Staccee, who lives in Italy and is visiting Spokane with her husband, Mickele Simone.

Not that this means anything to the neighbor. When your slumber is being shattered every 20 minutes by raccoons engaging in conjugal bliss with a canine cheering section, who gives a damn about international bloodlines?

Suffice it to say that Judy's neighbor, who just so happens to be a lawyer, was not amused.

Judy says the man telephoned her at 6:30 a.m. and lodged a rather stern, if not groggy, complaint. No litigious threats were uttered but Judy wasn't taking any chances. She attempted to outmaneuver the attorney by evoking the Sex-Crazed Raccoon Defense.

He wasn't buying it and asked her to control the animals.

That's no problem with the dogs. Tia has been banished to the garage and Grapa is like the typical spineless Democratic presidential candidate: a sleazy opportunist who will only howl if someone else does first.

But as for controlling these lovestruck critters, you may as well try to turn back a tornado. We are dealing with elemental urges that must be satisfied.

Judy's co-workers at the Century-21 Crane office on Grand say she can do a credible impression of the high-pitched keening noise made by the raccoons.

Over the telephone, however, the woman declined to demonstrate this unique talent.

"They are so noisy that I can be inside the house curling my hair and still hear them," was all she would say.

A call to the Washington Department of Wildlife quickly revealed that this tax-funded agency hasn't a clue when it comes to dealing with sexually boisterous raccoons.

Well, they do have one idea.

"She could probably charge admission and put the State Line operations out of business," says Madonna King with a laugh. "Now don't quote me on this."

Absolutely not. Madonna then referred me to someone she calls George "Silver-tongued" Coburn, the department's raccoon expert.

Raccoon expert? I don't think so.

George has a shocking lack of knowledge when it comes to the animal's sexual rampages.

"I've tried to stay out of the brush while this is going on," he says.

George does confirm that it is the right time of year for raccoons to swoon. It is nature's plan and in 63 days baby raccoons should be prowling about the town, on a never-ending quest for a free meal.

As for the carnal commotion, George has some good advice.

And that is to give these raccoons a break. It won't last forever (how could it at that pace?) and some spirited whoopee seems especially appropriate right now.

After all, says George the raccoon expert, "it's Valentine's Day."

Family takes homeless chicken under its wing

Say "chicken on the table" and most people will ask if it's baked or fried.

Except at the Muellers' north Spokane residence, where a Rhode Island red named Doo Dee rules the roost.

Doo Dee – yes, I'm talking about an honest-to-gawd chicken – doesn't live or act at all like your average barn-yard bird.

This pampered, year-old hen pecks spaghetti or Parmesan cheese bits off Pfaltzgraff china while perched on an antique oak high chair at the dinner table.

She snacks on lemon yogurt, sips bottled water, watches *Geraldo Live* on TV, rides in the car to the bank and each morning lays a brown egg in the laundry hamper.

Call her name and Doo Dee comes a-running like a friendly mutt. Stretching her auburn-feathered neck, she begs to have the fleshy red wattles on her throat scratched.

"She must have been a human in a previous life," speculates Pam Mueller, who often lets Doo Dee cling to her shoulder – even while driving the lawn tractor.

When a friend of the Muellers called to tell me about such cockamamie craziness, well, I thought I was getting my drumstick pulled.

A chicken roaming the house? No way. Not unless Doo Dee's owners were gap-toothed hill folk who don't know any better.

The Muellers are educated people, not kin of the dumb-cluck Clampetts. Herbert Mueller is a successful children's dentist. Pam teaches art lessons in her basement.

The Mueller estate is one classy coop, set on five river-lined acres in the posh Wandermere area. It is an immaculate, two-story white home with concrete lions on the porch.

The flowery Victorian interior – with wallpaper borders and stained glass windows – looks as if it were decked out by Martha Stewart.

"It's strange," says Sally Wittkopf, one of Pam's longtime pals. "You're sitting in the front room and suddenly this chicken comes flopping down the stairs."

The story of the Muellers and Doo Dee would be as charming as a Disney flick were it not for a very foul fact about fowls: "I sure wish they made Depends for chickens," sighs Pam.

You guessed it. Even the Einstein of chickens doesn't know the difference between a toilet and a carpet. Pam spends a good part of her day wiping up the McNuggets Doo Dee unloads at will.

"See, that isn't too bad," says Pam, removing a pile with a wad of Kleenex.

This complete lack of scatological sensitivity inspired Herbert to name the bird Doo Dee. Poor man. Herbert's fastidious nature isn't suited to having an incontinent critter in the house.

It gets weirder: One night, as the couple lay sleeping with Doo Dee, Herbert awoke to an unholy sensation. Upon closer inspection the groggy dentist realized the infernal chicken had left an unhappy ending on his arm.

Now when Pam brings Doo Dee in for a sleepover on cold nights, Herbert rejects the feather bed for a safer room.

"It's just easier that way," he says resolutely. "It boils down to it's either the chicken or me. And I'm sure it would be me."

Could there be something to this reincarnation business? The bird's origins are mottled in mystery. Last year [1996], Pam's mother-in-law, Thora, was walking up the driveway to her home near Gonzaga University when a strange noise stopped her.

She turned around to see she was being shadowed by a cheeping chick that followed her into the house. The chicken has never been afraid of people.

A neighborhood search produced no missing chicken reports. Unable to keep the bird in the city, Thora gave Doo Dee to Pam, who bestowed it with a lifestyle the average working stiff only dreams about.

"What I really want to know," asks Herbert, "is how long they live."

I called a true chicken expert and got some very good news for this hen-pecked husband.

"They apparently don't live too long," says James Kittredge, a counterman at the South Hill's Kentucky Fried Chicken franchise. "They come to us frozen in a box with their heads cut off."

Got a hatchet, Herb? No jury in the world will convict you.

They gave pup a name fit for a king

The good news is that Elvis is alive.

The bad news is that he's not quite paper trained.

You may think it strange to hear that the Clark family has named its new puppy after the one-and-only King of Rock.

But as I hope you'll see from my tail (cheap pun intended), there are a few things left in this universe that are truly meant to be.

Elvis would understand. Nobody seemed to be more in tune with the cosmic forces of destiny than Elvis – who was born 56 years ago this very day [January 8, 1991] in the small Mississippi town of Tupelo.

Elvis didn't let his dirt-poor beginnings or his slim chances of success stop him.

He had the lip. He had the look. He had Vaseline in his hair. Nothing could stand in his way.

"Elvis would make a fine name for a dog," I told my family as we fired up the Buick and headed across town to pick one out one Saturday afternoon. "After all, he wasn't nothin' but a hound dawg."

My son, Benjamin, enjoyed the reasoning but wasn't convinced.

"What if we pick out a girl dog?" he asked. "You can't name a girl dog Elvis, can you?"

I had to admit that you most certainly could not.

We'd been given the address for the puppies earlier after a neighbor had invited us over to see the tiny cockapoo she had just purchased.

For some inexplicable reason, my wife, Sherry, stroked the scruffy little dust mop and then announced that we, too, should get one.

I'm counting that as Elvis Miracle No. 1.

For the last 15 years, my wife has emphatically screamed "NO" to dogs. This is because in the early years of our marriage, we had two mutts I didn't clean up after.

Sherry has thrown those unscooped doggie doots in my face ever since.

Until Saturday, that is, when she suddenly decided that we had gone dogless too long.

I was still arguing for the name Elvis as we pulled outside the puppy house.

After all, I explained, this was Elvis' big weekend. There were Elvis impersonators at the hockey game. And in Graceland, there were four days of Elvis fun, ending tonight with a giant Elvis birthday banquet.

Who can understand this thing called Elvis?

In death he's become so much more alive. People keep seeing him in shopping malls and supermarkets.

So we entered the house, where Debbie Thackston led us to a cardboard box of puppies. Benjamin reached in and picked up a little male.

Then he stood up. Over his left shoulder, a velvet Elvis was smiling down at him.

Elvis Miracle No. 2.

My wife and I gawked at the big velvet painting. Then we gawked at each other. Then we turned so we wouldn't start laughing.

Our eyes ran smack dab into Elvis' face, beaming at us from a dozen commemorative plates.

Another Elvis picture hung on a different wall.

Elvis was everywhere.

"I've been a fan ever since I was 3," said Debbie. "That's when I took 10 silver dollars and bought an Elvis T-shirt and joined the Elvis Fan Club."

During the 1962 Seattle World's Fair, Debbie met the King while he was filming a movie. Debbie's father was good friends with the police officer assigned to protect Elvis.

"He gave me a kiss and a record album," she said. "When I went to his concert in Spokane, he gave me a scarf."

Debbie said she had a lot more Elvis stuff at her mother's house.

With a couple of miracles under our belts, it came to pass that Elvis moved in with the Clarks.

First thing, we gave him a bath and lathered him up with some "Love Me Tender" shampoo I had left from a traveling Elvis museum I once wrote about.

That got him all shook up, but he's recovered nicely with minimal doggie accidents to our hardwood floors.

Of course, there are certain problems that go with owning a dog named Elvis.

When he gets older, it just wouldn't seem right to have Elvis neutered. "That would be horrible," agreed Debbie.

And when I go out on the front porch and call his name, I'll never be sure who'll come crawling out of the bushes.

Unleashing a challenge for coroner

Lately, I've been trying to determine the intelligence of my dog, Elvis.

I've always thought of my pet as a dim bulb – about on the brain cell par with a fern or Spokane County Coroner Dexter Amend.

But an NBC *Dateline* segment on doggy IQ and recent events at the coroner's office have convinced me that I have sold Elvis way short.

On the show, an expert touted the poodle as the planet's second-smartest canine. Cocker spaniels didn't fare so badly, either, ranking 20th out of about 75 breeds.

Since Elvis is a cockapoo – a mixture of the aforementioned dogs – it seemed logical that he didn't come from the shallow end of the gene pool.

So I ran him through a battery of *Dateline* tests, which I will detail a bit later. (By the way, the border collie is the world's smartest breed.)

It turns out Elvis is one Rhodes scholar of a dog. Intellectual enough that I am announcing his candidacy for coroner in the next election.

Before you laugh, ask yourself: Could a common mutt do any worse than a cantankerous old coot like Dexter Amend?

I don't think so.

Sure, Elvis embarrasses himself with a lot of mindless, goofy yapping.

But Amend recently barked at a single mother, telling her she should go find a husband when she couldn't pay for her brother's cremation.

Around the house, Elvis is always blundering into the tables and chairs.

Amend once tripped over the body of a 3-year-old child while lecturing the boy's stunned and grieving parents on how the boy's organs could be harvested.

Elvis is a harmless friend to all.

Our coroner snaps at anybody in his way. Before he took office, Amend canned a longtime coroner's office secretary, presumably for being a Democrat.

Amend has a medical license. Elvis also is fully licensed.

My dog has rolled in a lot of foul substances on the lawn, but he's never come close to creating the kind of stink that Amend routinely leaves behind.

Amend took off on a bizarre homophobic tangent recently when he indicted gays because a young murder victim was sodomized.

Police complain Amend constantly plays *Quincy*, the 1970s TV coroner played by Jack Klugman, trying to guess how people died without having any facts. His death certificates are considered by many to be a joke.

Trust me. Elvis has sense enough to defer to pathologists and autopsy findings before ruling on any cause of death.

I know what you're thinking. You're thinking, "Yeah, Doug, Amend's a clod, but how do we know Elvis is the right dog to hold public office?"

I'm glad you asked.

On the *Dateline* program, scientists measured canine IQ by tying dynamite to dogs and then running them around a track until they exploded.

No, wait a minute. That's how *Dateline* scientists demonstrated the dangers of General Motors pickups.

During the show I watched, a fat guy in an ascot ran dogs through some weird experiments.

He threw a blanket over the dogs and timed how long it took them to shake it off.

He hid a yummy under a plastic cup to learn which dogs could figure out how to get the treat.

He tested dogs to see if they could remember where food was hidden.

Some dull-witted bowsers, like the poor basset hound, didn't have the gray matter to find their way out from under the blanket. Sounds like our County Commission, huh?

Elvis, however, was as sharp and crafty as Bill Clinton avoiding the draft. He aced every challenge in split seconds.

So as the first step in our campaign, we dare Amend to take the same tests. Because of his witless antics, it's time our unworthy opponent proved he has more smarts than a mop-haired cockapoo.

So far, the only thing this arrogant and tactless pit bull of a coroner has proved is that he shouldn't leave home without a muzzle.

Courtroom Follies

Chapter Fourteen

Once again, armed robber, killer walks out of court

It was as if fate had offered Gary Haman a reprieve.

For there, sitting once again in the judge's Coeur d'Alene courtroom, was Spokane resident Rodney D. Beck – armed robber, drunken and reckless driver, killer of Richard Greene.

Where had the time gone? Three years before, Haman had sat stone-faced, listening to Beck admit to running down the Newman Lake, Washington, man who had been pedaling his 10-speed bicycle home to attend a Father's Day barbecue with his wife and two children.

"It was a gut-wrenching case," agreed Peter Erbland, the Kootenai County deputy prosecutor who left a barbecue of his own to rush to the grisly scene near Post Falls. "Greene's bicycle looked like a pretzel. The body was gone by the time I got there, but there was blood everywhere."

Erbland said the case nearly went to trial, but that Beck, at the last minute, decided to plead guilty.

It was no wonder, the case against Beck was that good. There were even reports of how the defendant had, at times, thought it great sport to intentionally swerve his truck at bicyclists.

That, plus the fact Beck's pickup was the only vehicle on the four-lane road at the time of the accident had prosecutors initially contemplating charges of murder, rather than manslaughter.

Then there was the matter of Beck's criminal past.

Who could overlook the 13 convictions for speeding, including a drunken driving and a reckless driving citation? The day he killed Greene, Beck was on probation for an armed robbery and a burglary he had pulled months earlier in Spokane.

A condition of the probation was that Beck stop drinking. He didn't.

Minutes before he ran his truck over Greene, Beck had been boozing it up in a Coeur d'Alene tavern. When he got behind the wheel, Rodney Beck was gassed to the gills.

A few miles later, he plowed into Greene, instantly killing the man. Beck then over-corrected the steering wheel and spun his vehicle across the highway, where it rolled and finally landed upside down.

Idaho State Police investigators remember Beck well.

He was the guy who tried to keep them from finding the marijuana stash in his truck. He was the guy who showed no remorse for what he had done to Richard Greene.

Armed with all of this information and more, Judge Haman, on a winter's day in 1983, imposed a sentence that even caught the defense lawyers by surprise.

Five years probation, 180 days in jail.

"I'm still trying to recover from that," said Greene's widow, Maxine. "It's hard. The more I learn about the judicial system, the more numb I become.

"And there's not a day that goes by that I don't think about Richard."

So incomprehensible was Haman's sentence that the *National Enquirer* found it sensational enough to devote a scalding feature article, headlined: "Drunk Driver Kills Cyclist – And Gets a Slap on the Wrist."

"Such leniency," wrote the *Enquirer*, "is more suitable for shooting a deer out of season – not for killing another human being."

But three years have passed since Haman's outrageous sentencing.

And last Wednesday, there was the judge with a second chance, this golden opportunity to try to set things right, to make amends.

Beck was in court this time because several months ago he had tried to get some guns out of hock at a Spokane pawn shop. He knew having firearms was a violation of his probation, so when he filled out the federal form required in a firearms transaction, he checked the "No" box for the question that asks, "Have you ever been convicted of a felony?"

Nobody will ever accuse Rodney Beck of being a master criminal.

It didn't take long before the law caught up with Beck and hauled him back in front of Haman.

"You didn't forget about your convictions, did you Rodney, when you filled out the forms?" asked Erbland.

"No." Beck admitted, knowing he'd been caught flat.

So there it was, laid out as nice as can be.

Haman had only to say the words to order Beck to serve the two years remaining on his probation behind bars and thus salvage some belated justice.

Dream on.

Haman told Beck that if he paid a small fine within 90 days, he'd discharge the felon from any more Idaho probation. The felon was still on probation in Washington so why not let the authorities across the border worry about it?

Once again, it was the easiest way out.

"It was kind of like Haman was saying, 'Glad you came over here Rodney so we can get this business cleared up and reward you,'" mused one courtroom observer.

"It's just so ludicrous I can't fathom it anymore," said Craig Gilbert, who was bicycling with Greene the day he died. "What can this judge be thinking of?"

The *National Enquirer* minced few words when it branded Haman a "softie" and "spineless" judge before its millions of readers.

It was too lenient.

I think "wimp" has a nicer ring to it.

Idaho judge makes only slightly gigantic mistakes

My daddy, rest his soul, brought me up believing there is no such thing as being occasionally honest, partially pregnant or nearly dead.

Too bad he didn't live long enough to be enlightened by Judge Craig Kosonen.

On Monday, [December 13, 1993], the North Idaho jurist gave a Christmas gift to a three-time felon who only slightly raped a retarded woman.

"It was just marginally forcible. There was no actual intercourse," explained Santa Kosonen of why he sent 32-year-old Wallace resident David Sapp to a 180-day sex offender's program and not to a more suitable location such as the bottom of the Black Sea.

The judge reasoned that Sapp had trouble penetrating the woman and did stop after she said, "No."

Let's give credit where credit is due. Sapp didn't bludgeon the woman into pulp or carve her up with a steak knife.

Of course, Sapp's victim has the mental capacity of an 8-year-old, so she may not understand the subtle benefits of being raped by a gentleman.

Prosecutor Dan McGee is likewise confused. He asked Kosonen to slam-dunk Sapp with 20 years in the joint. He was so shell-shocked after the judge's action he could barely speak.

Who can blame him? If the considerate rapist behaves himself (which is likely since there are no retarded women to molest in the Cottonwood facility), Sapp could be out on probation in six months.

Women's groups and some jurors who convicted Sapp are understandably appalled. How, they wonder, could a judge come up with such nonsense?

Practice, people. Practice.

Let us journey back nine years, when Kosonen was just a mouse training to be a rat.

In April 1984, then-Magistrate Kosonen dismissed charges against two North Idaho yahoos who only slightly strung up a mentally ill man.

The victim was Keith Gilmore, a 36-year-old schizophrenic visiting his parents in Harrison, Idaho. Deeply religious, Gilmore liked to scribble biblical messages on note cards.

Walking barefoot and shirtless through the city park one Saturday, Gilmore dropped a card near some children. On the paper were words like "lust" and "carnal" and "angel."

The scared kids took the note straight to the local authorities: the owners of a nearby saloon.

Two macho guys heard about the weird man and decided to take action. They put Gilmore in a truck and drove to an isolated dirt road.

Sheriff's deputies found the terrified Gilmore with his head in a noose. They said he was standing on his tiptoes, pleading for his life. The attackers, who had thrown the rope over a branch, were pulling on the other end.

It takes a rare intellect to screw up such a simple case, but Kosonen rose to the challenge. In dismissing aggravated assault charges, he said the two citizens were merely trying to do their civic duty.

"I find it appropriate that they tried to find him (Gilmore) and hold him for police," said the magistrate.

A disbelieving Kootenai County prosecutor refiled charges. A year later, a jury took four hours to find the men guilty of aggravated assault.

As a District Court judge, Kosonen has even more opportunities to do harm. Take, for instance, his handling last April of killer Mickey Whitcomb.

After putting a bullet in his girlfriend's brain, the Avery, Idaho, man fired at her 13-year-old son but missed by inches. The boy played dead and survived.

Most people wouldn't buy a used car from such a creep, but Kosonen swallowed his sob story: The killer needed to get out of jail to take care of his sick father.

Kosonen gave him a two-week furlough on a $20,000 bond. A little later, it was discovered that Whitcomb was only slightly lying.

He really did want to get out of jail – but mainly to go to a bar.

Kosonen revoked bail when he discovered that Whitcomb had threatened his ex-wife. As police searched for the man, the frightened woman went into hiding. Fortunately, Whitcomb turned himself in without incident.

"It's a terrible thing for a judge to do that to the people out here," remarked Jim Crutcher, the ex-wife's boyfriend at the time.

Wrong, Jim – it's only slightly terrible.

Sitting down, men stood up for rights

As our nation's leaders discuss fiddling with the Constitution to prohibit flag burning, in Spokane the strange case of the two men who burned a judge prepares for trial.

Their case may never reach the U.S. Supreme Court or become a talk show topic. But it does pose a fascinating question about free symbolic speech.

Just like the guy who torched the flag, Glen Braunstein and Robert Newmeyer say they have used their First Amendment rights to inflame yet another sacred American symbol.

As a result, on February 17, 1988, Braunstein and Newmeyer were found in contempt and jailed by District Court Judge Daniel Maggs.

Their crime: refusing to stand as Maggs entered the courtroom.

"I have a lot of respect for the courtroom," says attorney Mary Schultz, who represents the two men and whose lawsuit against Maggs has been cleared for trial in federal court.

"But it's somewhat embarrassing to know that a judge's authority can be used to jail a spectator who refuses to go down on one knee."

To Braunstein and Newmeyer, obeying the old invocation to "all rise" is repugnant, tantamount to bowing before the king. Although they have spent thousands of hours sitting in on the judicial process as part of what they call the Citizens Bar Association (a constitutionalists' group), they have steadfastly refused bailiff commands to get to their feet.

There is, after all, no law saying anyone must rise. And most jurists at the Spokane County Courthouse are emotionally secure enough to ignore the silent, seated protests of these two men as much ado about nothing.

District Court Judge Daniel T. Maggs, however, is a judge of another gavel. When it comes to a decorum of his court-room, he is said to be a bit of a prig, a man who had scolded observers for wearing hats, for chatting and for a host of other petty infractions.

As for those who will not stand, well, that tradition-trashing set the judge's ego smoldering. And on the fateful day, it erupted into a four-alarm fire.

Bailiff: "All rise."

Maggs: "Now, Mr. Braunstein, I've noticed for the last several times that you've failed to stand when the court's called to order."

Braunstein: "I can't . . ."

Maggs: "Since you're not a defendant, you're only observing, you may leave my court or I will hold you in contempt."

Braunstein: "Does that mean I'll go to jail, your honor?"

Maggs: "Yes, sir."

Judge Maggs, as the official transcript goes on to show, went through basically the same spiel with Newmeyer, who was seated next to Braunstein. When it was all over, the two men found themselves arrested, booked, fingerprinted and sentenced to two days in the slammer.

The pair were no strangers to Maggs. He had warned Braunstein, in particular, a number of times about the consequences of not obeying him.

"He had bluffed us for a couple of years on this," says Braunstein. "I decided that, this time, I wanted it to stop there. If not, what's next? Do we start kissing the president's ring?"

A bit extreme, perhaps, but Braunstein's point is not without logic.

As Schultz says, an American's right of non-participation is the most elemental form of protest.

"There is nothing more benign, in my opinion, than refusing to go along with a tradition. All through your life, there are kids who don't want to go to graduation or sing along at the campfire. And so what? Does their non-participation harm anybody? Of course not."

At the heart of the issue, however, is whether or not the two men represented a disruptive influence on Maggs' court. If so, the judge does have the power to use a contempt order to remove troublemakers that are impeding the flow of justice.

The only problem with that argument is that nothing in the transcripts suggests Braunstein or Newmeyer were creating a disturbance. The whole episode seems to be precipitated by Maggs, who made a point of forcing the issue.

As Schultz says: "Aw, Maggs just got (bleeped) off and went overboard."

If that's true, these two so-called super-patriots may have the judge by the robes. Maggs' attorney – who declined to talk on the record about all of this – has offered to settle.

He has agreed to pay Schultz's fees if her clients will keep their mouths shut in front of the press and abide by an odd arrangement under which they will stay away from Maggs' courtroom at the times he is coming onto the bench.

In exchange, Maggs will ignore Braunstein and Newmeyer if they don't mark his exits with a standing ovation. The contempt record will be expunged as if the whole thing never happened.

No soap, says Schultz, who adds that the entire settlement offer misses the point of what happened.

"The problem is that Judge Maggs is in a position to do some damage to some folks," she says. "Maybe we can educate him so he doesn't do this to the next poor soul who comes along."

Judicial lunacy allows inmate to attend class

He strangled and slashed the throat of an elderly Sunnyside woman and buried the gasoline-soaked remains in her own flower bed.

He escaped from a mental hospital and later shattered the shoulder of a sheriff's deputy.

Now, big fog-brained keepers claim lunatic killer Phillip Arnold Paul, 32, is well enough to visit Spokane once a week – provided he is guarded at all times and takes his medication.

"I am so angry," says Helen Mottley, whose 78-year-old mother, Ruth was murdered by Paul in 1987. "Nobody should go through what my family had to go through."

Ruth Mottley, a retired educator, was the matriarch of Sunnyside. She founded the town's historical association and was recognized as one of Washington's 100 most influential women of the last century.

But voices jabbering inside Paul's skull told him Motley was a witch. The powerfully built former wrestler entered the woman's home on Emerald Road on April 25, 1987, and practically twisted her head off.

He sliced her neck with a pocketknife, soaked her in gasoline to throw search dogs from her scent and buried the body in a shallow grave.

Paul was found not guilty because of this insanity and was confined to Eastern State Hospital in Medical Lake. Paul needs biweekly injections of a drug to keep his demons at bay.

"He's the only paranoid schizophrenic – I've seen hundreds, maybe thousands of them – that frightened me," psychiatrist Frank Hardey testified during a 1988 deposition.

Yet on June 15, [1995] a Yakima Superior Court judge signed an order to let Paul attend an art class once a week in Spokane beginning August 2.

Dr. Al Miller, Eastern State Hospital's medical director, says Paul's treatment puts him in better touch with reality. "Obviously, he's not grossly psychotic at this time."

When Paul ventures out, he will pay his private guards with Social Security disability money.

"The damn Social Security money oughta be going to the state of Washington for his care," says Yakima County Prosecutor Jeff Sullivan.

There are a lot of things crazy about this.

For starters, Sullivan "very reluctantly" went along with Paul's conditional release. He did so, he says, because of the restrictions placed upon Paul's movements outside the hospital.

But Sullivan didn't bother to notify Mottley family members that Paul's release was being considered. Their objections at the hearing conceivably could have stopped the release.

"I apologize," concedes the prosecutor. "That was my responsibility and I dropped the ball."

That's not the only time officials have dropped the ball where Paul is concerned.

In 1990, his keepers let him wander the hospital grounds unsupervised. Paul just walked away.

Spokane Sheriff's Deputy Roger Knight caught Paul and found how vicious he can be. At the Spokane County Jail, Paul's transformation from meek prisoner to lunatic was lightning quick.

"He suddenly punches me in the head, picks me up and smashes me into the floor," says Knight, whose shoulder was reconstructed and will never be the same. Paul was pounding the officer's head into the floor when jailers pulled him off.

"I hope whoever guards him has good life insurance and medical benefits," adds the deputy.

No one is more upset by the system's handling of Paul than Southern Idaho rancher Marx Hintze.

In the spring of 1987, Paul drove off in the man's truck. He made it to Mackay, Idaho, where Hintze happened upon him sitting dazed in the pickup in the middle of a highway.

Hintze called a deputy, who arrested Paul and found several loaded handguns and a sawed-off shotgun in the truck.

Paul was taken to a mental facility in Blackfoot, but Custer County wanted him discharged because of the cost.

Hintze pleaded with officials not to let the inmate go. He mailed a registered letter to the institution, demanding Paul be kept because of the danger to society.

Instead, mental health workers gave Paul some drugs and released him to his mother, who took her sick son back to Sunnyside. Ten days later, Phillip Arnold Paul took care of that witch on Emerald Road.

No matter how strict the conditions, Hintze is incredulous that anyone would run the risk of putting Paul back into the community.

"I thought Washington had more smarts than that," says the rancher. "Keep him locked up. This guy's had his chance."

If only jury had seen killer's art

Hey, Mark Wayne Clark!

A jury has just awarded a sicko convict artist like you $8,550. Where will you spend your loot?

Disneyland?

Only after you complete your life sentence, pal.

Clark, 35, is a first-degree killer from the Seattle area [and not a relative of the author]. He has been warehoused inside Walla Walla's sprawling Washington State Penitentiary since his 1985 conviction.

That will remain his address until the felon's "earned release" date, which arrives in the year 2002.

Until then, Clark will be a convict with some means if last week's court decision isn't overturned on appeal.

I hope it is. Should this fiasco stand, it may cost taxpayers upward of $50,000 in damages and legal fees.

A U.S. District Court jury in Spokane found that prison officials interfered with Clark's First Amendment rights of artistic expression and then retaliated against him after he began making waves.

The penitentiary did make some mistakes.

A hearing officer wrongly told Clark he couldn't draw any more. Prisoners do have a constitutional right to paper and pen.

Clark also lost a 90-cent-an-hour job and was denied a transfer to a different prison, perhaps as punishment for making waves.

But managing a bunch of criminals is no cakewalk.

Had jurors been allowed to gaze upon the vile artwork that triggered all of this, they might have concluded the case differently.

Unfortunately, Clark's Seattle lawyer successfully argued to keep his client's inflammatory drawings from the jury.

That came as a major setback to the defendant's case, says Martin Wyckoff, one of the state attorneys who defended the prison.

"There's no doubt in my mind, those pictures were key," he says. "I'm sure the jurors had no idea the case they were ruling on."

Let me help.

Clark is an artist all right – if you like looking at naked little girls having sex.

Guards in 1992 discovered and carted off Clark's crude, but graphic, pen and ink drawings of a naked, pre-pubescent girl engaged in various sexual positions with an adult male.

In one scene a little girl in pigtails performs oral sex. In another she lies on top of the man. A portrait of a young nude girl was confiscated later.

This guy's a real Picasso, all right.

To be fair, not all of Clark's artwork is pornographic or even explicit. He does some greeting cards, some unicorns . . . .

Had he kept to that stuff there would be no need for a courtroom.

His sick stuff, however, is dynamite in a prison populated with child molesters and every kind of sex freak imaginable.

No wonder authorities revoked permission for Clark to use special art supplies. No wonder they repeatedly searched his cell.

Officials claim Clark was using his cell as a jailhouse store, trading adult magazines to other inmates for stamps.

"I'm still convinced the officers did nothing wrong," adds Wyckoff.

Sure, prison officials got in Clark's face. No question it made him an unhappy camper.

So what. Clark wasn't beaten or tortured as he probably would have been in the old, less-enlightened days of the penal system.

He may have suffered some inconvenience, but this guy didn't go to Walla Walla on the taxpayers' dime to draw dirty pictures or file lawsuits.

He got life for gunning down an unarmed West Seattle hairdresser, Daniel F. Conklin, in cold blood.

Two bullets to the head. One to the chest.

Clark carefully planned the killing and then bragged about what he'd done. He's lucky he didn't hang.

At his sentencing, Clark told the judge he would use his time behind bars to better himself.

He's got about seven years left to make good on that.

Just for Laughs

Chapter Fifteen

An ex-rocker cannot betray his brothers

A nice lady approached me the other day and asked if I'd sign her petition to help keep the Monsters of Rock from invading Spokane.

It seems a lot of decent, God-fearing folks believe that the coming infusion of senseless noise at Joe Albi Stadium could mean an end of civilization as we know it.

"This is a decent city," the woman informed me. "Let the Monsters of Rock go somewhere else to peddle their filth."

I declined her invitation to sign, of course. Being a newspaper columnist, I make it a habit never to get personally involved with political crusades, hostile takeovers, lynchings, bloodless coups, demonic possessions, Democratic caucuses, liquor store holdups, telethons or Holy Ghost revivals.

But what really stopped me from jotting my name on the petition was the unwritten Headbangers Code:

"Thou shalt not betray a brother rocker, ya dig?"

That's right. Few people are aware of this, but except for the fame, money, sex, drugs and tons of fabulous equipment, I was once a Monster of Rock.

It was 20 years ago today. Well, it was 20 years ago this month [July 1988] that The People Upstairs launched its ill-fated world tour with a debut concert at the Moses Lake Job Corps.

The People Upstairs was a local rock 'n' roll band. I played rhythm guitar and trumpet. We were all going to make millions and become stars and would have, too, except for the fact that we weren't very good.

301

But the beautiful, democratic thing about rock 'n' roll is that you don't have to be very good to get jobs. Loud and cheap are much more crucial.

At least, that's how The People Upstairs got to start its career.

The Job Corps, if you're not old enough to recall, was part of President Lyndon Johnson's War on Poverty. (Which, by the way, turned out to be as mishandled and stupid as the one he waged in Vietnam. But that's another story, too.)

At various Job Corps sites around the country, tough inner-city kids – kids on parole from dismembering family members or robbing entire supermarket chains – were deposited and taught to lead meaningful lives. In other words, the Job Corps was much like prison.

All members of The People Upstairs – Dave Schober, Gary Wilson, Lyle Hall and me – were very, very excited to find work, even it it was at an institution which contained people who might disembowel us with switchblades. Dave Schober's parents were also very very excited. For months, we had been driving the Schober household scooters with long basement practice sessions. The Schobers were understandably fatigued with hearing us blare out, "Gloooo-reee-yah, G-L-O-R-I-A, Gloooo-ree-yah!!!" over and over again with a distinctive People Upstairs tonal quality unfit for all but the hearing impaired or the dead.

In between practices we did what all Spokane rock bands did. We hung out at Hoffman's Music Center, acting smug and ogling guitar amplifiers that were larger than Norge appliances.

We also painted a sign on our bass drum and I even wrote a theme song for our band. "If the Monkees can do it, so can we," I told my fellow People Upstairsians.

Mercifully, time has all but erased memories of the song. The closest I can recollect is something like, "Here we coooooome, walking down your streeeeeet. We're The People Upstaaaaaairs and we're really neeeeeeat…"

We didn't have Spandex pants back then, but we did all go to Swabbies and buy pointy-toed Beatle boots, which were every bit as uncomfortable and foolish as anything Eddie Van Halen might put on.

So on a blazing July day, we packed up Dave Schober's white Chevy van and drove to Moses Lake. It was there I learned what an ugly job being a Monster of Rock can be.

My first clue came when one of the Job Corps cretins turned a sprinkler on our gear we had unloaded near the van. Not the best treatment for electrical equipment, as I discovered when my amplifier shorted out during "Love Potion No. 9." Schober spent the concert using a screwdriver to retune his organ every few minutes.

To top it off, the Job Corps internees hated us. They liked meaty East Coast soul. Our music was West Coast Wonder Bread. As a result, Job Corpsers kept turning on a juke box in protest until someone – and I'm not saying who – clipped the end off the juke's cord.

Knowing then that they were stuck with us, we made a pact. We would only play "House of the Rising Sun" and "Summertime" and they would let us leave Moses Lake alive.

It was an amicable arrangement, except that after playing eight trumpet renditions of "Summertime" my lip turned into a blister bigger than Fats Domino.

The only positive note came when I sang a romantic ballad called "Anita," another of my original masterpieces. That song went, "The night is approaching the wind is dying; Out in the distance the hounds are crying, Ah-neeee-taaaah..."

At the end of our concert, a fat girl with a cross tattooed on her forearm waddled up and looked me over with huge doe eyes. "Mah name's Anita," she said. "Will you sign mah autograph."

In disbelief, I grabbed for a pen. Now that's the kind of petition we Rock Monsters will always sign.

Accordion Joe has the answer for vacation fame

HOW I SPENT MY RECENT VACATION.
Chapter One: The setup.
So I pick up the telephone and a guy named Accordion Joe starts telling me how I should write him up in the newspaper.

This kind of thing happens all the time. There are glory hounds of all kinds out there who think we newspaper types have nothing better to do than act as personal publicist for every nut case that comes along.

"Look here Accordion Whoever-you-are," I try to explain, "we newspaper types have better things to do than act a personal publicists for every nut case that comes along."

"Besides," I add, "journalism is a very proper and dignified business. I have some very high standards as to who gets in my column and who doesn't."

I pause.

"And futhermore, I'm on vacation. I don't work on vacation; that's when I relax and try to do fun family things."

Accordion Joe tells me that he plans to play his accordion blindfolded while waterskiing on one ski.

"Er, what time do you want me there?" I say.
Chapter Two: Breaking the news.
"We're going to do what?" my wife says with one of those "my-parents-were-right-about-you" looks. "This our vacation time. Have you gone out of your mind?"

My daughter, Emily, who has seen Chevy Chase's *Vacation* movie three times, is more optimistic. "Why not?" she says. "After all, weeee're the Griswolds!"
Chapter Three: The big day.
Accordion Joe meets the Clark family at the Nine Mile Resort on Long Lake.

We have here a tall, 46-year-old man who should know better. Accordion Joe likes to say "right-on-dude" a lot and he looks like Bob Uecker, the former baseball player who plays the bumbler on *Mr. Belvedere* and assorted prime time beer commercials.

Accordion's last name is Jenkins, he claims, but he's also known as – and I'm not making this up – The Rhinestone Mailman.

Accordion Joe has brought his scrapbook, a three-ring binder filled with stuff that explains the odd nicknames, the musical exploits and just about everything else except what brand of tranquilizer he's supposed to be on.

"Right on, dude," says Accordion, yukking it up at my tranquilizer joke.

A Spokane area native, Accordion Joe now lives in Tacoma and works for the Kent Post Office, where he oftens plays accordion tunes for postal customers during his lunch hour. When he performs, he wears the mandatory accordion players' garb – an Elvis-style white jumpsuit plastered with sequins and musical notes. So far, there are no federal regulations to prevent this.

"I just hear a voice in my head that says 'Show Time,' and I know it's time to play," he says.

Which is sufficient explanation for today's outing. Accordion Joe had come to Spokane on a vacation to visit his sweet, aging mother, Helen. Then the voice went off and, well, that was the cue The Rhinestone Mailroom needed.

"I don't know why he does these things," says Helen, tossing up her hands.

Chapter four: Hidden motives.

Did I mention before that I hate accordions?

Let's be honest, if ever there was a musical instrument for nerds – next to bagpipes, that is – the accordion is it. These are the things bought by people who can't afford pianos, things mothers forced their children to play back in the '40's, when child abuse was legal.

If you don't believe me, I offer two words as incontrovertible proof: Myron Floren.

Little does Accordion Joe know that I have come to root for the lake, not for him.

Chapter five: The show always goes on.

Accordion Joe tells me about the time back in '79 when he got a construction company in Pullman to tie his feet together and suspend him 120 feet off the ground while he played, blindfolded, the song "Up, Up and Away." Another time, Accordion Joe climbed all 73 floors of the Seattle Seafirst Center while playing 50's and 60's music.

This is not normal and I tell him so. "If you only knew the half of it, dude," is his response.

Accordion Joe is finally in the water, holding his squeeze box above his head. His son, Rik is driving the family speedboat while wife, Brenda, acts as spotter. A band of vacationing Baptists have lined up on the dock to watch. One of them has a video camera. Baptists love anything having to do with immersion.

Accordion Joe gives the signal. Rik pulls the throttle. We're off.

Accordion Joe is up. He fastens the tow rope to a hook strapped around his waist. He pulls down his blindfold. He begins to play. Baptists are praying. Engine noise from the boat divinely intercedes, mercifully covering satanic accordion sounds.

Accordion Joe has succeeded, but all is not lost. Rik cuts the engine and, before Joe can save his instrument, they both slip under the waves.

He emerges, Long Lake gushing out of what was once an accordion.

Chapter six: A fitting touch.

On shore, Joe's accordion breaks into three pieces and falls to the ground. For no apparent reason, a large, white dog named Cody trots up and begins to eat it.

"Music critics," I tell Accordion Joe. "Everyone's a music critic."

He smiles. "You got that right, dude."

Dark forces tamper with Halloween

Halloween is getting scarier every year.

I'm not talking about those unearthly wails that emanate from weedy graveyards, those unexplained night bumping or those religious wackos who believe that leering jack-o'-lantern faces are really caricatures of Satan or Tammy Faye Bakker.

No, in the epic struggle between evil versus good fun, there are far darker forces at work than these.

I'm talking about – gasp! – well-intentioned adults.

A scientific report detailing the latest adult meddling into the spirit of this fine holiday has come from my 11-year-old son, Benjamin. Recently, he revealed to me that his fifth-grade Halloween party would this year be candy-free and that the following would be served: "Cheese, little crackers, sausages with toothpicks and green and black olives."

Aaaaarrrrggggggg!!!

That's not a Halloween party, that's a Republican fund-raiser.

"It's like getting underwear for Christmas," says my bummed-out Benjamin, and I have to agree.

Should this health-conscious trend continue, one can only imagine what foul, hideous party permutations the ghouls of Halloween future will conjure up.

Join me now as we peer into Doug's magic Halloween crystal ball.

Look! We see little children, all wearing wing-tipped shoes. Little Stepford children, who sit quietly in school and read from their latest L. L. Bean catalogs and listen to public radio.

After consuming sensible portions of brie and Perrier, the real merriment begins. A school district nurse arrives, and each child takes a fun-filled turn at having his or her cholesterol screened.

"What did you get for Halloween, Joel?" asks Joel's dad, Kevin. "A Snickers?"

"Better than that," says a proud Joel. "I got a 140 on my cholesterol, my high-density lipids look great and my triglycerides are way, way down."

Makes you shudder just to think about such a thing.

No, Halloween should remain exactly what it always has been: an infantile, sucrose-laden, tooth-rotting orgy of candy corns, jelly beans, gum drops and dozens of packages of (my personal favorites) the ever-popular Sugar Babies.

Face it, there is nothing at all redeeming about Sugar Babies or Halloween and let's keep it that way.

I'm tired of adults always horning into things, banning war toys for Christmas, fireworks for the Fourth and then sweets for Halloween. I'm tired of bank tellers and bartenders dressing up like hobgoblins or Nixon and smudging makeup on my paycheck or shot glass. I'm tired of food columnists telling me to eat oat bran.

I'm tired of, well, mostly I'm just very, very tired.

But somebody has to talk about these things. Somebody has to stick up for good, old-fashioned fun.

The role we adults should play on Halloween is to be as unobtrusive as possible.

If you're a parent with young children, it's perfectly permissible to shamble about in the night, keeping a watchful eye as your offspring beg their way from house to house like little homeless bag people.

And why not make a party of it? Join the other dads of the neighborhood like my good friend, Ray, who prefers that I always wear my large, blue parka on Halloween. The one with the big pockets that will hold six or seven cans of Budweiser to aid us in our nocturnal wanderings.

This is what Halloween is all about, not cheese and crackers and sausage and, for crying out loud, olives.

If you have no kids and you're over 15, stay home and help dole out the treats. Speaking of treats, I'm happy to say that all the news on the Halloween front this year is not bad.

A friendly worker at the PayLess Drug Store at South 4514 Regal told me her store still has packages left of the innovative Halloween treats – and I'm not making this up – "Boogers" candies.

"We're still working on selling out our first case," she said. "I haven't tried any, but they look pretty disgusting."

Made in Argentina and distributed by a New Jersey candy company, Boogers have the taste and consistency of Gummy Bears. Only they're shaped like, well, the name says it all.

But trust me on this. Give these out for Halloween and you'll be the trick-or-treat hit of the neighborhood. Oh, and keep some Bud on hand in case Ray and I show up.

Dr. Doug offers some prescriptions for sane holiday season

Christmas, as any shrink will tell you, is the craziest time of the year.

When you consider all the pressures – the office parties, the gift giving, the flying reindeer – why, it's no wonder the streets are crawling with yuletide yoyos.

Nobody knows this better than husband and wife psychologists Dr. Larry and Dr. Mary Weathers. After all, this couple has made a fine living treating my readers for years.

But even Dr. Larry and Dr. Mary need a breather. To avoid the Christmas mad rush (or rush of the mad), they've decided to close down their Spokane practice for the holidays and go skiing.

In their absence, they have written a self-help pamphlet called *The 12 Pitfalls of Christmas* and left me in charge.

And why not? As Dr. Larry said in the beginning of our interview: "We only see our patients an hour a week but you see them (through the magic of newsprint) all the time."

So before you take that long walk off a short pier, I give you Dr. Larry's and Dr. Mary's *The 12 Pitfalls of Christmas*, with special analysis from Dr. Doug.

Too much to do: Trying to cram holiday activities on top of an already busy schedule can make you bonkers. Make a list of your priorities and stick to them, says Dr. Mary. Dr. Doug says you neurotics should not hold back. Sign up to bake cookies for church the same night you baby-sit for friends while they shop. Keep it up and by Christmas, you'll be getting the rest you need at Eastern State Hospital.

Overspending: Don't try to impress people by buying big-ticket presents, says Dr. Larry. It's better to pick out less expensive, meaningful gifts. Dr. Doug says to look for business advertising "No payments until February." Then spend all your money there. Who knows? The world might end by February and who wants to go with cash available on your charge cards?

Child custody: Divorced parents need to remember that Christmas is for kids. Learn to share. Don't let a paternal tug-of-war destroy your kid, says Dr. Mary. Dr. Doug says if you treat your kids well, they will grow up and feel guilty if they don't buy you fabulously expensive gifts.

Football: Most wives hate it. Real men love it. Dr. Larry says compromise is the answer. Couples should agree on specific times when a man can do "his football gladiator ritual" in peace. Dr. Doug says thoughtful husbands should cut back on football and watch more hockey, basketball and professional bowling.

Overeating: What's Christmas without cholesterol? But if you have more rolls than a baker, stand as far away from the food table as possible, says Dr. Mary. Dr. Doug says never put anything into your mouth that's larger than your head.

Drinking too much: Dr. Larry advises alternating booze with soda pop and other non-alcoholic drinks. Dr. Doug endorses alternating beer with rum cake and rum cake with Sterno, which is a pleasant change of pace.

Relatives: Both Dr. Larry and Dr. Doug agree that it's best not to have any. "My relatives like warm climates," says Dr. Larry. "I guess you can see why I'm here in Spokane."

Loneliness: Christmas can be lonely if you're trying to live up to expectations set by old *The Waltons* TV episodes. Dr. Mary says people without family or friends should go to a ballet or see a movie. Don't sit around and be miserable. Dr. Doug says he'd be glad to put lonely people in touch with his lousy relatives.

The Old Times: Longing for the good old days can be very intense at Christmas. To combat such sentimental drivel, start some new traditions, says Dr. Larry. If you think the good old days were good, says Dr. Doug, just remember that Nixon got pardoned, but Old Yeller got shot. How's that for justice?

Religious conflicts: The religious nature of Christmas produces a lot tension. Tolerance is the key, says Dr. Mary. Don't forget that people have the right to believe in whatever they want. Dr. Doug advises watching an hour of Jimmy Swaggart's show. That should take your mind off religion for the rest of the year.

Excessive sympathy for the poor: With so many worthy causes, it's easy for the guilt feelings to flow. Before you get carried away, make out a budget so you can see what you can afford to give. Dr. Doug says anyone with spare cash can mail it to: Dr. Doug's Christmas Graft Fund, *The Spokesman-Review*, 99210.

Year-end blues: Many people experience a tremendous letdown after Christmas and New Year's. Dr. Mary says to set reasonable goals for the coming year and plan some special activities for January. Dr. Doug has a cure for the blues, too. Turn the tube to a sports station, hunker down in a chair and sip a tall Sterno on the rocks.

Oh, and take the phone off the hook. You never know when a relative might call.

U.S. *judge's shower stall christened*

A fresh bar of soap. A jet blast of warm water.

Ahhhhh . . .

Nothing like an invigorating shower to restore odor in the court.

Even better when the shower you're standing under is in the controversial private bathroom of federal bankruptcy Judge John Klobucher.

Taxpayers are in a lather about the $6,688 they paid to add a fiberglass shower stall and refurbish the judge's personal water closet.

Klobucher's new bathroom was part of the $7.6 million renovaton of Spokane's vintage downtown post office, a two-year project that ended up costing a million bucks more than expected.

Being somewhat of a taxpayer, I decided to visit His Honor's third-floor office Wednesday morning [July 28, 1993] and see how it feels to come clean in a judge's chambers.

"You want to take a shower?" asked Ellie Iverson, Klobucher's secretary. "Nobody's ever made that request to me before."

When the laughter died, Iverson and her 61-year-old boss generously agreed, provided I use my own soap and towels and didn't do anything weird.

No problem. Cranking the faucet, I slid under the soothing judicial spray and immediately broke into a spirited chorus of "I Fought the Law" followed by "Slip Sliding Away."

This, I'm proud to announce, was a precedent-setting shower. Not even Klobucher has played "Here Come Da Suds" inside his one-piece plastic stall.

The judge didn't get a lot for our money.

"My bathroom is the tackiest job in the whole post office renovation," bemoans Klobucher.

Members of the construction crew made such a mess of the tile floor they finally had to cover it with carpet squares.

Workers chipped and cracked a number of wall tiles and then crudely glued them back together.

They somehow managed to lose the judge's medicine cabinet. He got a nice antique oak mirror in its place, but now Klobucher keeps his toothbrush and aspirin bottle in a sack under the sink.

The crew broke his toilet paper dispenser. It was replaced with one of those hideous, industrial-strength metal boxes that hold two jumbo rolls.

Which brings us to Klobucher's commode.

This is hardly a throne fit for a man who is paid to sit in judgment of others.

This is a lidless jail cell toilet, the kind tattooed inmates flick their cigarette butts into and then flush by stomping the chrome lever with their feet.

Klobucher's $6,688 bathroom is more Motel 6 than Taj Mahal.

"You'd better bring your sunglasses," he says sarcastically, "because I don't want you to be dazzled when you see this glorious bathroom."

Like the public, the judge also wonders where the money went. A private citizen wouldn't accept this kind of work, he adds. "But I didn't bitch about it."

Klobucher says he wanted a shower for those occasions when he spends the night in his chambers, delving into mysteries of juris and prudence.

"If I'd known there wasn't a shower in my bathroom I never would have taken the job," says Klobucher, his tongue firmly in this cheek.

Although shower stalls are allowed in the guidelines for judges, Klobucher nearly didn't get one. He says it was on the plans and later taken off to cut costs.

The contractors then asked Klobucher if he would move to another floor during one phase of the renovation. The judge agreed with a provision: install the stall.

"Now that you've had your shower, do you feel like putting on the robes and dispensing a little justice?" Klobucher asks.

He's right. Getting yourself zestfully clean is a wonderful way to start a legal career.

Most of the lawyers I know could use a good, long shower.

With one at his command, perhaps the Showering Judge will have his robes made of black terry cloth. That way he can jump straight from the bath to the bench.

"I hadn't thought of that," says Klobucher. "But you don't need to wear anything under the robes."

Hear ye. Hear ye. It is a wise judge who understands grime and punishment.

Follicle farming very tough in fallow field

For some mysterious reason, any baldness remedies that arrive at the newspaper are quickly forwarded to my desk.

I can't figure out the connection, but . . . Wait a minute. I just saw my column photograph.

My gawd, call the cops. Somebody stole my haaaiiiir!!!

Let me confess something you may not have noticed. I'm a follicly-challenged guy.

Or as my friends lovingly say: "Put a hat on, baldo. The glare's hurting our eyes!"

Well, no more shots across the brow for this baldo. Thanks to a miracle of modern merchandising, I soon may have more mane than Mister Ed.

I am testing an amazing new treatment called – don't laugh – Hair Farming.

I heard about Hair Farming through a press release mailed to *The Spokesman-Review* from a New York public relations firm. Here's the part that got my pulse a-pounding: "After just 20 minutes of Hair Farming," the release states, "you will see hair that was not previously visible."

The only uncomfortable thing about Hair Farming is training a herd of tiny cows to fertilize your forehead without dribbling in your eyes.

Ha, ha. Just kidding. You'll be glad to hear that Hair Farming doesn't involve livestock, tractors or toothless hicks named Jeb who wear bib overalls and splat tobacco on your head.

Hair Farming is a simple process that consists of several secret ointments and easy-to-follow directions. It's also expensive. A six-month supply of Hair Farming products runs $859.95. The brochure says the average program costs between $1,000 and $2,000.

"We have the answer to (male) pattern baldness," boasts Jacqueline Sable, the Pompano, Florida, woman who invented what she calls "a product that can end hair loss in the human race."

Sable's theory, if I may paraphrase, is that we chrome domes are the way we are because pour hair follicles are stopped up like clogged kitchen drains.

Her Hair Farming elixirs promise to unplug the tiny openings like Drano in the sink. Suddenly – "SPROING!" – hairs that haven't seen daylight since the Nixon administration are sprouting up like Jack's beanstalk.

"Thick coarse hairs, not peach fuzz," promises Sable, who talks about one subject who actually sproinged out a 10-inch hair after a session.

The last 10-inch hair I found was in my burrito at a cheap cafe.

Sable sent me a Hair Farming starter kit free so I could check it out for journalistic purposes.

I took the glop to the auto shop where I get my head buffed. Actually, Gary Swift at Hair's Image in the Paulsen Building graciously agreed to apply the liquids while Sable talked him through it over the telephone.

Getting Hair Farmed is a slippery but not unpleasant process that took about an hour.

"I don't see any difference," said Swift, who squinted at my head as carefully as an astronomer scanning the heavens for signs of alien life.

Sable claims Swift didn't find any new growth because he didn't know what to look for. "I told him to call me back," she adds angrily in a later conversation.

I dunno, Jackie, a new 10-incher would be hard for even Ray Charles to miss. Besides, Swift has cut my hair for years. He knows every pathetic barren patch.

I'll give Sable credit for persistence. She wants me to keep on Hair Farming and checking the mirror for success.

"By Monday you'll have lots of new hair," she says. "This is for real. It's my pride that's on the line here."

I hope I do turn into a human chia pet. (Keep checking my column photo for signs of progress.)

But even if I end up a failed farmer, I'll come out on top. I can always get Willie Nelson to stage a Hair Aid benefit concert for me.

Or maybe I'll apply for some of those federal agricultural subsidies you always hear people grousing about. Wouldn't that be baldo heaven – getting paid to NOT grow hair.

Draft board lets you shirk with pride

After 42 years of shirking my patriotic duty, I'm thinking of enlisting.

No, I'm not joining the Army. Uncle Sam doesn't want any near-sighted old goobers like me to keep the evil Hun at bay.

What I have in mind is much, much less dangerous. I've picked up the paperwork to join the draft board.

You heard me, the draft board. I could hardly believe my eyes the other day when a concerned co-worker handed me the following shocking item he ripped out of this newspaper.

It read:

"Tonight! Wisconsin's Best Stripper, Alyssa Alps, Appearing at the Deja Vu Club."

Oops. Wrong item.

The one I'm talking about read:

"Selective Service System – Board members needed for Local Draft Board. . . Call Connie . . ."

Draft board? This came as quite a surprise. The last time I thought about the draft board was 25 years ago, when I studied very hard to stay in college and keep my student deferment.

(**Editor's Note**: We will pause briefly to allow those who bravely served their country to fill their medal-encrusted chests with air and shout: "Clark, you are a good-for-nothing, yellow-bellied, draft-evading WEASEL!")

But I'm an honest weasel. I graduated from high school in 1969 and frankly, from all the newspaper and television accounts, Southeast Asia looked problematic.

Jumping back to the present, I didn't know we still had a draft board. Men 18 years old still are required to register with the Selective Service, but the United States did away with the draft in 1973.

Before another draft could start up again many unlikely and politically charged events would have to take place:

(1) Congress would have to pass a law, which would (2) have to be signed by President Clinton, who would (3) drop his pen and start giggling hysterically because, (4) let's face it, when it comes to dodging the draft Bill Clinton makes me look like (5) General George Patton.

So I called Connie to ask why we need a draft board when we don't even have a draft.

After a lengthy conversation, this young woman not only convinced me that having a draft board was extremely vital to the nation's security, but it was also something I should become part of.

"We have to be ready," she warned.

For instance: if Canadians ever come storming over the border after our beer, we'd need to draft a huge force of bartenders to serve them.

Until that happens, the main function of a draft board member appears to be – (yawn) – waiting around.

"If you need something not to do, this is it," says a draft board member who asked not to be identified for fear of being yelled at by Connie.

"Plus you get a certificate and neat little pin."

Draft board members are nominated by the governor and appointed by the president, which is a pretty impressive way to pad the old resume.

You don't get paid anything, but that seems fair since the amount of meaningful work a draft board member performs is about on a par with city street department administrators. (You know those crackerheads who ran out of de-icer during the recent ice storm.)

Draft board members get together for a few hours every year to talk about what they might do if there really was a draft. In the event of war, the draft board decides whether certain hardships cases, divinity students or future presidents should stay home or become Canadians.

The amazing thing is how difficult it is to get on the draft board.

An applicant must fill out a form guaranteeing that he (a) has a pulse and (b) has never dismembered anyone or at least any family members.

After that, a person must wait for an opening that usually comes when someone on the draft board moves away or dies of boredom.

Right now, for example, all 15 seats on the three area draft boards are filled. Connie is looking for people with even less ambition: backup draft board members.

It takes a rare individual who is willing to wait a long period of time for a chance to do absolutely nothing.

Finally, a job I am qualified to perform.

Ban squirt guns? Boston mayor has water on the brain

You can have my water gun after you pull my cold, drenched finger off the trigger.

That's what I say to Boston Mayor Raymond Flynn and all the other left-wing, water wienies who want to take away America's right to squirt.

Flynn made headlines in June 1992 when he asked Boston merchants to yank Super Soaker squirt guns off their shelves.

Flynn was reacting to the death of a 15-year-old Boston kid who was shot in the wake of a water fight.

The mayor also carped that some youths had used their Soakers to spray noxious liquids like bleach.

Lord deliver us from well-intentioned clods like Flynn.

Ban water guns? No way. Peace through superior water power is the very sump pump of life in a free society.

Anybody who says different is all wet. Or should be.

Paul Rieckers will say amen to that. He telephoned last week to suggest a way Spokane could cash in on Mayor Flynn's nutball proposal. Rieckers wants Flynn to gather up all of Boston's contraband Super Soakers and send them here.

"For God's sake, we need the moisture," says Rieckers, who has lived here since 1947. "And because we're in a drought, we'll send Boston our fireworks."

Not a bad idea. Even with the recent rain, we're still drier than a mummy's undies, and Flynn didn't say a word against fireworks. Rieckers is on target when he says that Flynn's fuss over squirt guns is laughable.

"The Super Soakers shoot one shot at a time," he adds. "That means they're a semi-automatic weapon. What I worry about are all those people armed with fully automatic garden hoses."

True enough. Water fights are usually won by whoever grabs the hose. I know. Waging war with water has played a big part in my life.

Every summer, the Clarks engage in the following ritual: I drive my kids to the nearest toy store and arm them to the teeth with the very latest in water-fighting technology.

Naturally, I buy a weapon for myself. You can never be too careful.

Several years ago we discovered long, tubular things that looked like they were designed for giving enemas to cattle. They were called Blasters. You filled them from a pail and then expelled the water with a hard push on the plunger.

Next came battery-powered machine guns that shot water bursts through an electric pump. Zee, zee, zee . . . Those were followed by water shotguns. You pumped a slide to fire them, just like the old Model 12 Winchester.

This year, despite Mayor Flynn's crybaby plea, the Clarks have embraced Super Soakers.

But as much as I look forward to each summer's new mode, no squirt gun has ever delivered the pure soaking satisfaction as the one I used during Doug's Last Stand.

I was 12 when it happened. On the day school let out, half our class met in Preston Macy's back yard for the summer's first water war.

Looking for an advantage, I sneaked next door and pulled my granddad's old weed sprayer out of his garage. Unfortunately, I didn't think to wash it out before filling it with water. So Lord knows what kind of hellish cocktail I spewed on my friends that day.

What mattered to me was that it would shoot a pressurized stream if you pumped air into it with the wooden handle. Thus armed, I hauled the heavy metal tank to the top of the lava rock overlooking Preston's yard.

From the weed sprayer I created a stockpile of 30 water balloons. When my arsenal was complete, I surveyed the soggy battle raging below.

Howling like wildebeest in heat, I unleashed a deadly air assault. The sky rained water balloons that day. I picked off my pals in a frenzy of great splooshing glee.

They froze like deer in the headlights. Then scattered like Tokyo residents in a Godzilla movie.

Victory was mine. I laughed. I hooted.

I ran out of water.

It dawned on me suddenly what the phrase "high and dry" was all about.

Alone on my rocky Alamo, out of water, I watched as the slobbering Huns began to climb with squirt guns, water balloons and buckets of water in their hands.

I can't recall exactly what happened when they reached me. But I do know one thing: Mayor Flynn would have been positively horrified.

Vasectomy – Ooohh, I hate it when that happens

My buddy Big Al Bluford shambled toward me like a man astride an invisible Shetland pony.

"Yesterday was V-Day," he hissed in a pain-stricken voice normally associated with severe snakebite victims or someone who has been forced to listen to Jim Nabors sing.

Then he skewered his ashen face into something resembling a clenched fist and focused a lone, bleary eye on a vague spot somewhere below his belt.

"It's all over," he mumbled sadly, shaking his head. "And it wasn't a bit pretty."

I gazed at my bovine friend with queasy empathy.

"I know just how you feel, Big Al."

I did, too.

Let's face it. For generations, women have cornered the market on intimate talk. They have shared a camaraderie of suffering never before experienced by men.

Get a couple of gals together and, invariably, the discussion will turn to things we males have lumped under a mysterious heading called "Female Troubles."

Hysterectomies, 49-hour labors, pelvic exams, prolapsed whatchamacallits, menopausal jim-jams, premenstrual hobgoblins and a litany of other embarrassing horror stories are told with such graphic detail as to shame a stevedore.

Men, on the other hand, are mostly empty-headed louts who love to sprawl around tables full of beers and speculate endlessly on such meaningful subjects as the Niners' cocaine consumption or whether O. J. Simpson will ever learn to speak English.

This is all changing.

Ever since wives discovered that vasectomies were perfect ways to get back at their husbands for putting them through childbirth, more and more of us big bruisers can be seen cowering together in office corridors, nattering about "Male Troubles" and what indignities we've endured.

"Ya shoulda seen it," Bluford muttered. "First I had to climb on this long table without mah pants on and the doctor started puttin' this cold antiseptic stuff all over mah lower parts down there, which about sent me through the freaking roof."

Big Al paused.

"I tol' the doc, 'You keep puttin' that cold stuff on me an it'll take ya another hour afore ya can start again.'"

At this point, my Cro-Magnon friend had so amused himself with the subtlety of his joke that he forgot his postsurgical miseries and began to laugh.

A big mistake for one in Big Al's precarious condition.

He only managed a "har" of an intended "har-de-har-har" when the first shock wave reached those tender, abused "lower parts" he'd been speaking of. When it comes to vasectomies, parts is definitely not parts.

The 40-megaton burst of pain would've killed an ordinary man.

I patted Big Al on a massive shoulder and watched while he did a pathetic doubled-over duck walk toward the elevator and home.

All right, I admit it.

Men are basically sissies.

Compared to what women go through, we've had it knocked. But even the most liberated babe would have to feel a smattering of pity for the nation's vasectomized masses – a half million of us a year according to *The American Journal of Public Health*. That's 40 million total worldwide, which makes it one of the most popular forms of birth control.

Other than an occasional "Turn your head and cough, please," males aren't used to being prodded and poked in places nature surely intended for nicer treatment. So there you lay, shivering from fear, on the surgeon's table whilst you entrust to someone you hardly know the things you have grown to hold most dear.

Lying on that lonely slab, I discovered what a wimp I really was.

A regular macho guy, I wanted to believe that, like James Bond, I could bear up under torture. Whatever the cost, I figured, my country was safe.

The vasectomy affords one a rare opportunity to see that this notion is total horse twaddle.

Let me tell you, when somebody starts doing a fandango on your mangos, the national secrets are going to pour forth like wine.

Of course the entire procedure doesn't last more than an epoch or two and is no more painful than, say, having your lungs ripped out with a wire coat hanger.

After an unbearable recovery in which one discovers why God created icebags, there is the little matter of – ahem – verification.

After all, one must know if one's money (vasectomies average $451 a pop) was well spent.

Let us forego any clinical details on collection techniques. It is enough to say that a sperm sample must be taken to your physician for analysis.

Hoping to avoid public humiliation, I wrapped the tiny specimen jar into a shopping bag and stuffed the bag into a Samsonite suitcase.

Then I donned a wig and false moustache and drove to Dr. Cutzit's office.

"May I help you?" asked the pretty, 19-year-old receptionist.

"Yes, I'm Doug Clark and (lowering my voice) here's my ssppsppspmmm saamppp for analysis."

"Your what?"

(Slightly louder, but still hushed.)

"Here's my sperm sample for analysis."

The girl, looking at the luggage I had brought her, began to giggle uncontrollably. Then she stood up and bellowed at someone in the back room.

"Clark's here with his SPERRRRM SAAAAAAMPLE!!!!"

My face the color of your average stop sign, I turned to the crowded waiting room – filled with guffawing patients – and bowed as gracefully as I could.

Then I rode my own invisible pony out the door.

About the Author

Doug Clark, 46, is lead guitar player for The Spam-Tones, a rock 'n' roll band known more for its tradition of giving away Spam to exuberant dancers rather than the quality of its music. Because paying gigs are scarcer than albino Sinatra impersonators, Clark wisely has kept his day job writing three columns a week for *The Spokesman-Review* newspaper in Spokane, Washington, since 1985.

Clark's columns have earned him a score of journalism honors, including a Peter Tobenkin Award from Columbia University for human rights writing, three National Society of Newspaper Columnists Awards, and a Best in the West Award. A Spokane native, Clark lives with Sherry, his beloved wife of 25 years, their wonderful children, Ben and Emily, and a disobedient cockapoo named Elvis.